If you're serious about success, it's time to *Concentrate!*

Each guide in the *Concentrate* series shows you what to expect in your law exam, what examiners are looking for, and how to achieve extra marks.

* Written by experts
* Developed with students
* Designed for success

For a full list of titles available and forthcoming please visit the website

Don't miss the **Concentrate apps**!

Download the apps from the iTunes app store for your iPad, iPhone, or iPod touch. Hundreds of multiple choice questions with feedback, helping you to study, learn and revise, anytime, anywhere.

If you're struggling with your course or worried about exams, don't panic, just *concentrate!*

For a wealth of online resources including diagnostic ... and cases, and ... nt feedback visit:

Buy ...
you ...
book ...
online ...
from O...

...oncentrate/

D0318743

www.oxfordtextbooks.co.uk/law/revision

New to this edition

- Content fully updated with recent developments in the law

- New problem solving flow charts

- Coverage of Regulation 492/2011 on freedom of movement for workers within the Union

- New case law coverage including *Mangold* (Case C-144/04) and *Courage and Crehan* (Case C-453/99)

EU Law
Concentrate

3rd edition

Sylvia Hargreaves

Former Associate Dean, Nottingham Law School

Matthew J. Homewood

Principal Lecturer in EU Law, Nottingham Law School

OXFORD
UNIVERSITY PRESS

OXFORD
UNIVERSITY PRESS

Great Clarendon Street, Oxford, OX2 6DP,
United Kingdom

Oxford University Press is a department of the University of Oxford.
It furthers the University's objective of excellence in research, scholarship,
and education by publishing worldwide. Oxford is a registered trade mark of
Oxford University Press in the UK and in certain other countries

First edition 2009
Second edition 2011

Impression: 1

British Library Cataloguing in Publication Data

Data available

ISBN 978-0-19-965425-3

Printed in Great Britain by
Ashford Colour Press Ltd, Gosport, Hampshire

Contents

Table of cases   vii
Table of primary legislation   xv
Table of secondary legislation   xvii

1   Origins, institutions, and sources of law   1

2   Supremacy, direct effect, indirect effect, and state liability   21

3   Preliminary rulings: Article 267 TFEU   45

4   Direct actions in the Court of Justice of the European Union: Articles 258–260, 263, 265, 277, and 340 TFEU   62

5   Free movement of goods   88

6   Free movement of persons   117

7   EU competition law: introduction and Article 101 TFEU   155

8   EU competition law: Article 102 TFEU   177

Outline answers   A1
Glossary   A12
Index   A17

Table of cases

UK Cases

Bulmer Ltd and another v Bollinger SA and Others [1974] 2 CMLR 91 . . . 57

Chiron Corporation v Murex Diagnostics [1995] All ER (EC) 88 . . . 54

Commissioners of Customs and Excise v Samex ApS [1983] 3 CMLR 194 . . . 58, A3

NUT and Others v The Governing Body of St Mary's Church of England (Aided) Junior School and Others [1997] ICR 334; [1997] IRLR 242; [1997] ELR 169 . . . 33

R v Stock Exchange, *ex parte* Else (1982) Ltd [1993] 2 CMLR 677 . . . 58, A3

European cases and decisions

ABG Oil, Re OJ (1977) . . . 178, 181, 185

ACEC/Berliet (Commission Decision) OJ 1968 L 201/7, [1968] CMLR D35 . . . 170, 171, 172, 175, A9

Adams v Commission (Case 145/83) [1985] ECR 3539 . . . 80, A4

Ahlström & Ors v Commission (Woodpulp) (Cases C-89, 104, 114, 116–117, 125–129/85) [1993] ECR I -1307 . . . 156, 164, 174

AKZO Chemie v Commission (Case C-62/86) [1991] ECR I-3359 . . . 179, 190, 191, 196, A11

Allué and Coonan v Universita degli studi di Venezia (Case 33/88) [1989] ECR 1591 . . . 136

Alpine Investments BV v Minister of Finance (Case C 384/93) [1995] ECR I-1141 . . . 140

Amministrazione delle Financze dello Stato v Simmenthal (Case 106/77) [1978] ECR 629 . . . 26, 41, A2

Amylum NV v Council and Commission (Isoglucose) (Cases 116 & 124/77) [1979] ECR 3497 . . . 79, 81, 86, A4

Angonese v Cassa di Risparmio di Bolzano SpA (Case C-281/98) [2000] ECR I-4139 . . . 135

Anker, Ras and Snoek v Germany (Case C-47/02) [2004] 3 CMLR 14 . . . 136

Arsenal Football Club v Reed (Case C-206/01) [2002] ECR I-10273 . . . 50

Avello v Belgian State (Case C-148/02) [2003] ECR I-11613 . . . 130

Bacardi-Martini SAS v Newcastle United Football Club (Case C-318/00) [2003] ECR I-905 . . . 52

Baumbast v Secretary of State for the Home Department (Case C-413/99) [2002] ECR I-7091 . . . 122, 124, 128, 150, A8

Bayerische HNL Vermehrungsbetriebe GmbH v Council and Commission (Cases 83 & 94/76, 4, 15 & 40/77) [1978] ECR 1209 . . . 79, 81, 83, 85, 86, A4

Becker v Hauptzollamt Münster-Innerstadt (Case 8/81) [1982] ECR 53 . . . 33, A2

Bethell v Commission (Case 246/81) [1982] ECR 2277 . . . 77

Bettray v Staatssecretaris van Justitie (Case 344/87) [1989] ECR 1621 . . . 122, 133, 150, A7

Bleis v Ministère de l'Education Nationale (Case C-4/91) [1991] ECR I-5627 . . . 136

Bonsignore v Oberstadtdirektor of the City of Cologne (Case 67/74) [1975] ECR 297 . . . 145, 147, 148, 153, A8

Brasserie de Haecht SA v Wilkin (No 1) (Case 23/67) [1967] ECR 407 . . . 166, 175, A9

Brasserie du Pêcheur v Germany and R v Secretary of State for Transport *ex parte* Factortame Ltd and Others (Joined Cases C-46 & 48/93) [1996] ECR I-1029 . . . 37, 38, 43, 81, 82, A2, A4

British Leyland plc v Commission (Case 226/84) [1986] ECR 3263 . . . 179, 188, 189, 195, A11

Broeckmeulen v Huisarts Registratie Commissie (Case 246/80) [1981] ECR 2311 . . . 50–1

Brown v Secretary for State for Scotland (Case 197/86) [1988] ECR 3205 . . . 126

Campus Oil Ltd v Minister for Industry and Energy (Case 72/83) [1983] ECR 2727 . . . 109

Table of cases

✱✱✱✱✱✱✱✱✱✱✱✱

Carpenter v Secretary of State for the Home Department (Case C-60/00) [2002] ECR I-6279 . . . 130

Casagrande v Landeshauptstadt München (Case 9/74) [1974] ECR 773 . . . 129

Castelli v ONPTS (Case 261/83) [1984] ECR 3199 . . . 136

CECED (Commission Decision) OJ 2000 L187/47 [2000] 5 CMLR 635 . . . 171, 172, 176, A9

Centre Public d'Aide Sociale de Courcelles v Lebon (Case 316/85) [1987] ECR 2811 . . . 127

Chemial Farmaceutici SpA v DAF SpA (Case 140/79) [1981] ECR 1 . . . 91, 96, 113, A6

Chevally v Commission (Case 15/70) [1972] ECR 975 . . . 78

CIA Security International SA v Signalson SA (Case C-194/94) [1996] ECR I-2201 . . . 33

CILFIT Srl v Ministero della Sanita (Case 283/81) [1982] ECR 3415 . . . 46, 47, 54, 55, 56, 58, 60, A3

Collins v Secretary of State for work and pensions (Case C-138/02) [2004] ECR I-2703 . . . 134

Commission v Belgium (Case 77/69) [1970] ECR 237 . . . 66

Commission v Belgium (Case 149/79) (Public Employees) [1980] ECR 3881 . . . 122, 135, 151

Commission v Belgium (Case 132/82) (Customs Warehouses) [1983] ECR 1649 . . . 93, 94, 113, A6

Commission v Belgium (Case 1/86) [1987] ECR 2797 . . . 65, 83

Commission v Belgium and Luxembourg (Cases 90–91/63) [1964] ECR 625 . . . 68

Commission v Council (ERTA) (Case 22/70) [1970] ECR 263 . . . 71

Commission v Denmark (Case 252/83) (Re Insurance Services) [1986] ECR 3713 . . . 141

Commission v Denmark (Case 302/86) (Danish Bottles) [1988] ECR 4607 . . . 104, 114, A6

Commission v France (Case 167/73) (French Merchant Seamen) [1974] ECR 359 . . . 69, 84, 122, 135, 151

Commission v France (Case 168/78) (French Taxation of Spirits) [1980] ECR 347 . . . 96

Commission v France (Case 232/78) [1979] ECR 2729 . . . 68, 84

Commission v France (case 90/79) (Reprographic Machines) [1981] ECR 283 . . . 97

Commission v France (Case 243/84) [1986] ECR 00875 . . . 97

Commission v France (Case 307/84) [1986] ECR 1725 . . . 136

Commission v France (Case 220/83) [1986] ECR 3663 . . . 141

Commission v France (Case C-265/95) (Spanish Strawberries) [1997] ECR I-6959 . . . 65, 101

Commission v France (Case C-1/00) [2001] ECR I-9989 . . . 67, 70

Commission v France (Case C-304/02) [2005] ECR I-6263 . . . 69

Commission v France (Case C-121/07) [2008] ECR I-9159 . . . 69

Commission v Germany (Case 314/82) (Health Inspection Service) [1984] ECR 1543 . . . 93

Commission v Germany (Case 178/84) (Beer Purity Laws) [1987] ECR 1227 . . . 104, 105, 110

Commission v Germany (Case 205/84) (Re Insurance Services) [1986] ECR 3755 . . . 141

Commission v Germany (Case 18/87) (Animal Inspection fees) [1988] ECR 5427 . . . 93, 94

Commission v Germany (Case C-325/00) [2002] ECR I-9977 . . . 100

Commission v Greece (Case C-391/92) [1995] ECR I-1621 . . . 97, 106, A5, A6

Commission v Ireland (Case 55/79) (Excise Payments) [1980] ECR 481 . . . 96

Commission v Ireland (Case 113/80) (Restrictions on Importation of Souvenirs) [1981] ECR 1625 . . . 103, 107, 108, 111, 114

Commission v Ireland (Case 249/81) ('Buy Irish' Campaign) [1982] ECR 4005 . . . 100

Commission v Ireland (Case 206/84) (Re Co-insurance services) [1986] ECR 3817 . . . 141

Commission v Italy (Case 7/61) (Re Ban in Pork Imports) [1962] CMLR 39 . . . 109

Commission v Italy (Case 7/68) (Export Tax on Art Treasures, No. 1) [1968] ECR 423 . . . 111

Commission v Italy (Case 24/68) (Statistical Levy) [1969] ECR 193 . . . 93, 94, A6

Commission v Italy (Case 101/84) (Re Transport Statistics) [1985] ECR 2629 . . . 68, 84

Commission v Italy (Case 225/85) [1987] ECR 2625 . . . 136

Commission v Italy (Case C-283/99) [2001] ECR 4363 . . . 136

Commission v Jégo-Quéré (Case C-263/02P) [2004] ECR I-3425 . . . 71, 76, 85

Commission v Luxembourg (Case C-473/93) [1996] ECR I-3207 . . . 136

Commission v United Kingdom (Case 128/78) (Tachographs) [1979] ECR 419 . . . 68, 84

Commission v United Kingdom (Case 170/78) (Excise Duties on Wine) [1980] ECR 417; [1983] ECR 2265 . . . 97

Commission v United Kingdom (Case 40/82) (Imports of Poultry Meat) [1982] ECR 2793 . . . 108, 110, 112

Commission v United Kingdom (Case 207/83) (Origin Marking of Goods) [1985] ECR 1202 . . . 100

Commission v United Kingdom (Case C-246/89R) [1989] ECR 3125 . . . 69

Conegate Ltd v Customs and Excise Commissioners (Case 121/85) [1986] ECR 1007 . . . 109

Cooperatieve Vereniging 'Suiker Unie' UA v Commission (the Sugar Cartel cases) (Cases 40–8, 50, 54–6, 111, 113, 114/73) [1975] ECR 1663 . . . 164

Costa v ENEL (Case 6/64) [1964] ECR 585 . . . 25–6, 41, 53, 59, A2

Courage Ltd v Crehan (Case C-453/99) [2001] ECR I-06297 . . . 161

Cowan v Le Trésor Public (Case 186/87) [1989] ECR 195 . . . 123, 142, 152

Criminal Proceedings against Donatella Calfa (Case C-348/96) ECR I-11 . . . 146, 152, A8

Criminal proceedings against Karl Prantl (Case 16/83) [1984] ECR 1299 . . . 102, A5

Criminal Proceedings against Lynne Watson and Alessandro Belmann (Case 118/75) ECR 11850 . . . 129

Criminal Proceedings against Webb (Case 279/80) [1981] ECR 3305 . . . 141

Cristini v SNCF (Case 32/75) [1975] ECR 1085 . . . 122, 136, 151

Da Costa en Schaake NV v Nederlandse Belastingadministratie (Cases 28-30/62) [1963] ECR 31 . . . 46, 55, 56, 58, 60, A3

Defrenne v Sabena (Case 43/75) [1976] ECR 455 . . . 22, 29, 30, 42, A2

Denkavit v France (Case 132/78) [1979] ECR 1923 . . . 94, 95, 113, A6

Deutsche Apothekerverband v 0800 DocMorris NV (Case C-322/01) [2003] ECR I-14887 . . . 110

Deutschmann v Germany (Case 10/65) [1965] ECR 469 . . . 95

D'Hoop v Office national de l'emploi (Case C-224/98) [2002] ECR I-6191 . . . 130, A8

Diatta v Land Berlin (Case 267/83) [1985] ECR 567 . . . 128

Dillenkofer v Germany (Cases C-178-9, 188-190/94) [1996] ECR I-4845 . . . 38

Dorsch Consult Ingenieurgesellschaft v Bundesbaugesellschaft Berlin (Case C-54/96) [1997] ECRI-4961 . . . 51

Dumortier Frères v Council (Cases 64 & 113/76, 167 & 239/78, 27, 28 & 45/79) [1979] ECR 309 . . . 79, 83, 86, A4

Dzodzi v Belgium (Cases C-297/88 & C-197/89) [1990] ECR I-3763 . . . 46, 58, 60, A2, A3

Eau de Cologne v Provide (Case C-130/88) [1989] ECR 3891 . . . 52

Emmott v Minister for Social Welfare (Case C-208/90) [1991] ECR I-4269 . . . 40

Eridania v Commission (Cases 10&18/68) [1969] ECR 459 . . . 78

Etablissements Consten SA and Grundig – Verkaufs GmbH v Commission (Cases 56 & 58/64) [1966] ECR 299 . . . 156, 162, 165, 166, 168, 173, 174, 175, A9

Eternach and Moritz v Minister van Onderwijs en Wetenschappen (Cases 389/87 and 390/87) [1989] ECR 723 . . . 128

Eurofix & Bauco v Hilti AG (1989) . . . 178, 179, 182, 183, 184, 185, 190, 192, 195, 196, A10, A11

Table of cases

****

European Parliament v Council (Case 13/83) [1985] ECR 1513 . . . 77

Europemballage Corp and Continental Can Co Inc v Commission (Case 6/72) [1973] ECR 215 . . . 178, 183, 184, 194, A10

Foglia v Novello (No 1) (Case 104/79) [1980] ECR 745 . . . 46, 51, 59, A3

Foglia v Novello (No 2) (Case 244/80) [1981] ECR 3045 . . . 46, 51, 52, 59

Ford España SA v Estado español (Case 170/88) [1989] ECR 2305 . . . 94

Förster v Hoofddirectie van de Informatie Beheer Groep (Case C-158/07) judgment of 18 November 2008 . . . 126

Foster v British Gas (Case C-188/89) [1990] ECR I-3133 . . . 22, 32, 33, 42, A1

Foto-Frost v Hauptzollamt Lübeck-Ost (Case 314/85) [1987] ECR 4199 . . . 57

Franca Ninni-Orasche v Bundesminister für Wissenschaft, Verkehr und Kunst (Case C-413/01) [2004] 1 CMLR 19 . . . 122, 132, 150, A7

Francovich and Bonifaci v Republic of Italy (Cases C-6/90 and C-9/90) [1991] ECR I-5357 . . . 23, 36, 37, 42, A2

Fratelli Costanzo v Comune di Milano (Case 103/88) [1989] ECR 1839 . . . 33, A2

Gebhard v Consiglio dell'Ordine degli Avvocati e Procuratori di Milano (Case C-55/94) [1995] ECR I-4165 . . . 123, 139, 151

Geddo v Ente Nazionale Risi (Case 2/73) [1974] ECR 865 . . . 98, 112, A5, A6

Geraets-Smits v Stichting Ziekenfonds and HTM Peerbooms v Stichting CZ Groep Zorgverzekeringen (Case C-157/99) [2001] ECR I-6155 . . . 140

Germany v European Parliament and Council (Tobacco Advertising) (Case C-376/98) [2000] ECR I-8419 . . . 63, 76

Grad v Finanzamt Traunstein (Case 9/70) [1970] ECR 825 . . . 31

Gravier v City of Liege (Case 293/83) [1985] ECR 593 . . . 126

Groener v Minister for Education (Case 379/87) [1989] ECR 3967 . . . 122, 135, 151

Grzelczyk v Centre Public d'Aide Sociale d'Ottignies-Louvain-la-Neuve (Case C-184/99) [2001] ECR I-6193 . . . 122, 124, A8

Harz v Deutsche Tradax GmbH (Case 79/83) [1984] ECR 1921 . . . 34

Hennessy/Henkell (Commission Decision) OJ 1980 L 383/11, [1981] 1 CMLR 601 . . . 168, A9

Hilti v Commission (Case T-30/89) [1991] ECR II-1439 . . . 178, 179, 182, 183, 184, 185, 190, 192, 195, 196, A10, A11

HM Customs and Excise v Schindler (Case C-275/92) [1994] ECR I-1039 . . . 141

Hoeckx v Centre Public d'Aide Sociale de Kalmthout (Case 249/83) [1985] ECR 973 . . . 136

Hoekstra (née Unger) v Bestuur der Bedrijfsvereniging voor Detailhandel en Ambachten (Case 75/63) [1964] ECR 177 . . . 131

Hoffmann-La Roche & Co AG v Commission (Case 85/76) [1979] ECR 461 . . . 178, 179, 186, 189, 195, A10, A11

Höfner and Elser (Case C-41/90) [1991] I-1979 . . . 156, 162, A8

Hugin Kassaregister AB v Commission (Case 22/78) [1979] ECR 1869 . . . 178, 179, 182, 194, A10, A11

Huls AG v Commission (Case C-199/92P) [1999] ECR I-4287 . . . 164

Humblot v Directeur des Services Fiscaux (Case 112/84) [1985] ECR 1367 . . . 95, 97, 113, A6

IAZ International Belgium NV v Commission (Cases 96–102, 104, 105, 108 & 110/82) [1983] ECR 3369 . . . 156, 163, 173

IBM v Commission (Case 60/81) [1981] ECR 2639 . . . 71, 84

Imperial Chemical Industries Ltd v Commission (Dyestuffs) (Case 48/69) [1972] ECR 619 . . . 156, 163, 168, 174

International Chemical Corporation v Amministrazione Finanze (Case 66/80) [1981] ECR 1191 . . . 49, A11

Internationale Handelsgesellschaft GmbH (Case 11/70) [1970] ECR 1125 . . . 26, 41, A2

Inzirillo v Caisse d'Allocations Familiales de l'Arondissement de Lyon (Case 63/76) [1976] ECR 2057 . . . 136

Irish Creamery Milk Suppliers Association v Ireland (Cases 36 & 71/80) [1981] ECR 735 . . . 48, A3

Istituto Chemioterapico Italiano SpA and Commercial Solvents Corporation v Commission (Cases 6 & 7/73) [1974] ECR 223 . . . 179, 183, 192, 193, 194, 196, A11

Jégo-Quéré v Commission (Case T-177/01) [2002] ECR II-2365 . . . 63, 75, 76, 85

John Walker v Ministeriet for Skatter (Case 243/84) [1986] ECR 875 . . . 96

Johnston v RUC (Case 222/84) [1986] ECR 1651 . . . 33, A2

Keck and Mithouard (Cases C-267 & 268/91) [1993] ECR I-6097 . . . 89, 91, 105–6, 110, 112, 114, A5, A6

Kempf v Staatssecretaris van Justitie (Case 139/85) [1986] ECR 1741 . . . 122, 132, A7

Köbler v Austria (Case C-224/01) [2003] ECR I-1039 . . . 39, 43, 56, 60, A2, A3

Konsumentombudsmannen (KO) v De Agostini (Svenska) Förlag AB ECR I-3843 . . . 106, A6

Konsumentombudsmannen (KO) v TV Shop i Sverge AB (Cases C-34-6/95) [1997] ECR I-3843 . . . 106

Krohn v Commission (Case 175/84) [1986] ECR 1299 . . . 83

Kühne & Heitz v Productschap voor Pluimvee en Eieren (Case C-453/00) [2004] ECR I-837 . . . 49

Laboratoires Pharmaceutiques Bergaderm SA and Goupil v Commission (Case C-352/98P) [2000] ECR I-5291 . . . 39, 81, 82, 86, A4, A5

Lair v Universität Hannover (Case 39/86) [1988] ECR 3161 . . . 126

Lawrie-Blum v Land Baden-Württemberg (Case 66/85) [1986] ECR 2121 . . . 122, 131, 136, 150, A7

Leonesio v Italian Ministry of Agriculture (Case 93/71) [1972] ECR 287 . . . 22, 30, A2

Levez v Jennings (Case C-326/96) [1998] ECR I-7835 . . . 40

Levin v Staatssecretaris van Justitie (Case 53/81) [1982] ECR 1035 . . . 122, 131, 150, A7

Luisi and Carbone v Ministero del Tresoro (Cases 286/82 and 26/83) [1984] ECR 377 . . . 142

Lütticke v Commission (Case 4/69) [1971] ECR 325 . . . 79, 80, 85, A4

Lütticke (Alfons) GmbH v Hauptzollamt Saarlouis (Case 57/65) [1966] ECR 205 . . . 95, A6

Lyckeskog (Case C-99/00) [2002] ECR I-4839 . . . 54, 60, A3

McNicholl v Ministry of Agriculture (Case 296/86) [1988] ECR 1491 . . . 68

Magill see RTE v Commission (Case T-69/89) [1991] ECR II-485

Mangold (Werner) v Rudiger Helm (Case C-144/04) [2005] ECR I-09981 . . . 32

Marleasing SA v La Comercial Internacional de Alimentación SA (Case C-106/89) [1990] ECR I-4135 . . . 23, 35, 42, A1, A2

Marshall v Southampton & South West Hampshire Area Health Authority (Case 152/84) [1986] ECR 723 . . . 22, 31, 33, 34, 41, 42, A1, A2

Marsman v Rosskamp (Case 44/72) [172] ECR 1243 . . . 137

Meilicke v ADV/ORGA AG (Case C-83/91) [1992] ECR I-4871 . . . 46, 52, 59, A3

Messner (Case C-265/88) [1989] ECR 4209 . . . 129

Metro-SB-Grossmärkte GmbH & Co KG v Commission (No 1) (Case 26/76) [1977] ECR 1875 . . . 157, 169, 175

Métropole Télévision (M6) and Others v Commission (Case T-112/99) [2001] ECR II-2459 . . . 157, 169, 175, A9

Microsoft Corporation v Commission (Case T-201/04) [2007] ECR II-1491 . . . 186, 190, 192

Ministre de l'Intérieur v Olazabal (Case C-100/01) [2002] ECR I-10981 . . . 145, 148, 149, 154

Table of cases

****

Morson and Jhanjan v Netherlands (Cases 35 & 36/82) [1982] ECR 3723 . . . 130

Municipality of Differdange v Commission (Case 222/83) [1984] ECR 2889 . . . 63, 74, 84, A4

Nederlandsche Banden-Industrie Michelin NV v Commission (Case 322/81) [1983] ECR 3461 . . . 178, 179, 185, 190, 194, A10, A11

Netherlands State v Reed (Case 59/85) [1985] ECR 1283 . . . 127

Oebel (Case 155/80) [1981] ECR 1993 . . . 104, A6

Officier van Justitie v Sandoz BV (Case 174/82) [1983] ECR 2445 . . . 110

O'Flynn v Adjudication Officer (Case C-237/94) [1996] ECR I-2617 . . . 137

Orfanopoulos and Oliveri v Land Baden-Württemburg (Joined cases C-482/01 and C-493/01) [2004] ECR I-5257 . . . 145, 146, 147, 153, A8

Oscar Bronner GmbH & Co KG v Mediaprint Zeitungs- und Zeitschriftenverlag GmbH & Co KG and others (Case C-7/97) [1998] ECR I-779 . . . 179, 192

Outokumpu Oy (Case C-213/96) [1998] ECR I-1777 . . . 96

Paolo Faccini Dori v Recreb Srl (Case C-91/92) [1994] ECR I-3325 . . . 32, A2

Paraiki-Patraiki v Commission (Case 11/82) [1985] ECR 207 . . . 63, 74, 75, 84, A4

Plaumann v Commission (Case 25/62) [1963] ECR 95 . . . 63, 74, 75, 76, 85, A4

Politi v Italian Ministry of Finance (Case 43/71) [1971] ECR 1039 . . . 22, 30, 50, A2

PreussenElektra AG v Schleswag AG (Case C-379/98) [2001] ECR I-2099 . . . 111

Procureur du Roi v Dassonville (Case 8/74) [1974] ECR 837 . . . 91, 98, 99, 100, 102, 106, 112, 113, 114, A5, A6

Procureur du Roi v Royer (Case 48/75) [1975] ECR 497 . . . 122, 125, 129, 133, 151, A7

Pronuptia de Paris GmbH v Pronuptia de Paris Irmgard Schillgalis (Case 161/84) [1986] ECR 353 . . . 157, 168, 169, 175, A9

Prym-Werke (Commission Decision) OJ 1973 L296/24, [1973] CMLR D250 . . . 170, 171, 175

Pubblico Ministerio v Ratti (Case 148/78) [1979] ECR 1269 . . . 22, 31, 42, A1, A2

Pupino (Case C-105/03) [2005] ECR I-5285 . . . 23, 35, A1, A2

R v Bouchereau (Case 30/77) [1977] ECR 1999 . . . 144, 145, 146, 148, 153, A8

R v Henn and Darby (Case 34/79) [1979] ECR 3795 . . . 109

R v HM Treasury, *ex parte* British Telecommunications (Case C-392/93) [1996] ECR I-1631 . . . 38, 39, 43, 50, A2

R v Immigration Appeal Tribunal, *ex parte* Antonissen (Case C-292/89) [1991] ECR I-745 . . . 122, 133, A7

R v Immigration Appeal Tribunal and Singh, *ex parte* Secretary of State for the Home Department (Case C-370/90) [1992] ECR I-4265 . . . 130

R v London Borough of Ealing & Secretary of State for Education, *ex parte* Bidar (Case C-209/03) [2005] ECR I-2119 . . . 126

R v Ministry of Agriculture, Fisheries and Food, *ex parte* Hedley Lomas (Ireland) Ltd (Case C-5/94) [1996] ECR I-2553 . . . 39, 43, A2

R v Pieck (Case 157/79) [1980] ECR 2171 . . . 147

R v Secretary of State for Transport, *ex parte* Factortame Ltd (II) (Case 213/89) [1990] ECR I-2433 . . . 26, 27, 41, A2

R v Secretary of State for Transport, *ex parte* Factortame Ltd III and Others (Joined Cases C-46 & 48/93) [1996] ECR I-1029 . . . 23, 38, 39, 41, 50, A2, A4

R v Thompson (Case 7/78) [1978] ECR 2247 . . . 109

Reina v Landeskreditbank Baden-Württemberg (Case 65/81) [1982] ECR 33 . . . 136

Rewe-Zentral AG v Bundesmonopolverwaltung für Branntwein (Case 120/78) [1979] ECR 649 (Cassis de Dijon) . . . 89, 91, 102–5, 107, 108, 111, 112, 115, 143, A5, A6

Rewe-Zentral. nanz v Landwirtschaftskammer Bonn (San Jose Scale) (Case 4/75) [1975] ECR 843 100, 110, 114, A5

Reyners v Belgium (Case 2/74) [1974] ECR 631 . . . 138

Rheinmühlen-Düsseldorf v Einfuhr-und Vorratsstelle für Getreide und Futtermittel (Case 146/73) [1974] ECR 139 . . . 46, 58, 60, A2, A3

Roquette Frères v Council (Case 138/79) [1980] ECR 3333 . . . 63, 76

RTE v Commission (Case T-69/89) [1991] ECR II-485; BBC v Commission (Case T-70/89) [1991] ECR II-535; ITP Ltd v Commission (Case T-76/89) [1991] ECR II-575; (Cases C-241 & 242/91P) Radio Telefis Eireann v Commission [1995] ECR I-743 Decisions upheld on appeal to the ECJ in RTE & ITP v Commission (Joined Cases C-241 & 242/91P) [1995] ECR I-743 . . . 178, 179, 184, 192, 194, 195, A11

Rutili v Ministre de l'Intérieur (Case 36/75) [1975] ECR 1219 . . . 145, 146, 148, 154

Safir v Skattemyndigheten i Dalarnas Lan (Case C-118/96) [1998] ECR I-1897 . . . 140

Säger v Dennemeyer & Co Ltd (Case C-76/90) [1991] ECR 241; [1992] ECR I-4221 . . . 123, 141, 152

Sala v Freistaat Bayern (Case C-85/96) ECR I-2691 . . . 124, 149, A8

Sayag v Leduc (Case 9/69) [1969] ECR 329 . . . 80

Schmidberger v Austria (Case C-112/00) [2003] ECR I-5659 . . . 101

Schöppenstedt Aktien-Zuckerfabrik v Council (Case 5/71) [1971] ECR 975 . . . 80, 81, 82, 85, A4, A5

Schutzverband gegen unlauteren Wettbewerb v TK-Heimdienst Sass GmbH (Case-254/98) [2000] ECR I-151 . . . 107

Sealink/B and I–Holyhead: Interim Measures (Commission Decision) [1992] 5 CMLR 255 . . . 178, 179, 185, 192, 194, A11

Secretary of State for the Home Department v Akrich (Case C-109/01) [2003] ECR I-9607 . . . 127, 130

Seda Kucukdeveci v Swedex GmbH & Co KG (Case C-555/07) [2010] ECR I-00365 . . . 32

SFEI v Commission (Case C-39/93P) [1994] ECR I-2681 . . . 71

Sociaal Fonds voor de Diamantarbeiders v Chougol Diamond Co (Cases 2 and 3/69) [1969] ECR 211 . . . 92, 93, 94, 113, A6

Société Technique Minière v Maschinenbau Ulm GmbH (STM) (Case 56/65) [1966] ECR 235 . . . 156, 157, 165, 167, 174, 175, 179, 193, 196, A8, A9

Society for the Protection of Unborn Children Ltd v Grogan (Case C-159/90) [1991] ECR I-4685 . . . 140

Sotgiu v Deutsche Bundespost (Case 152/73) [1974] ECR 153 . . . 135

Star Fruit Company v Commission (Case 247/87) [1989] ECR 291 . . . 66, 83

Steymann v Staatssecretaris van Justitie (Case 196/87) [1988] ECR 6159 . . . 122, 132, 150, A7

T Port v Bundesanstalt für Landeswirtschaft und Ernährung (Case C-68/95) [1996] ECR I-6065 . . . 78

Tankstation 't Heukske vof and J.B.E Boermans (Joined Cases C-401/92 & C-402/92) [1994] ECR I-2199 . . . 106, A6

Telemarsicabruzzo SpA v Circostel (Cases C-320, 321, 322/90) [1993] ECR I-393 . . . 53, 59, A3

Tetra Pak International SA v Commission (Case C-333/94P) [1996] ECR I-5951 . . . 179, 191, A11

Thieffry v Conseil de l'Ordre des Avocats α la Cour de Paris (Case 71/76) [1977] ECR 765 . . . 123, 139, 151

Torfaen Borough Council v B&Q plc (Case 145/88) [1989] ECR 3851 . . . 104, 106, A6

Trajhetti del Mediterraneo SpA v Italy (Case C-173/03) [2006] ECR I-5177 . . . 39, 57

Transocean Marine Paint v Commission (Case 17/74) [1974] ECR 1063 . . . 63, 77

Trojani v Centre public d'aide social de Bruxelles (Case C-456/02) [2004] ECR I-7574 . . . 122, 133, 150

Table of cases
****

UK v Council (Case C-84/94) [1996] ECR I-5755 . . . 63, 77

Unilever Italia SpA v Central Food SpA (Case C-443/98) [2000] ECR I-7535 . . . 33

Union de Pequeños Agricultores v Council (UPA) (Case 50/00 P) [2002] ECR I-6677 . . . 63, 75–6, 85

United Brands Co v Commission (Case 27/76) [1978] ECR 207 . . . 178, 179, 181, 182, 184, 185, 188, 189, 190, 192, 194, 195, A10, A11

Vacuum Interrupters Ltd (Commission Decision) OJ 1977 L 48/32, [1977] 1 CMLR D67 . . . 166, 168, 174, A9

Van Binsbergen v Bestuur van de Bedrijfsvereniging voor de Metaalnijverheid (Case 33/74) [1974] ECR 1299 . . . 123, 138, 140, 152

Van Duyn v Home Office (Case 41/74) [1974] ECR 133 . . . 22, 31, 42, 145, 146, 152, A1, A2

Van Gend en Loos v Nederlandse Administratie der Belastingen (Case 26/62) [1963] ECR 1 . . . 22, 25, 28, 29, 30, 41, 49, 55, 58, 60, A1, A2

Vatsouras & another v Arbeitsgemeinschaft Nürnberg 900 (Cases C-22 & 23/08) . . . 134

Vlassopoulou v Ministerium für Justiz (Case 340/89) [1991] ECR I-2357 . . . 139

Volk v Établissements Vervaecke Sprl (Case 5/69) [1969] ECR 295 167 . . . A9

Von Colson and Kamman v Land Nordrhein-Westfalen (Case 14/83) [1984] ECR 1891 . . . 23, 34, 35, 42, A1, A2

Wagner Miret v Fondo de Garantira Salaria (Case C-334/92) [1993] ECR I-6911 . . . 23, 35, A1, A2

Walter Rau Lebensmittelwerke v de Smedt PvbA (Case 261/81) [1982] ECR 3961 . . . 101, 104, 105, 112, 113, A5

Werner Mangold v Rudiger Helm (Case C-144/04) [2005] ECR I-09981 . . . 32

Wouters v Netherlands Bar (Case C-309/99) [2002] ECR I-1577 . . . 156, 163, 173

Zhu and Chen v Secretary of State for the Home Department (Case C-200/02) [2004] ECR I-9925 . . . 130

Zückerfabrik Süderdithmarschen v Hauptzollamt Itzehoe (Case C-143/88) [1991] ECR I-415 . . . 57

Table of primary legislation

UK Statutes

European Communities Act 1972 . . . 27
  s 2(1) . . . 26
  s 2(4) . . . 27

Merchant Shipping Act 1988 . . . 37, 38

Sex Discrimination Act 1975 . . . 41

European primary legislation

Constitutional Treaty 2004 . . . 8

EC Treaty . . . 4, 5, 6, 7, 8, 24, 64, 120
  see also Treaty on European Union;
   Treaty on the Functioning of the
   European Union
ECSC Treaty 1951 . . . 3, 4, 5
EEC Treaty 1957 . . . 3, 4, 5, 6, 25
EU Charter of Fundamental Rights . . . 18
Euratom Treaty 1957 . . . 4, 5

Maastricht Treaty *see* Treaty on European
  Union

Reform Treaty *see* Treaty of Lisbon 2007

Single European Act 1986 . . . 5, 16, 113

Treaty of Amsterdam 1997 . . . 5, 7, 8
Treaty on European Union . . . 5–6, 4, 8, 10, 11,
  17, 18, 69, 120
  Art 4 . . . 65, 101
  Art 14 . . . 14
  Art 15 . . . 11
  Art 16 . . . 12, 13
  Art 17 . . . 13–14
  Art 18 . . . 11
  Art 19 . . . 15
Treaty on the Functioning of the European
  Union . . . 8, 10, 11, 17, 24, 47, 73, 89, 92, 120,
  121, 134, 158, 180
  Art 3 . . . 122
  Art 4 . . . 25, 34, 36, 122
  Art 18 . . . 118, 121, 123, 124, 126, 138, 142,
   148, 149, 152, 154, A6, A7

Art 20 . . . 121, A6, A7
Art 21 . . . 118, 121, 122, 124, 129, 130, 137,
  150, A6, A7
Art 26 . . . 92, A5, A6, A7
Art 30 . . . 28, 29, 41, 68, 89, 90, 92, 93, 94, 95,
  113, 159, A5, A6
Art 34 . . . 30, 89, 90, 91, 98, 99, 101, 102, 103,
  104, 106, 107, 110, 112, A5, A6
Art 35 . . . 30, 98, 107, A5
Art 36 . . . 89, 90, 107–12, 159, A6
Art 45 . . . 30, 118, 121, 122, 125, 130, 137, A7
Art 45(1) . . . 118, 131
Art 45(2) . . . 118, 131, 134, 135, 151, A7
Art 45(3) . . . 118, 130, 131, 144, 145, A7
Art 45(4) . . . 118, 122, 135, 136
Art 49 . . . 30, 119, 121, 123, 125, 137, 138, 139,
  142, A7
Art 49(3) . . . A6
Art 51 . . . 138
Art 52 . . . 119, 130, 138, 144, 145
Art 56 . . . 30, 119, 121, 123, 130, 137, 138, 140,
  141, 142, A7
Art 57 . . . 119, 140
Art 62 . . . 119, 138, 144, 145
Art 90 . . . 77
Art 101 . . . 30, 155, 156, 157, 158, 159, 160,
  161, 166, 177, 180, 193, A9
Art 101(1) . . . 156, 158, 162, 163, 164, 165,
  166, 167, 168, 169, 170, 171, 172, 173, 174,
  176, A8, A9
Art 101(1)(a)–(e) . . . 157, 168
Art 101(2) . . . 157, 158, 162
Art 101(3) . . . 157, 158, 162, 168, 169, 170,
  172, A9
Art 102 . . . 30, 155, 158, 159, 160, 161, 177–96,
  A10
Art 102(c) . . . 189
Art 102(d) . . . 190
Art 110 . . . 89, 91, 94, 95, 96, 97, 159, A5
Art 110(1) . . . 91, 95, 96, 97
Art 110(2) . . . 91, 95, 96, 97
Art 114 . . . 113, A6
Art 115 . . . 113, A6
Art 153 . . . 77
Art 157 . . . 29, 42
Arts 223–234 . . . 14–15
Art 235 . . . 11

Table of primary legislation
****

Art 236 . . . 11
Arts 237–43 . . . 12–13
Arts 244–250 . . . 13–14
Arts 251–257 . . . 15
Art 258 . . . 62, 64, 65, 66, 67, 68, 69, 70, 83
Art 259 . . . 62, 64, 65, 70
Art 260 . . . 62, 64, 65, 69
Art 260(3) . . . 69
Art 263 . . . 15, 62, 63, 64, 67, 70, 76, 78, 80, 84, 161
Art 263(2) . . . 76
Art 265 . . . 62, 66, 77, 78
Art 266 . . . 78
Art 267 . . . 15, 45, 47–60, 64, 76, A3
Art 267(1) . . . 45, 46
Art 267(2) . . . 46, 53, 55, 57, 58, A2, A3
Art 267(3) . . . 46, 53, 54, 55, 57, A2, A3
Art 277 . . . 62, 64, 78, 80, 81, 82
Art 278 . . . 69
Art 279 . . . 69
Art 288 . . . 17, 27, 30
Art 289 . . . 17, 19, 73
Art 290 . . . 17, 73
Art 294 . . . 19

Art 298(2) . . . 19
Art 340 . . . 39, 62, 64, 79, 80, 83, 85, 87, A4, A5
Treaty of Lisbon 2007 . . . 8–11, 12, 13, 14, 15, 17, 18, 24, 47, 62, 64, 70, 72, 73, 89, 120, 158, 180
Treaty of Nice 2001 . . . 5, 7, 14, 16, 59
Treaty of Paris *see* ECSC Treaty (1951)
Treaty of Rome *see* EC Treaty; EEC Treaty; Treaty on the Functioning of the European Union

French legislation

Code du Travail maritime 1926 (France) . . . 135

International legislation

European Convention on Human Rights . . . 11, 18
    Art 8 . . . 130, 147, 153

Irish legislation

Irish Consitution . . . 135, 151

Table of secondary legislation

Directives

Directive 64/221 . . . 31, 42, 144, 146, 148

Directive 68/151 . . . 35, 42

Directive 68/360 . . . 121, 137

Directive 70/50 . . . 91, 98, 99, 112, A5
Art 2 . . . 99
Art 3 . . . 99

Directive 73/148 . . . 142

Directive 76/207 . . . 31, 32, 34, 42
Art 6 . . . 34, 42

Directive 79/7 . . . 40

Directive 80/97 . . . 35

Directive 80/987 . . . 36

Directive 83/189 . . . 33

Directive 89/48 . . . 143

Directive 89/646 (Second Banking
Directive) . . . 52

Directive 90/364 . . . 121, 124, A7

Directive 90/365 . . . 121, 124, A7

Directive 90/366 . . . 121, 124, A7

Directive 90/531 . . . 39, 50

Directive 92/51 . . . 143

Directive 98/34 . . . 33

Directive 99/42 . . . 143

Directive 2003/88/EC (Working Time) . . . 77

Directive 2004/30 . . . 122

Directive 2004/38 . . . 31, 117, 118, 120, 121, 123,
125, 126–30, 131, 133, 134, 137, 138, 142, 144,
145, 147, 149, A7, A8
Recital 3 . . . 125
Art 2 . . . 119, 127
Art 2(2)(b) . . . 127
Art 3 . . . 127
Arts 4–6 . . . 125
Art 5 . . . 118, 127, 129
Art 5(1)–(2) . . . 134
Art 6 . . . 118, 127
Art 7 . . . 118, 127
Art 7(1) . . . 128, 134
Art 7(1)(a) . . . 125, A7
Art 7(1)(b)–(c) . . . 126

Art 7(1)(d) . . . 125, 126, 134
Art 7(2) . . . 125, 134
Art 7(3) . . . 133
Art 7(4) . . . 127
Art 8 . . . 129
Art 8(4) . . . 126
Art 9 . . . 129
Art 12(1)–(3) . . . 128
Art 13(1)–(2) . . . 128
Art 14 . . . 118, 122
Art 14(3) . . . 125
Art 14(4) . . . 134
Art 14(4)(b) . . . 125, A7
Art 16 . . . 129, 134
Art 22 . . . 145, 149
Art 23 . . . 129
Art 24 . . . 119, 129, 134, A7
Art 24(2) . . . 125, 126
Art 27 . . . 144, 145, 146, 147, 148, A7
Art 28 . . . 147, A7
Art 29 . . . 145, 147, 149
Art 30 . . . A7
Art 31 . . . 149, A7
Art 32 . . . 149, A7
Art 33 . . . 147
Art 35 . . . 130

Directive 2005/36 . . . 119, 143

Directive 2006/123 . . . 143–4
Art 16 . . . 144

Directive 2008/78 . . . 32

Regulations

Regulation 1612/68 . . . 131, 151
Art 3 . . . A7
Art 3(1) . . . 135
Art 4 . . . 135, 151
Art 7 . . . 136

Regulation 2790/99 . . . 172, 173

Regulation 1/2003 . . . 155, 158, 159, 160, 161,
170, 180

Regulation 330/2010 . . . 155, 157, 158, 165, 172,
173, 176, A8, A9
Art 2 . . . 172
Art 4 . . . 172, 173
Art 5 . . . 173

Table of secondary legislation

✳✳✳✳✳✳✳✳✳✳✳✳

Regulation 492/2011 . . . 118, 122, 129, 134, 135, 137, A7
    Arts 1–6 . . . 135
    Arts 7–9 . . . 136
    Art 10 . . . 129, 131

Other material

European Road Transport Agreement . . . 71

Guidance on enforcement priorities in applying Article 82 EC to abusive exclusionary conduct by dominant undertakings, 2009 . . . 193

Guidelines on the application of Article 81(3) of the Treaty, 2004 . . . 167, 170
    para 85 . . . 171
    para 105 . . . 172

Guidelines on the effect on trade concept contained in Articles 81 and 82 of the Treaty, 2004 . . . 167, A9

Notice on agreements of minor importance, 2001 . . . 157, 167, A9

Notice on co-operation within the network of competition authorities, 2004 . . . 160

Notice on the definition of the relevant market, 1997 . . . 183

Notice on the handling of complaints by the Commission
    para 16 . . . 161

Notice on immunity from fines and reduction of fines in cartel cases, 2002 . . . 164

Statute of the Court
    Art 46 . . . 83

#1

Origins, institutions, and sources of law

The examination

Some courses may cover the origins and institutions of the EU and the sources of EU law as introductory topics and exclude these matters from direct examination. Others may examine areas that typically give rise to academic debate, for instance the power relationship between the EU institutions and democracy within the institutions. You are unlikely to be asked for purely descriptive historical accounts, but may encounter questions about the development of the original economic and political aims of the EU or its evolving 'variable geometry'. Problem questions in this area are unlikely.

Key facts

- The European Economic Community (EEC) was created by the **European Community Treaty** (the **EEC Treaty** or **Treaty of Rome**), signed by the six original Member States in 1957.

- The **EEC Treaty** set up the **common market**, now known as the **internal market**, in which goods, persons, services, and capital move freely between Member States.

- The **Treaty on European Union 1992** created the European Union (EU), incorporating the EEC, together with two new policy areas, Co-operation on Justice and Home Affairs and Common Foreign and Security Policy. The EEC was renamed the 'European Community' (EC) and the **EEC Treaty** the '**EC Treaty**'.

- Over the years, further Treaties agreed by the Member States have amended the two founding Treaties, effecting changes to the institutions and law-making procedures of the EC and EU and adding new policy areas.

- From six original states, the EU has expanded to a membership of 27 and further enlargement is planned.

- The principal EU institutions are the European Council; the Council; the European Commission; the European Parliament; and the Court of Justice of the European Union.

- The **Treaty of Lisbon** amended the two founding Treaties, and replaced all references to the 'European Community' with 'European Union'. Together, the two amended Treaties (the **Treaty on the Functioning of the European Union (TFEU)** (formerly called the **EC Treaty**) and the **Treaty on European Union**) constitute the Treaties on which the EU is founded.

Origins

The European Community

The EEC

The EEC was created by the **Treaty of Rome (EEC Treaty)**, signed by France, Germany, Italy, Belgium, the Netherlands, and Luxembourg in 1957. In the preamble to the Treaty, the founding states expressed the desire to 'lay the foundations of an ever closer union among the peoples of Europe' and, through a pooling of resources, 'to preserve and strengthen peace and liberty'.

Impetus for European integration

The events leading up to the founding of the EEC can be traced back through the first half of the twentieth century, during which Europe had suffered the devastating effects of two major wars. There was a strong desire for lasting peace and, as Europe finally emerged from war, greater European political and economic cooperation were seen as the means to achieve this. After the Second World War (1939–1945), the vision of European integration moved towards reality. The political landscape had changed dramatically as the Soviet Union pursued an expansionist policy, gaining control over the Eastern European states, including the former East Germany. Amidst mutual fear and suspicion, the communist East and the capitalist West entered the period known as the Cold War. As long as Western Europe remained divided, it was vulnerable to the effects of Soviet power and expansionism.

The founding states were driven by high ideals, political motivation, and economic objectives. The cost and physical devastation of warfare had left western national economies weak. As part of a defence strategy against the Soviet threat, the USA had bolstered these economies with massive financial aid, particularly to the former West Germany, through the Marshall Plan. Then, in 1957, the **EEC Treaty** established a common market to promote across the Member States a harmonious development of economic activities, a continuous and balanced expansion, an increase in stability, and an accelerated raising of the standard of living.

First steps: ECSC Treaty, 1951

The first stages of formal European economic integration pre-date the **EEC Treaty**, going back to the adoption of the **European Coal and Steel Community Treaty 1951 (the ECSC Treaty or Treaty of Paris)**. The original blueprint for the **ECSC Treaty** was set out in the Schuman Plan of 1950. This envisaged linking the French and German coal and steel industries, under the control of a High Authority operating at a **supranational** level, in other words above and independently of the two governments. Supranational control over coal and steel production would remove national capability for armament production and reduce the likelihood of war.

The **ECSC Treaty**, signed in Paris by France, Germany, Italy, Belgium, the Netherlands, and Luxembourg, created a common market in coal and steel, regulated by four institutions, including a High Authority with decision-making powers. The **ECSC Treaty** expired in 2002, when its functions were incorporated within the **EC Treaty**.

Next steps: EEC and Euratom Treaties, 1957

The **EEC Treaty** extended economic integration beyond coal and steel, creating a **customs union** incorporating the free movement of goods between Member States and a **common customs tariff** to be applied to goods entering the EEC. The core framework was a common market, now known as the 'internal market', entailing gradual removal of barriers to trade, free movement rights for workers and the self-employed, and prohibition of anti-competitive practices. Common policies in agriculture and transport were introduced.

Alongside the **EEC Treaty**, the founding states also signed the **European Atomic Energy Community Treaty (the Euratom Treaty)**, which regulated nuclear power. The **EEC and Euratom Treaties** were signed in Rome in 1957 and are sometimes referred to, together, as the '**Treaties of Rome**'. Given its legal and economic significance, the **EEC Treaty** is frequently referred to as the '**Treaty of Rome**'.

The **EEC Treaty** set up the institutions of the EEC: the Assembly (now the European Parliament), Council, Commission, and the European Court of Justice. This framework remains in place today, although the respective institutions' functions and powers, considered presently, have evolved over the years.

The European Union

The **Treaty on European Union (TEU)**, signed at Maastricht in 1992, created the European Union (EU), a new entity incorporating the existing Communities, and amended the existing Treaties.

Revision tip

Questions requiring pure description of EC and EU origins are unlikely, but familiarization with the history will help you contextualize EU law.

Enlargement

EEC membership remained unchanged, at six states, until the UK, Denmark, and the Republic of Ireland joined in 1973. Then followed the accessions of Greece (1981) and Spain and Portugal (1986). With the reunification of Germany, East Germany was assimilated in 1990. In 1995 Austria, Finland, and Sweden joined what had by then become the EU, followed by Cyprus, the Czech Republic, Estonia, Hungary, Latvia, Lithuania, Malta, Poland, Slovakia, and Slovenia in 2004. The Union was enlarged yet further, to a membership of 27, when Romania and Bulgaria joined in 2007. Currently, Croatia are an acceding state whilst Turkey, Macedonia, Montenegro, Iceland, and Serbia are candidate countries. The other countries of the Western Balkans, Albania, Bosnia and Herzegovina, and Kosovo have been promised the prospect of EU membership and are known as potential candidates.

Development

The amending Treaties

Later Treaties amended the founding Treaties. With regard to the **EEC Treaty**, the most significant amending Treaties were the **Single European Act 1986** and the **TEU 1992**. The **Treaty of Amsterdam 1997** and the **Treaty of Nice 2001** amended both the **EC Treaty** and the **TEU**. Various Accession Treaties, adopted as new members joined the EU, made the necessary amendments to the **EC Treaty** concerning, for instance, increased membership of the EU institutions.

Single European Act 1986

The principal aim of the **Single European Act 1986 (SEA)** was to complete the internal market by removing remaining barriers to trade by the deadline of 31 December 1992. The **SEA** introduced a new 'cooperation' procedure, which enhanced the European Parliament's role in law-making, and extended EEC competencies to economic and social cohesion, research and technological development, and environmental protection.

Treaty on European Union 1992

Creation of the EU

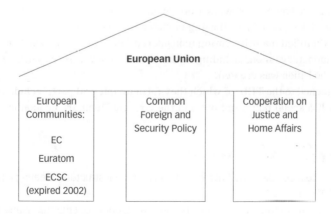

Figure 1.1 The three pillars of the EU

Development

✳✳✳✳✳✳✳✳✳✳✳

Following protracted ratification processes in some Member States, the **TEU** came into effect on 1 November 1993. The **TEU** was much more than an amending Treaty. As well as introducing changes to the **EC Treaty**, it created the EU.

The EU was set up as a three-pillar structure, comprising the three Communities (the first pillar), a Common Foreign and Security Policy (the second pillar), and Co-operation on Justice and Home Affairs (the third pillar). The three Communities, along with their governing Treaties, remained intact within the larger edifice of the EU.

This structure was devised to allow Member States to cooperate within new policy areas – Common Foreign and Security Policy and Justice and Home Affairs – outside the mechanisms of the Community Treaties. Although the second and third pillars shared the Community institutions, decision-making within these pillars was based on national autonomy, resting largely with the Council, representing the Member States. Here, the other Community institutions had a limited role in decision-making. Except in limited circumstances, the European Court of Justice had no jurisdiction in matters within the second and third pillars.

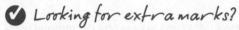 *Looking for extra marks?*

Decision-making under the second and third pillars of the **TEU** is described as **intergovernmental**, since it entailed agreement between the Member States acting as independent sovereign states. By contrast, decision-making within the Community framework had significant 'supranational' elements, for here the institutions, acting partly or entirely independently of the Member States, had a key role.

Amendments to the (renamed) EC Treaty

The **TEU** renamed the **EEC Treaty** the '**EC Treaty**', reflecting the fact that the activities of the EEC (renamed the 'EC') now went beyond its original economic goals.

The European Parliament's powers were enhanced, particularly through the introduction of the co-decision procedure allowing Parliament to veto (block) proposed legislation in certain areas. Qualified majority voting (considered later) was extended. The timetable for economic and monetary union, including a common currency, was set out. The new status of citizenship of the Union was created.

Protocols attached to the **TEU**, of which they form an integral part, included the protocols granting the UK a social policy opt-out and the UK and Denmark economic and monetary union opt-outs.

Looking for extra marks?

The **TEU** established a complex and fragmented constitutional structure, creating a Europe of 'variable geometry'. The three pillars were incorporated within the overarching new entity, the EU. The Community institutions were shared within this framework, but whilst the supranational elements of decision-making were contained entirely in the first pillar, the second and third pillar processes were intergovernmental. Complexity and fragmentation were further manifested in the opt-out protocols, giving rise to the description 'two-speed' Europe.

Treaty of Amsterdam 1997

It was intended that the **Treaty of Amsterdam** (which entered into force on 1 May 1999) would begin a process of restructuring the EU institutions in preparation for enlargement to 25 Member States. In fact, this was not achieved. Restructuring was put on hold, to be taken up later by the **Treaty of Nice**. However, this Treaty did achieve the reform of the EC legislative process, considered later.

The **Treaty of Amsterdam** moved provisions across the three-pillar structure of the EU. A new Title was inserted into the **EC Treaty**, headed 'Visas, Asylum and Immigration' and the relevant elements of the third pillar were moved here. The remaining Title in the third pillar was renamed 'Police and Judicial Co-operation in Criminal Matters'. The strictly intergovernmental character of the third pillar was being broken down, notably as the European Court of Justice and the European Parliament acquired enhanced roles under this pillar.

This transfer of provisions, together with the extension of supranational elements into previously intergovernmental areas of Union activity, seemed to herald a more integrated EU legal order. However, other provisions introducing 'closer cooperation' (later reformulated and renamed 'enhanced cooperation' by the **Treaty of Nice**) indicated movement the other way, towards further fragmentation. 'Closer cooperation' allowed Member States, using the institutions and mechanisms of the EC and EU, to cooperate more closely in areas falling within the general scope of the Treaties but which were not yet covered by EC legislation. This meant that some Member States could choose to cooperate, as a small group, in specific areas. Morcover, further opt-outs were incorporated. Whilst following a change of government the UK's social policy opt-out was no longer necessary and was repealed, the UK, Ireland, and Denmark secured opt-outs on border controls.

The **Amsterdam Treaty** renumbered all the articles of the **EC Treaty** and the **TEU**. It should be noted that all pre-Amsterdam texts, including pre-dating case law, use the pre-Amsterdam numbering.

Treaty of Nice 2001

The focus now on enlargement and the business left uncompleted by the **Treaty of Amsterdam**, the **Treaty of Nice** was signed in 2001. After rejection and then acceptance in Irish referenda in 2001 and 2002 respectively, this Treaty eventually entered into force on 1 February 2003. The **Treaty of Nice** addressed important institutional issues in preparation for the accession of ten new Member States in 2004 relating, for instance, to qualified majority voting, the co-decision procedure, and the composition of the institutions. This chapter returns to these matters presently. 'Closer cooperation' was renamed 'enhanced cooperation', the latter requiring, significantly, the participation of a minimum of only eight Member States, rather than 'a majority', as previously under the **Treaty of Amsterdam**.

Failed Constitutional Treaty

In a 'Declaration on the Future of the Union', the Nice summit called for a deeper and wider debate on the future of the EU. That call was echoed at the 2001 Laeken summit, which resolved to convene a 'Convention on the Future of Europe' to draft a Constitutional Treaty. Following considerable debate and amendment the 'Treaty establishing a Constitution for Europe' was eventually signed in Rome in October 2004. This Treaty would have replaced the founding Treaties, setting out the institutional and substantive provisions of the EU in a single document. In 2007 the Constitutional Treaty was abandoned in the face of widespread criticism and opposition, including rejection in the 2005 French and Dutch referenda.

Treaty of Lisbon 2007

Following abandonment of the Constitutional Treaty, a new amending Treaty, the **Treaty of Lisbon (the 'Reform Treaty')** was signed in December 2007. After a protracted ratification process, including rejection and then acceptance in Irish referenda of June 2008 and October 2009 respectively, the **Treaty of Lisbon** entered into force on 1 December 2009. Unlike the failed Constitutional Treaty, the **Treaty of Lisbon** did not replace but amended the **EC Treaty** and the **TEU**, though it incorporates many of the provisions of the abandoned Constitutional Treaty.

The **Treaty of Lisbon** renamed the **EC Treaty** the '**Treaty on the Functioning of the European Union' (TFEU)** and replaced all references to the 'Community' with 'Union'. The amended **TEU** and the **TFEU**, with their various protocols, now together constitute the Treaties on which the Union is founded and are the primary source of EU law. Their provisions, together with secondary legislation (regulations, directives, decisions), international agreements entered into by the EU, and the case law of the Court of Justice of the European Union make up the body of law known as **European Union Law**.

Institutional changes

The **Lisbon Treaty** introduced institutional changes, such as the elevation of the European Council to a full Union institution, the creation of new positions of President of the European Council and High Representative of the Union for Foreign Affairs and Security Policy, and the limitation of the European Parliament's maximum membership to 750. These and other changes are addressed later.

Streamlining law-making

EU law-making was streamlined through adjustments to **qualified majority voting (QMV)**, to be introduced from 2014, preventing a very small number of the larger Member States from vetoing (blocking) proposed legislation. QMV became the standard system, and was extended to further policy areas including immigration, asylum, and judicial cooperation in civil matters. Unanimity is still required in areas such as tax, foreign policy, defence, and social security.

The European Council acquired new – and controversial – powers. By unanimous vote, it can propose amendments to certain parts of the EU Treaties, with adoption following ratification by Member States. Previously, such changes could only be effected by an amending Treaty. More controversially still, the Treaty permits the European Council, again acting unanimously, to amend the Treaties so as to allow QMV to operate in certain areas previously requiring unanimity.

Legislative procedures

Co-decision (renamed the 'ordinary legislative procedure') – involving the participation of the European Commission, the Council, and the European Parliament – became the standard legislative procedure and was extended to new areas, including the free movement of **third country nationals**, economic and monetary union, and the common agricultural policy. The other legislative procedures ('special legislative procedures'), requiring decisions by the Council, and in some cases involving only consultation with Parliament, continue to apply, for instance, to areas of foreign and security policy and tax.

Role of national parliaments

National parliaments can scrutinize and submit opinions on proposed EU legislation, allowing them to ensure that **subsidiarity** is applied. Subsidiarity requires that decisions be taken as closely as possible to the citizen and that action at EU level, rather than at national, regional, or local level, is justified. If one-third of national parliaments requested it, a proposal would have to be reviewed. If a majority opposed a proposal, with the backing of the Council or the Parliament, it would have to be abandoned.

Areas of competence

The EU has **competence** (power) to adopt policies and legislation only in the areas specified in the Treaties. As specified by the **Lisbon Treaty**, the EU retains exclusive competence (decisions must be made at EU, not national, level) in certain areas, for instance the customs union and the competition rules. The EU and national governments retain joint competence in other areas, for instance agriculture and consumer protection, with new joint competencies, such as aspects of the environment and public health. National governments retain some areas of exclusive competence (with the EU having competence to coordinate activity), for instance industry, culture, and tourism.

Development

✳✳✳✳✳✳✳✳✳✳✳✳

Citizens' initiative

This allows for at least one million citizens from different Member States to directly request the Commission to initiate proposals within an area of EU competence.

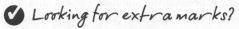 **Looking for extra marks?**

It could be argued, with justification, that the **Treaty of Lisbon** has enhanced democracy and transparency in the EU. The extension of co-decision and its renaming as the 'ordinary legislative procedure' represents both a significant conceptual development and a very tangible increase in the Parliament's role in law-making. The opportunity for national parliaments to submit opinions on legislative proposals has given them a new, formal role in the legislative process. Through the citizens' initiative, Union citizens can request the Commission to initiate proposals. The listing of areas of competence clarifies the respective powers of the EU and the Member States.

External relations

With the **Lisbon Treaty**, the EU acquired legal personality (previously held by the EC but not the EU), allowing it to conclude international agreements and join international organizations. A new High Representative of the Union for Foreign Affairs and Security Policy coordinates external policy, assisted by a new European External Action Service. The appointee is Vice-President of the Commission and chairs the Foreign Affairs Council.

Common Foreign and Security Policy

The intergovernmental character of decision-making on Common Foreign and Security Policy remained unchanged, with all action requiring the Council's unanimous approval. However, Member States or the High Representative, not the European Commission, propose initiatives. Subject to specific national defence policies, for instance on neutrality, Member States now have an obligation to assist should another Member State become the victim of armed aggression. A new 'solidarity clause' requires EU/Member State joint action should a Member State become the target of a terrorist attack or suffer a natural or man-made disaster.

Area of Freedom, Security, and Justice

All the remaining **TEU** third-pillar provisions on Justice and Home Affairs were moved to the **TFEU** into a section entitled 'Area of Freedom, Security and Justice'. Here, most new legislation is adopted by the 'ordinary legislative procedure', with QMV in the Council. The Court of Justice will gradually acquire jurisdiction and, after five years, will have jurisdiction over all matters in this area.

Justice and Home Affairs matters were extended to include common policies on asylum, immigration, and external border control, cooperation between police and judicial authorities in cross-border criminal matters, and judicial cooperation in cross-border civil matters.

✅ *Looking for extra marks?*

By moving the remaining elements of Justice and Home Affairs from the **TEU** to the **TFEU**, the **Treaty of Lisbon** dismantled what remained of the EU's three-pillar structure. More significantly still, the changes shifted much decision-making in this area from an intergovernmental basis to a European, supranational basis. Denmark, Ireland, and the UK regarded this as an unacceptable transfer of national sovereignty and negotiated opt-outs.

Human and fundamental rights

The **Lisbon Treaty** provides for the EU's accession to the **European Convention on Human Rights**, binding the Court of Justice to interpreting EU law in accordance with it. The **TEU** was amended to recognize the EU **Charter of Fundamental Rights**, giving it the same legal value as the Treaties, but with opt-outs for Poland and the UK.

Renumbering

The **Lisbon Treaty** renumbered the provisions of the **TEU** and the **EC Treaty** (now the **TFEU**). This book uses the new numbering, with reference to the old numbering only when necessary for clarity or where the context demands it.

Institutions

The principal EU institutions are the European Council; the Council; the European Commission; the European Parliament; the Court of Justice of the European Union; the European Central Bank; and the Court of Auditors. Other bodies include the Committee of the Regions, the Economic and Social Committee, and the Committee of Permanent Representatives.

European Council (Articles 15 TEU; 235–236 TFEU)

The European Council, which has a broad non–legislative role, consulting on topical political issues and defining general policy direction for the EU, comprises the Heads of State or Government of the Member States. Its meetings are known as 'European summits'.

The **Treaty of Lisbon** created the new role of President of the European Council. Elected by the European Council by qualified majority for two and a half years, the President, who is not allowed to hold national office whilst holding the Presidency, ensures the preparation and continuity of the European Council's work, in cooperation with the President of the Commission, and reports to the European Parliament. European Council meetings are held four times a year. The President of the Commission is a full member of the European Council (**Article 15 TEU**).

The new role of High Representative of the Union for Foreign Affairs and Security Policy was also created. The post-holder, elected by the European Council by qualified majority, conducts the EU's common foreign and security policy (**Article 18 TEU**).

Council (Articles 16 TEU; 237–243 TFEU)

Presidency

The Presidency of the Council is held by each Member State, in rotation, for six months. Before taking office, a Member State sets the programme for its Presidency.

Composition

The Council comprises ministers of the Member States, its membership changing according to the matter under discussion. So, for instance, if agricultural matters are under consideration, the Council comprises national Ministers of Agriculture. The General Affairs Council ensures consistency in the work of the different Council configurations. Each configuration is chaired by the relevant minister of the Member State holding the Presidency, except for the Foreign Affairs Council which, under **Treaty of Lisbon** amendments, is chaired by the High Representative of the Union for Foreign Affairs and Security Policy. Council members represent national interests. By contrast, as noted later, members of the Commission are required to act independently of national governments.

Powers

The Council has final power of decision on the adoption of secondary legislation, exercised jointly with the European Parliament where ordinary legislative procedure applies. The Council can generally act only on a Commission proposal, but can require the Commission to frame draft legislation in any specific area. The Council can delegate power to the Commission to enact regulations. Its work is prepared by the Committee of Permanent Representatives (COREPER), which considers legislative proposals drafted by the Commission and helps set the agenda for Council meetings. The Council Secretariat provides administrative support.

Voting

Voting in the Council is by unanimity, simple majority, or qualified majority, depending on the Treaty requirement for the particular matter. When unanimity is required, it can be difficult to press ahead with legislation, as any one state has power of veto (to block the legislation). For that reason, the amending Treaties have continued to extend majority voting to more areas of EU activity.

The **Treaty of Lisbon** retained unanimous voting for certain areas, such as common foreign, security and defence policy, taxation, and social security. Simple majority voting is rarely used, but Treaty amendments have gradually extended the use of qualified majority voting. QMV is required for the adoption of legislation in many areas, including most internal market measures and other areas such as the environment, agriculture, competition, consumer protection, asylum, immigration, and judicial cooperation in civil and criminal matters.

QMV currently operates as a system of weighted votes. The larger the Member State, the more votes it holds, ranging from 29 (for Germany, France, and the UK) down to three (for Malta). From the total of 345 votes distributed across the 27 Member States, a qualified majority comprises 255 votes (73.91%), provided a majority of Member States have voted in favour (for Commission proposals) or two-thirds have voted in favour (in other cases). Additionally, a member of the Council may request verification that the majority states constitute at least 62% of the EU's total population. If not, the legislation cannot be adopted.

Under **Lisbon Treaty** amendments, from 2014, a qualified majority (to be known also as a 'double majority' under a system of double majority voting (DMV)) would be reached when at least 55% of Member States agreed to a proposal (currently 15 out of 27 Member States) and these states represented at least 65% of the EU population (72% where the proposal does not emanate from the Commission or the High Representative). A blocking minority must include at least four Member States, failing which a qualified majority will be deemed attained. Between 2014 and 2017, a Member State will be able to request that a vote by qualified majority be taken according to the method applied pre-2014 (**Article 16 TEU**).

It is intended that a Council decision will set out a revised 'Ioannina' compromise, whereby a small number of Member States can delay the adoption of legislation by qualified majority, the Council being required to undertake further discussion in an attempt to address their concerns.

 ✔ *Looking for extra marks?*

Currently under QMV the distribution of votes is based loosely on Member States' population size. Over the years the definition of qualified majority and the allocation of votes have been hotly disputed, the smaller states fearing domination by the larger states and the latter often claiming that the smaller states were over-represented.

QMV creates a particular dynamic in Council decision-making. Ministers representing different national interests across different policy areas frequently seek to 'trade' their agreement in one area in return for support from other Member States in other areas.

European Commission (Articles 17 TEU; 244–250 TFEU)

Commissioners must be completely independent, neither seeking nor taking instructions from their governments, and Member States must not seek to influence them.

Appointment and removal

Commissioners are nominated by the President-elect of the Commission and the European Council followed by approval, as a body, by the European Parliament. They are appointed for a renewable five-year term. Parliament can remove the entire Commission by vote of censure but has no power to remove individual Commissioners. The Court of Justice may, on application by the Council or Commission, compulsorily retire a Commissioner for failure to perform his/her duties or for serious misconduct. Additionally, the President of the Commission can require a Commissioner to resign. The President is nominated by the European Council and elected by Parliament.

Composition

There is one Commissioner for each of the Member States.

Following **Lisbon Treaty** amendments, the number of Commissioners will equal the number of Member States until 2014, and then comprise two-thirds the number of Member States, unless the European Council were to decide otherwise (**Article 17 TFEU**). In negotiations following the Irish rejection of the **Lisbon Treaty** in 2008, the European Council stated that it would take the necessary decision to maintain the current composition of one Commissioner per Member State.

Commissioners' portfolios are allocated by the President and cover policy areas such as trade, competition, environment, and fisheries. The Commission is supported by a staff of around 25,000, based largely in Brussels, and organized into administrative departments known as Directorates-General – for instance, the Directorate-General for Competition – each headed by a Director-General. This bureaucracy is frequently referred to as 'the Commission'.

Role

The Commission acts as 'guardian' of EU law, bringing actions against Member States or individuals in breach. It formulates policy, proposes legislation, partakes in discussions on the framing of legislation by the Council and Parliament, and performs an executive role, implementing the Council's policy decisions, under delegated powers. The Commission also manages the EU's budget. The **Treaty of Lisbon** made no significant changes to the Commission's functions.

European Parliament (Articles 14 TEU; 223–234 TFEU)

Membership and functioning

The European Parliament has its seat in Strasbourg and a secretariat in Luxembourg, with certain sessions and committee meetings taking place in Brussels. Members of the European Parliament (MEPs) are directly elected in the Member States. Following the June 2009 elections, 736 MEPs were appointed, in accordance with the **Treaty of Nice**.

Under **Lisbon Treaty** amendments, by 2014 the number of MEPs will be fixed at a maximum of 750, plus the President. The European Council, with the Parliament's consent, will determine the number of MEPs and the seats allocated to Member States, on the basis of population size and 'degressive proportionality' (MEPs representing the larger Member States by population will represent more people than the smaller states), none having more than 96 nor less than 6 MEPs (**Article 14 TEU**).

Powers

Originally, Parliament's participation in the legislative process was purely advisory and consultative. With the amending Treaties, Parliament's powers increased. Notably, where the ordinary legislative procedure applies as is now the case in many policy areas, Parliament's approval must be obtained before legislation can be adopted.

Parliament exerts control over the executive through its right to approve the Commission and to dismiss the entire Commission. It also has powers of scrutiny, including the ability to question Commissioners orally or in writing, and the power to reject the annual budget. The **Treaty of Lisbon** increased Parliament's powers still further by the extension of co-decision (now ordinary legislative procedure) to more policy areas.

Revision tip

Think about the composition and powers of the Council, Commission, and Parliament and the extent to which it can be argued that a democratic deficit exists.

Court of Justice of the European Union (Articles 19 TEU; 251–257 TFEU)

The Court of Justice, the General Court (formerly known as the Court of First Instance), and the specialized courts (formerly the judicial panels) are now collectively referred to as the Court of Justice of the European Union (**Article 19 TEU**).

Court of Justice

The Court of Justice's task is to ensure that, in the interpretation and application of the Treaties, the law is observed. It has jurisdiction to give **preliminary rulings** on the interpretation of EU law under **Article 267 TFEU** and to review the legality of acts of the institutions under **Article 263 TFEU**. The Court of Justice is not bound by its own decisions, but nevertheless seeks to maintain consistency in its judgments.

The Court consists of one judge from each Member State and eight Advocates-General (A-Gs), chosen 'by common accord' of Member State governments from persons whose independence is beyond doubt and who possess the qualifications required for the highest judicial office in their respective jurisdictions. Appointments, which are scrutinized by a panel established under the **Lisbon Treaty**, including former judges of the Court of Justice and judges of national supreme courts, are for six years and are staggered to provide partial replacement every three years. A-Gs assist the Court by giving reasoned opinions. Although these do not bind the Court and are not always followed, they carry considerable weight. Where no new points of law are raised, the Court's Statute permits it to reach a determination without an A-G's submission.

The Court sits in plenary session for cases of exceptional importance; as a Grand Chamber of 13 judges when a Member State or institution that is a party to the proceedings so requests; and, in the majority of cases, in chambers of three or five judges.

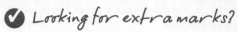

The Court of Justice has played a key role in the development of EU law, using its jurisdiction crea-tively in ground-breaking decisions, for instance in establishing the principles of direct effect and state liability, upholding the fundamental principles of the free market and furthering the rights of individuals.

General Court

The Court of First Instance (now known as the General Court) was set up under the **Single European Act 1986** to reduce the Court of Justice's workload. Since then, its jurisdiction has been extended to include most **direct actions** (annulment actions, actions for failure to act, damages actions), the power to give preliminary rulings and to hear appeals from the judi-cial panels. The General Court comprises at least one judge from each Member State and sits as a full court or in smaller chambers. One judge may act as A-G in complex cases.

Specialized courts

Judicial panels, now known as specialized courts, were established by the **Treaty of Nice**. They may be set up by the Council to hear certain classes of action at first instance. Appeal lies to the General Court and, if there is a serious risk to the consistency of EU law, the Court of Justice may exceptionally review the General Court's decision. An EU Civil Service Tribunal has been set up under these provisions to hear staff cases.

Court of Auditors

This body performs budgetary functions, auditing expenditure and producing an annual report for the European Parliament.

Economic and Social Committee and Committee of the Regions

These are advisory bodies that must be consulted on proposed legislation concerning mat-ters within their respective remits.

Sources of law

Acquis communautaire

This term is applied to the entire body of EU law, including all the forms of law described in this section.

Treaties

Following the entry into force of the **Treaty of Lisbon**, the **TEU** and the **TFEU** together constitute the Treaties on which the Union is founded and are the primary source of EU law.

Various protocols and declarations are annexed to the Treaties. Protocols are integral to the Treaties and possess Treaty status. By contrast, declarations are not binding but may inform or assist the interpretation of EU law.

Secondary legislation

The EU institutions enact secondary legislation – **regulations, directives, decisions** – under powers conferred by the Treaty. These acts of the institutions supplement Treaty provisions, many of which are framed as broad policies or principles. Following **Lisbon Treaty** amendments, a distinction is made between 'legislative acts' (adopted under legislative procedures) and 'non-legislative acts' (adopted by the Commission under delegated powers) (**Articles 289–290 TFEU**).

Regulations

Regulations are detailed forms of secondary legislation. A regulation is defined in **Article 288 TFEU** as having 'general application . . . binding in its entirety and directly applicable in all Member States'. This means that regulations apply to all governments, institutions, and individuals without the need for any national implementing legislation.

Directives

Article 288 TFEU describes a directive as 'binding as to the result to be achieved, upon each Member State to which it is addressed'. . . but leaving 'to the national authorities the choice of form and methods'. This means that Member States are required to implement directives, which are set out in general terms, through the adoption of detailed measures, normally legislation. Directives specify the deadline by which implementation must be completed.

Decisions

These are addressed to Member States or to specified individuals, for instance Commission decisions addressed to businesses concerning breaches of competition law.

Recommendations and opinions

Unlike regulations, directives, and decisions, recommendations and opinions are not legally binding.

Case law

The Court of Justice's decisions are binding on Member States, including national courts. As will be noted throughout this book, many of the Court's decisions concern the interpretation of the Treaties and secondary legislation. In formulating its judgments, the Court draws upon general principles such as human or fundamental rights, equality, **proportionality** and **legal certainty**.

General principles of law

Human and fundamental rights

The EU legal order embraces recognition of human rights. The **Lisbon Treaty** provided for the EU's accession to the **European Convention on Human Rights**, its fundamental rights constituting general principles of EU law. The amended **TEU** recognizes the EU **Charter of Fundamental Rights**, giving it the same legal value as the Treaties, but with opt-outs for Poland and the UK.

Equality

The principle of equality or non-discrimination permeates EU law and is set out, for instance, in Treaty provisions relating to equal pay for men and women in employment and non-discrimination on grounds of nationality.

Proportionality

This general principle requires that actions taken or measures adopted, whether by Member States or the EU institutions, go no further than is necessary to achieve their objective.

Legal certainty, non-retroactivity, and legitimate expectation

The concept of legal certainty incorporates the requirement that the distinction between what is lawful and unlawful should be reasonably clear. Within this general principle, **non-retroactivity** dictates that the law should not impose penalties retroactively; the principle of **legitimate expectation** requires that law or action must not breach the legitimate expectations of those who are affected by it.

International agreements entered into by the EU

These also form part of the *acquis communautaire*.

Law-making process

Legal base

Secondary legislation is adopted by the EU institutions under Treaty powers. The **legal base** of a particular legislative measure is the Treaty article conferring the power to legislate in the relevant policy area. The Treaty article forming the legal base also sets out the procedure and the voting requirements in the Council – unanimity, simple majority, or qualified majority – for the adoption of the legislation.

Legislative procedures

Ordinary legislative procedure (Articles 289, 294 TFEU)

The ordinary legislative procedure was first introduced as the co-decision procedure by the **TEU** and entails two readings of proposed legislation. At first reading, Parliament delivers its opinion to the Council, with any suggested amendments. If these are approved, the measure may be adopted. If not, at second reading, Parliament considers the Council's common position, including any proposed Council amendments which must have been adopted unanimously. If Parliament rejects the common position, the measure is not adopted. If it proposes further amendments, these are referred to the Council and Commission, which deliver their opinion. If the Council approves all the amendments, the measure can be adopted. If not, a meeting of the Conciliation Committee, comprising MEPs and Council members or their representatives, is convened. If a joint text is approved, this can be adopted. Otherwise, the measure is not adopted.

The vast majority of secondary legislation is now adopted by the ordinary legislative procedure.

Special legislative procedure (Article 298(2) TFEU)

The special legislative procedure applies in respect of specified areas provided for by the Treaties. Thus, the adoption of a regulation, directive, or decision by the Parliament with the participation of the Council (consent) or by the Council with the *participation of the Parliament* (consultation). The meaning can only really be ascertained by looking at the provision in question.

Revision Tip

Ensure that you can trace the development of the European Parliament's power in the legislative process.

Revision Tip

Online **Table of Equivalences**: you will find it helpful to refer to this table as you work through the book.

Exam question

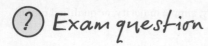

(?) Exam question

Essay question

The EU has been criticized as 'undemocratic'. Critically evaluate the accuracy of this assessment by reference to the composition of the EU institutions and their respective powers in relation to law-making within the EU.

An outline answer is available at the end of the book.

Scan here

Scan this QR code image with your mobile device to see a full answer to this question or log onto www.oxfordtextbooks.oc.uk/orc/concentrate/

#2

Supremacy, direct effect, indirect effect, and state liability

Supremacy, direct effect, indirect effect, and state liability are key concepts within the EU legal order. It would be surprising to encounter an EU law examination that did not include at least one question in this area. Problem questions typically concern individuals who are seeking to invoke EU law in the national court because it gives them better rights than any national provision. Questions may also require application of the principle of state liability, concerning damages claims by individuals against a Member State for non-implementation of a directive or other EU law infringements. Because of the particular difficulties surrounding the direct effect of directives, these are likely to figure prominently, as indeed they do in the case law. Essay questions may ask you to analyse the development of the doctrines of supremacy, direct effect, indirect effect, and state liability and the significance of the Court of Justice's activism in this area.

Overview: direct and indirect effect

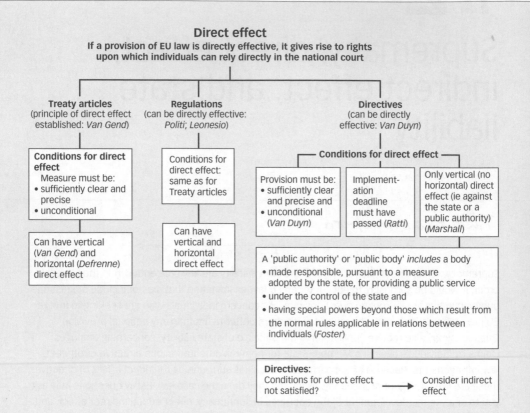

Direct effect
If a provision of EU law is directly effective, it gives rise to rights upon which individuals can rely directly in the national court

Treaty articles
(principle of direct effect established: *Van Gend*)

Conditions for direct effect
Measure must be:
- sufficiently clear and precise
- unconditional

Can have vertical (*Van Gend*) and horizontal (*Defrenne*) direct effect

Regulations
(can be directly effective: *Politi*; *Leonesio*)

Conditions for direct effect: same as for Treaty articles

Can have vertical and horizontal direct effect

Directives
(can be directly effective: *Van Duyn*)

Conditions for direct effect

Provision must be:
- sufficiently clear and precise and
- unconditional (*Van Duyn*)

Implement-ation deadline must have passed (*Ratti*)

Only vertical (no horizontal) direct effect (ie against the state or a public authority) (*Marshall*)

A 'public authority' or 'public body' *includes* a body
- made responsible, pursuant to a measure adopted by the state, for providing a public service
- under the control of the state and
- having special powers beyond those which result from the normal rules applicable in relations between individuals (*Foster*)

Directives:
Conditions for direct effect not satisfied? → Consider indirect effect

Overview: direct and indirect effect

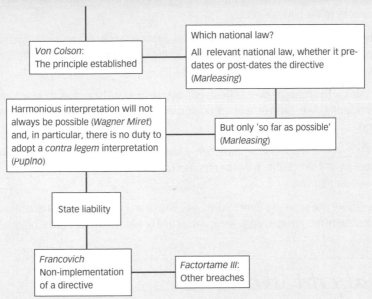

Indirect effect
National law must be interpreted in accordance with relevant EU law
Indirect effect can overcome the limitations of direct effect, notably in relation to directives

Von Colson:
The principle established

Which national law?
All relevant national law, whether it pre-dates or post-dates the directive (*Marleasing*)

Harmonious interpretation will not always be possible (*Wagner Miret*) and, in particular, there is no duty to adopt a *contra legem* interpretation (*Pupino*)

But only 'so far as possible' (*Marleasing*)

State liability

Francovich
Non-implementation of a directive

Factortame III:
Other breaches

Key facts

- The doctrine of supremacy dictates that EU law takes precedence over conflicting provisions of national law.

- If a provision of EU law is directly effective, it gives rise to rights upon which individuals can rely directly in the national court.

- Treaty articles and regulations are capable of direct effect both vertically (against the state and public bodies) and horizontally (against individuals) and are directly effective if they are sufficiently clear, precise, and unconditional.

- Directives are capable of direct effect, but only vertically. To be directly effective they must be sufficiently clear, precise, and unconditional and the implementation deadline must have passed.

- If an EU measure is not directly effective, a claimant may be able to rely on it through the application of indirect effect, which requires national law to be interpreted in accordance with relevant EU law.

- State liability gives rise to a right to damages where an individual has suffered loss because a Member State has failed to implement a directive or has committed other breaches of EU law.

Treaty of Lisbon

The **Treaty of Lisbon** amended the **EC Treaty** and renamed it the **Treaty on the Functioning of the European Union (TFEU)**, replaced all references to 'European Community' and 'Community law' with 'EU' and 'EU law' respectively, and changed the numbering of Treaty articles. Note that pre-Lisbon case law uses the previous terminology and Treaty numbering. This chapter uses the term 'EU' and the new Treaty numbering throughout, placed in brackets where they appear in the case summaries.

'EU law'

Treaty provisions, secondary legislation (regulations, directives, decisions), international agreements made by the EU, and the case law of the Court of Justice make up the body of law known as 'EU law'.

Revision tip

Remember: with the entry into force of the **Lisbon Treaty**, the EU is founded on the **TEU** and the **TFEU**.

Sovereignty and the supremacy of EU law

Sovereignty

Originally, it was thought that the founding Treaties, like other international treaties, bound Member States with respect to international obligations, but allowed them to exercise **national sovereignty** internally, determining the domestic legal effects of their international obligations.

Early in the European Community's development, the Court of Justice overturned this view. In *Van Gend en Loos v Nederlandse Administratie der Belastingen* (Case 26/62) the Court declared that 'The Community constitutes a new legal order in international law, for whose benefit the states have limited their sovereign rights, albeit within limited fields'. *Costa v ENEL* (Case 6/64) reiterated this statement: 'By contrast with ordinary international Treaties, the **EEC Treaty** has created its own legal system which became an integral part of the legal systems of the Member States'. By creating the Community, Member States had limited their sovereign rights and, within the areas covered by the Treaties, transferred powers to the Community. The corollary of the sovereignty of the Community (now EU) legal order is the **supremacy** of EU law.

Doctrine of supremacy

There is no express Treaty reference to supremacy. The Court of Justice has developed this doctrine, holding repeatedly that supremacy is implied in the Treaty. **Article 4 TEU** (ex **Article 10 EC**) requires Member States to take all measures to ensure fulfilment of Treaty obligations and to abstain from measures that could jeopardize Treaty objectives. Supremacy dictates that EU law takes precedence over conflicting provisions of national law.

....

Costa v ENEL (Case 6/64) [1964] ECR 585

The Court of Justice considered whether national legislation post-dating the Treaty and conflicting with it should take precedence. The Court affirmed that, by establishing the Community, Member States accepted a permanent limitation on their sovereign rights, creating a body of law binding their nationals and themselves. The integration of [EU] law into national law makes it impossible for subsequent national law to take precedence over [EU] law.

. . . .

The Court went further in *Internationale Handelsgesellschaft GmbH* (Case 11/70), holding that [EU] law takes precedence over all forms of national law, including national constitutional law. Moreover, national courts must set aside national provisions that conflict with [EU] law.

. . . .

Amministrazione delle Finanze dello Stato v Simmenthal (Case 106/77) [1978] ECR 629

An Italian magistrates' court asked whether it should disapply national legislation which the Court of Justice had already found to violate [EU] law. At that time, only the Italian Constitutional Court could declare national provisions invalid. The Court of Justice held that national courts must apply [EU] law in its entirety. Any conflicting national law must be set aside, whether prior or subsequent to the [EU] rule.

. . . .

National procedural rules must not interfere with an EU law right, even where that right has not been definitively established.

. . . .

R v Secretary of State for Transport, ex parte Factortame Ltd (II) (Case 213/89) [1990] ECR 1-2433

Spanish fishermen's claim that the UK **Merchant Shipping Act 1988** breached [EU] law was the subject of a reference to the Court of Justice (*Factortame I*). In *Factortame II* the applicants sought an interim injunction in the English court setting aside the relevant provisions, pending the outcome of *Factortame I*. Under the UK doctrine of **parliamentary sovereignty**, the English court had no power to suspend an Act of Parliament. The Court of Justice held that the full effectiveness of [EU] law would be impaired if a national rule could prevent the grant of interim relief in relation to [EU] rights. The national court must set aside that rule.

. . . .

Incorporation of EU law

The national incorporation of EU law depends broadly on whether a Member State embraces a monist or dualist view of the relationship between international and national law. In **monist systems**, such as the French system, EU law becomes binding from ratification, with no need for incorporating measures. In **dualist systems**, international law is not binding internally until it is incorporated by domestic statute. In the UK's dualist system EU law is incorporated by the **European Communities Act (ECA) 1972. Section 2(1)** provides:

All such rights, powers, liabilities, obligations and restrictions . . . created or arising by or under the Treaties . . . are without further enactment to be given legal effect . . .

National recognition of supremacy

Supremacy would be meaningless without acceptance by national courts. In general, the supremacy of EU law is now recognized across the Member States. In the UK, the relevant provision is **s 2(4) ECA 1972**:

> . . . any enactment passed or to be passed . . . shall be construed and have effect subject to the foregoing provisions of this section . . .

The supremacy debate in the UK has centred around two different views of **s 2(4)**. Are the courts simply required to construe national law, so far as possible, to be consistent with EU law, or to give priority to EU law in cases of conflict? Lord Bridge's view in *Factortame II* is thought to represent the current UK position:

> Under the terms of the **1972 Act** it has always been clear that it is the duty of a UK court, when delivering final judgment, to override any rule of national law found to be in conflict with any directly enforceable rule of [EU] law . . .

Through the doctrines of direct effect, indirect effect, and state liability, the Court of Justice has created a framework of principles through which supremacy is accorded to EU law.

Direct effect

Distinguishing 'direct applicability' and 'direct effect'

Directly applicable (or 'self-executing') provisions of EU law are part of national law and automatically binding, without further enactment. Regulations are directly applicable and of general application (**Article 288 TFEU**). They are automatically incorporated into the national legal order. Similarly, Treaty provisions are directly applicable. Their national validity was established through ratification of the Treaties. By contrast, directives are not directly applicable, since they require implementation into national law.

If a provision of EU law has **direct effect**, individuals (natural persons and businesses) can enforce it in the national court.

Revision tip

Always explain the meaning of 'direct effect'. You could use this definition.

Directly applicable EU law is not necessarily directly effective, but provisions that are not directly applicable (ie provisions of directives) are capable of direct effect. Whilst any provision of EU law is capable of direct effect, this is not automatic. Direct effect is subject to the conditions laid down by the Court of Justice. Confusingly in the past, 'directly applicable' has been used by some UK courts and the Court of Justice to mean 'directly effective', though this now occurs less frequently. This chapter uses the current generally accepted convention, using 'directly effective' to mean EU law which is directly enforceable by individuals in national courts.

The principle of direct effect is not contained in the Treaties but has been developed by the Court of Justice. Treaty articles, regulations, decisions, and directives are capable of direct effect.

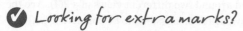 **Looking for extra marks?**

Direct effect is especially important where a Member State has failed to meet its obligation to implement an EU measure or where the implementation is partial or defective. This relates, in particular, to directives.

Treaty articles

Creation of the principle of direct effect

In *Van Gend* the Court of Justice created the principle of direct effect and held that Treaty articles are capable of direct effect.

Van Gend en Loos v Administratie der Belastingen (Case 26/62) [1963] ECR 1

Van Gend brought proceedings in the Dutch court seeking refund of a customs duty charged on its import of ureaformaldehyde from Germany into the Netherlands, claiming that the duty infringed an **EC Treaty** provision (now **Article 30 TFEU**) concerning the free movement of goods. The national court asked the Court of Justice whether Member States' nationals may, on the basis of a Treaty article, enforce rights before the national court. It was argued that claims concerning Member States' infringements of [EU] law could be brought only in enforcement proceedings by the Commission or other Member States, directly in the Court of Justice. The Court disagreed, holding that the Treaty is not only an agreement creating obligations between Member States. EU law imposes obligations upon individuals and confers on them legal rights. [**Article 30**] was capable of creating 'direct effects in the legal relations between the Member States and their citizens'. Direct effect not only provided a mechanism for the enforcement of individuals' [EU] rights but also an additional means of supervision of Member States' compliance with [EU] obligations.

✔ **Looking for extra marks?**

The doctrines of direct effect and supremacy are immensely significant. Together, they require national courts to apply EU law at the suit of individuals (provided the necessary conditions are met), in priority over any conflicting provisions of national law. National courts must disapply national measures that conflict with directly effective provisions of EU law.

Conditions for direct effect

In *Van Gend*, the Court of Justice then moved on to consider the direct effect of the Treaty article in question.

Van Gend contd

The Court declared that [**Article 30**] contained a clear and unconditional prohibition whose implementation required no legislative intervention by Member States. The fact that Member States were the subject of this negative obligation did not mean that individuals could not benefit from it. It followed from the spirit, general scheme, and wording of the Treaty that [**Article 30**] was directly effective, creating individual rights which national courts must protect.

This statement of the defining characteristics of directly effective Treaty articles was applied by the Court of Justice in numerous subsequent decisions. These provided an early formulation of the conditions to be satisfied: the measure must be sufficiently clear and precise and unconditional and its implementation must not be dependent upon any implementing measure. In its developing case law, the Court of Justice applied the conditions increasingly loosely, relaxing and eventually disregarding the third condition. In *Defrenne*, for instance, it was argued that the former **Article 119 EC** (now **Article 157 TFEU**) could not be directly effective because it could not be fully implemented without [EU] and national measures defining its scope.

Defrenne v Sabena (Case 43/75) [1976] ECR 455

Defrenne, who had worked as an air hostess for the Belgian airline Sabena, sought to rely on [**Article 157**] in an equal pay claim against her former employer. This provision requires Member States to uphold the principle of equal pay for equal work for men and women. The Court of Justice recognized that the complete implementation of this aim, in relation to both direct and indirect discrimination, may involve the adoption of national or [EU] measures providing elaboration of the criteria to be applied. Nonetheless, the provision was held capable of judicial enforcement in cases of direct discrimination.

Accordingly, to be directly effective, a Treaty article must be sufficiently clear, precise, and unconditional.

Vertical and horizontal direct effect of Treaty provisions

In *Van Gend* the Court of Justice held that Treaty provisions can be invoked by individuals against the state, in other words they can have **vertical direct effect**. However, could Treaty articles be invoked horizontally, by an individual against another individual?

This question, unresolved in *Van Gend*, was addressed in *Defrenne*. The Court of Justice's finding was unequivocal: 'the prohibition on discrimination between men and women applies not only to the action of public authorities, but also extends to all agreements which are intended to regulate paid labour collectively, as well as contracts between individuals'. The principle that Treaty provisions are capable of **horizontal direct effect** (as well as **vertical direct effect**) was established.

Since **Van Gend** and **Defrenne** numerous Treaty articles have been held to be vertically and horizontally directly effective, including provisions establishing the fundamental principles of the EU internal market. These are explored later: **Articles 28, 29 EC** (now **Articles 34, 35 TFEU**) (free movement of goods); **Articles 39, 43, 49** (now **Articles 45, 49, 56 TFEU**) (free movement of workers and rights of establishment and to provide services); **Articles 81, 82** (now **Articles 101, 102 TFEU**) (competition law).

Revision tip

Always explain the meaning of 'vertical' and 'horizontal' direct effect. Refer to **Van Gend** and **Defrenne**.

Regulations

Article 288 TFEU sets out the defining characteristics of **regulations**: 'A regulation shall have general application. It shall be binding in its entirety and directly applicable'. As already indicated, 'direct applicability' denotes the automatic incorporation of a measure into the national system, without the need for further enactment. Additionally, regulations are capable of vertical and horizontal direct effect, subject to the same conditions as are applied to Treaty articles (*Politi v Italian Ministry of Finance* (Case 43/71); *Leonesio v Italian Ministry of Agriculture* (Case 93/71)).

Directives

Direct effect

Unlike Treaty articles and regulations, **directives** are not directly applicable, but require **implementation** by Member States. This means that they must be incorporated into national law. Originally, it was believed that directives could not be directly effective, since a directive 'shall be binding as to the result to be achieved, upon each Member State to which it is addressed, but shall leave to the national authorities the choice of form and methods' (**Article 288 TFEU**).

 ✔ *Looking for extra marks?*

Article 288 appears to suggest that directives are not intended to operate as law within national systems, since that is the role envisaged for the relevant national implementing measures. Directives are addressed to Member States and seem not to affect individuals directly. They were widely seen as giving Member States broad discretion in implementation, being binding only as to the result to be achieved and insufficiently precise to fulfil the **Van Gend** criteria.

Despite these factors, the Court of Justice hinted in *Grad v Finanzamt Traunstein* (Case 9/70) and confirmed in *Van Duyn* that directives can have direct effect.

Van Duyn v Home Office (Case 41/74) [1974] 1337

Van Duyn, a Dutch national, challenged the UK immigration authorities' decision to refuse her entry on public policy grounds. She wished to come to the UK to work for the Church of Scientology, which the UK regarded as socially harmful. Under **Directive 64/221** (now incorporated into **Directive 2004/38**) any restriction of free movement on public policy grounds must be based exclusively on the individual's personal conduct. Van Duyn argued that her membership of the Church of Scientology did not constitute 'personal conduct' and, since the UK had not implemented **Directive 64/221**, she sought to rely on this directive in the English court. The Court of Justice held that Van Duyn could invoke the Directive before the national court, thus establishing the principle that directives are capable of direct effect.

Van Duyn established that, to be directly effective, directives must be sufficiently clear, precise, and unconditional. Later, in *Pubblico Ministero v Ratti* (Case 148/78) one further condition was applied. A Member State's obligation to implement becomes absolute only when the time limit for implementation has expired. A directive cannot be directly effective until its implementation deadline has passed.

 **Looking for extra marks?**

It would be unfair to permit a directive to be invoked against a Member State until its obligation to implement had become absolute. By the same token, it would be unfair to allow a Member State to rely on its failure to implement a directive to escape obligations arising under it.

Vertical and horizontal direct effect

Van Duyn, concerning a claim against the UK authorities, confirmed that directives can have vertical direct effect, but the question remained as to their potential horizontal direct effect. Can an individual rely on a directive against another individual? *Marshall* provided the answer.

Marshall v Southampton & South West Hampshire Area Health Authority (Case 152/84) [1986] ECR 723

Marshall sought to rely on the **Equal Treatment Directive 76/207** to challenge, as discriminatory, her employer's compulsory retirement policy. Although her claim was vertical, since the Health Authority was held to be part of the state (though it acted here in the capacity of an employer), the Court of Justice considered the issue of horizontal direct effect of directives. It held that directives can only be invoked vertically, against the state or a public authority.

Direct effect
****

The Court of Justice has been firm in reiterating this finding in later cases, notably in *Paolo Faccini Dori v Recreb Srl* (Case C-91/92).

> ### Revision Tip
> Directives: considering direct effect? Explain and discuss the conditions, citing the authorities. Problem questions: apply the conditions to the facts.

✔ Looking for extra marks?

The Court's refusal to permit directives to be invoked horizontally is frequently criticized as anomalous and unfair. In the employment context, for instance, individuals employed by the state or a public body can invoke rights under a directive against their employer, whilst those working for private employers cannot.

The Court's response to criticism is placed within the context of the EU legal order. This requires rights under directives to be enshrined in national implementing measures, upon which claimants can rely in national courts. Moreover, only Member States, not individuals, should be held accountable for a state's failure to implement directives.

Werner Mangold v Rudiger Helm (Case C-144/04) is seen to complicate things in this regard. In this case the Court appeared to provide for the horizontal direct effect of a directive (**2000/78**) even before the expiration of the transposition period. However, closer consideration of the case reveals that the horizontal direct effect allowed was based upon the underlying fundamental principles of EU law (non-discrimination). Whilst questions remain, it is clear from *Mangold* and subsequent case law (*Seda Kucukdeveci v Swedex GmbH & Co KG* (Case C-555/07)) that the basic position that directives are incapable of horizontal direct effect remains.

Whilst still maintaining this view, the Court of Justice has mitigated its harsh effects by creating the doctrines of indirect effect and state liability. The Court has also defined the scope of 'vertical' claims broadly, through a generous interpretation of 'public body'.

Broad interpretation of 'public body'

Whilst in many cases 'the state' is identified without difficulty, the meaning of 'public authority' or 'public body' is less clear. The point is crucial for claimants, since a finding that a claim is horizontal precludes absolutely direct reliance on a directive. *Foster* addressed the scope of 'public body'.

....

Foster v British Gas (Case C-188/89) [1990] ECR I-3133

Foster sought to rely on the **Equal Treatment Directive 76/207** to challenge her employer's different compulsory retirement ages for men and women. Considering the nature of the defendant, British Gas, the Court of Justice held that entities against which a directive can be invoked include

'. . . a body, whatever its legal form, which has been made responsible, pursuant to a measure adopted by the State, for providing a public service under the control of the state and has for that purpose special powers beyond those which result from the normal rules applicable in relations between individuals'.

Foster provides a three-limbed test for 'public body', or 'emanation of the state': (1) a body made responsible by the state for providing a public service; (2) under state control; (3) with special powers for that purpose, beyond those normally applicable between individuals. The test refers to those bodies that are 'included' within the scope of 'public body', so appears not to be intended as a legal definition, though bodies that satisfy all three elements clearly qualify. Other entities could well qualify as public bodies too. Indeed, in *NUT and Others v The Governing Body of St Mary's Church of England (Aided) Junior School and Others [1997]*, Schiemann LJ rightly drew attention to the often misunderstood point that it was clear '... from the wording of the Court's judgment in *Foster* ... that the formula there used was not intended to be an exclusive formula'.

In *Foster*, the Court of Justice referred to previous decisions indicating that directives can be invoked against tax authorities (*Becker v Hauptzollamt Münster-Innenstadt* (Case 8/81)), local or regional authorities (*Fratelli Costanzo v Comune di Milano* (Case 103/88)), authorities responsible for public order and safety (*Johnston v RUC* (Case 222/84)), and public health authorities (*Marshall*).

Revision tip

Direct effect of directives? Consider the wide scope of 'public body'.

Revision tip

Problem questions: apply *Foster* and associated authorities to the facts ensuring that the non-exclusivity of the *Foster* test is recognized.

'Incidental' effect of directives

On occasion, the Court of Justice has accorded 'incidental' effect to directives, notably in actions between private parties where one party has relied on a directive to challenge successfully the applicability of national legislation, resulting in an incidental adverse impact on the other party. Such cases are rare. Most are based on **Directive 83/189** (replaced by **Directive 98/34**) concerning the notification of national technical standards to the Commission (for instance *CIA Security International SA v Signalson SA* (Case C-194/94) and *Unilever Italia SpA v Central Food SpA* (Case C-443/98)). Whilst the Court has implicitly allowed horizontal direct effect in these cases, it has stressed that there is no departure from the basic position that directives are incapable of horizontal direct effect (*Unilever*).

Indirect effect

The principle established

By maintaining steadfastly that directives are not capable of horizontal direct effect, the Court of Justice has created apparently arbitrary distinctions, for instance in the employment context. This was brought into sharp focus by two cases decided shortly before *Marshall*, *Von Colson* and *Harz v Deutsche Tradax GmbH* (Case 79/83). In both cases, the women claimants, whose job applications had been rejected, sought to invoke **Article 6 of the Equal Treatment Directive 76/207**. In *Von Colson,* the claim was vertical, against the German prison service. In *Harz* the claim was horizontal, against Deutsche Tradax, a private company. The horizontal/vertical distinction was starkly presented. The Court of Justice created a novel solution in *Von Colson.*

....

Von Colson and Kamman v Land Nordrhein-Westfalen (Case 14/83) [1984] ECR 1891

The German court had found that sex discrimination had occurred but that national law limited compensation to the reimbursement of travel expenses. **Article 6 of Directive 76/207** requires Member States to introduce measures allowing individuals to pursue sex discrimination claims by judicial process. The Court of Justice held that the measures must be 'sufficiently effective to achieve the objective of the directive' and that the national provision would not satisfy this requirement. However, **Article 6** was not sufficiently precise to be directly effective. Nonetheless, Member States must, under (former) **Article 5 EC** (now **Article 4 TFEU**) take all appropriate measures to fulfil their [EU] obligations. The national court must interpret the national law in the light of the wording and purpose of the Directive.

....

This is the principle of **indirect effect**: national law must be interpreted in accordance with relevant EU law.

Revision tip

Always explain the meaning of 'indirect effect'. You could use this definition.

✓ *Looking for extra marks?*

Indirect effect is a vitally important principle for individuals who cannot rely directly on EU law either because the relevant provision is not sufficiently clear, precise, and unconditional or, more commonly in practice, because their claim is horizontal and concerns rights contained in a directive.

Which national law?

The national legislation in *Von Colson* and *Harz* had been adopted to implement **Directive 76/207**. Neither judgment determined whether indirect effect must be applied to national law that is not intended to perform this function, including national provisions pre-dating a directive. *Marleasing* addressed these issues.

⋯⋯⋯

Marleasing SA v La Comercial Internacional de Alimentación SA (Case C-106/89) [1990] ECR I-4135

Certain provisions of Spanish company law conflicted with the **Company Law Directive 68/151**, which Spain had not implemented. The parties were private companies and so, on the basis of **Marshall**, the Directive did not have direct effect. As in **Von Colson**, the Court of Justice referred to Member States' duty under the Treaty to ensure the fulfilment of [EU] obligations. National courts must, as far as possible, interpret national law, whether adopted before or after a directive, in the light of the wording and purpose of the directive.

⋯⋯⋯

Marleasing confirmed that indirect effect has wider scope than *Von Colson* had made apparent. It applies to both pre- and post-dating national legislation and, by implication, also to national legislation not intended to implement EU law. On the other hand, the judgment envisages limits to the duty of consistent interpretation, since national courts must interpret national law in accordance with EU law only 'so far as possible'. *Wagner Miret* recognized the limits.

⋯⋯⋯

Wagner Miret v Fondo de Garantira Salaria (Case C-334/92) [1993] ECR I-6911

The Court of Justice accepted that Spanish provisions relating to a compensation scheme for workers, but not senior managers, made redundant on their employers' insolvency, could not be interpreted in line with **Directive 80/97** to allow senior management staff entitlement to the scheme's benefits under national law.

⋯⋯⋯

In particular, indirect effect does not extend to *contra legem* **interpretations**. A national court has no duty to interpret national provisions against their clear meaning (*Pupino* (Case C-105/03)).

Revision tip

Problem questions: is there national legislation and a directive? Can the national provisions be interpreted in line with the directive and why?

✅ Looking for extra marks?

It is frequently suggested that, by creating indirect effect, the Court of Justice gave directives horizontal direct effect 'by the back door'. This argument certainly has some force. However, *Marleasing* established that indirect effect has limitations, since the duty of consistent interpretation is not absolute. A national court is obliged to interpret national law in line with EU law only 'so far as possible'. As such, as *Wagner Miret* recognized, other remedies exist to fill this lacuna.

State liability

Overcoming the limitations of direct and indirect effect

Clearly, the limitations of direct effect and indirect effect, especially in relation to directives, can have a significant impact on individuals' ability to benefit from EU law rights. The Court of Justice confronted these shortcomings in *Francovich*, developing a third principle, **state liability**. This provides a right to damages where a Member State has breached EU law, causing loss to the applicant.

Francovich: the principle established

Francovich established the principle of state liability. Here the applicants, who had been made redundant when their employer became insolvent, could not rely directly or indirectly on a directive which they claimed afforded them rights.

....

Francovich and Bonifaci v Republic of Italy (Cases C-6/90 & C-9/90) [1991] ECR I-5357

Directive 80/987 required Member States to ensure that schemes were in place to guarantee funds covering unpaid wages when employees were made redundant on their employers' insolvency. Italy had failed to implement the Directive, so no scheme had been set up. The applicants, who were owed wages in these circumstances, sought to rely on **Directive 80/987** to claim compensation from the Italian state. The Court of Justice held that the relevant provisions were insufficiently clear to be directly effective. However, the full effectiveness of [EU] law would be impaired if individuals could not obtain redress when their rights were infringed by a state's breach of [EU] law. Moreover, under **Article 5 EC** (now **Article 4 TEU**) Member States must take all appropriate measures to fulfil their [EU] law obligations. Consequently, they must make good any loss or damage caused to individuals through their breaches of [EU] law.

....

Thus, the Court of Justice established the principle of state liability. Italy, in failing to implement **Directive 80/897**, had not fulfilled its Treaty obligations. Francovich, who had suffered loss as a result, could bring proceedings directly against the state.

Damages for non-implementation of a directive: the conditions

The individual's right to damages is, however, subject to conditions.

....

Francovich contd

The Court of Justice declared that the conditions attached to a right to damages depend upon the nature of the breach of [EU] law. Where a Member State fails to implement a directive, there is a right to damages provided three conditions are satisfied:

- the result prescribed by the directive entails the grant of rights to individuals;
- it must be possible to identify the content of those rights from the directive; and
- there must be a causal link between the Member State's failure and the loss suffered by the individual.

Revision tip

Remember the three *Francovich* conditions so that you can set them out and (for problem questions) apply them.

Francovich left a number of questions unresolved. It was unclear whether damages would be available where a state's breach arose not from non-implementation but from incorrect or incomplete implementation, or indeed from any other kind of infringement. *Brasserie du Pêcheur* and *Factortame III* provided clarification.

Brasserie du Pêcheur and *Factortame III*: other kinds of breach

Whereas *Francovich* involved non-implementation of a directive, *Brasserie du Pêcheur* and *Factortame III* concerned the adoption and retention, by Germany and the UK respectively, of national legislation that infringed the Treaty.

Brasserie du Pêcheur v Germany and R v Secretary of State for Transport, ex parte Factortame Ltd and Others (Joined Cases C-46 & 48/93) [1996] ECR I-1029

Brasserie du Pêcheur, a French brewery, had been prevented from exporting its beer to Germany because of German 'beer purity' legislation imposing strict content and labelling requirements. *Factortame III* concerned the **Merchant Shipping Act 1988**, which prevented the applicants, Spanish fishermen, from fishing in UK territorial waters. The Court of Justice had already found that the legislation breached Treaty provisions on the free movement of goods (the 'beer purity' laws) and the right of establishment (the **1988 Act**). The applicants sought damages for their losses.

The Court of Justice held that the right of individuals to rely on directly effective Treaty provisions before national courts is only a minimum guarantee, in itself insufficient to ensure the complete implementation of the Treaty. The Court pointed out that, in the absence of direct effect, *Francovich* provides a right to damages where a Member State has failed to implement a directive. The Court reasoned that individuals should also be able to obtain redress in the event of a state's direct infringement of [an EU] provision. It would be irrelevant which organ of the state was responsible for the breach – the legislature, judiciary, or executive.

Damages for other breaches: the conditions

The Court then specified the conditions under which a right to reparation would arise.

....

Brasserie du Pêcheur and Factortame III contd

Reiterating its **Francovich** statement, the Court declared that the conditions under which a Member State's liability gives rise to a right to reparation depend on the nature of the breach. Where [EU] law allowed Member States a wide discretion, as in the present case, a right to damages would arise, provided three conditions were satisfied:

- the rule of law infringed must be intended to confer rights on individuals;
- the breach must be sufficiently serious; and
- there must be a direct causal link between the breach and the damage sustained.

The 'decisive test' for a 'sufficiently serious breach' is whether the Member State has 'manifestly and gravely disregarded the limits on its discretion'. In its assessment, the court may take a number of factors into account. These are the 'clarity and precision of the rule breached, the measure of discretion left by that rule to the national or [EU] authorities, whether the infringement and the damage caused was intentional or involuntary, whether any error of law was excusable or inexcusable, the fact that the position taken by [an EU] institution may have contributed towards the omission, and the adoption or retention of national measures or practices contrary to [EU] law'.

....

When *Factortame III* returned to the House of Lords, that court, applying the conditions, decided that the adoption and retention of the **Merchant Shipping Act** was a sufficiently serious breach by the UK, since it was an infringement of clear and unambiguous [EU] provisions.

Subsequently in *Dillenkofer v Germany* (Cases C-178–179, 188–190/94) the Court of Justice held that non-implementation of a directive amounted, in itself, to a sufficiently serious breach.

> *Revision tip*
>
> Remember the *Factortame III* conditions and the factors indicating a 'sufficiently serious breach'.

Expansion of state liability

BT established that liability can arise as a result of incorrect implementation of a directive. Here, however, the breach was not sufficiently serious and there was no right to damages.

....

R v HM Treasury, ex parte British Telecommunications (Case C-392/93) [1996] ECR I-1631

The UK had implemented **Directive 90/531**, but incorrectly. BT, which claimed it had suffered loss as a result, sought damages from the UK. The Court of Justice found that there was no right to damages. The UK's error was excusable because the provisions of the Directive were unclear.

....

As indicated in *Factortame III,* liability can arise from acts of the national executive and judicial decisions, as well as from acts of the legislature. *Hedley Lomas* concerned an administrative act.

....

R v Ministry of Agriculture, Fisheries and Food, ex parte Hedley Lomas (Ireland) Ltd (Case C-5/94) [1996] ECR I-2553

The Ministry had refused licences for the export of live animals to Spain for slaughter, claiming that Spanish slaughterhouses did not comply with [EU] law. The Court of Justice held that the Ministry acted, without justification, in breach of Treaty provisions on the free movement of goods. This infringement constituted a sufficiently serious breach by the UK and there was a right to damages.

....

Köbler extended state liability to a decision of a court of last instance.

....

Köbler v Austria (Case C-224/01) [2003] ECR I-1039

Köbler, an Austrian university professor, had been refused a length-of-service pay increment because he had not completed the requisite 15 years' service in Austrian universities. He claimed that the refusal infringed [EU] free movement provisions. The national court had found the refusal to be justified. Köbler argued that this court had wrongly interpreted [EU] law and brought a damages action against Austria. The Court of Justice, finding that the national court's interpretation of [EU] law was incorrect, held that an erroneous interpretation of [EU] law by a court of last instance can give rise to state liability, though in this case the breach was not sufficiently serious.

....

Köbler established liability in cases of 'intentional fault and serious misconduct' by a court of last instance. More recently in *Traghetti del Mediterraneo SpA v Italy* (Case C-173/03), the Court of Justice appeared to extend liability somewhat further by declaring that it could not rule out liability for damage caused by 'manifest errors' of interpretation of [EU] law by a court of last instance.

✔️ Looking for extra marks?

In *Bergaderm* (Case C-352/98P) the Court of Justice aligned the principles relating to state liability and EU liability, reiterating its declarations in *Factortame III*. *Bergaderm*, which concerned a claim under **Article 288 EC** (now **Article 340 TFEU**), is considered later.

Procedure and remedies in national courts

National procedural autonomy

Although direct effect, indirect effect, and state liability are immensely significant for the protection of individuals' EU law rights in national courts, the full effectiveness of these remedies depends upon national procedural rules which, in principle, fall outside the Court of Justice's jurisdiction. The Court has accepted the principle of national procedural autonomy in designating the courts having jurisdiction and in determining procedural rules.

At the same time, it has imposed limits on this autonomy, insisting that the principles of effectiveness and equivalence be applied in national proceedings concerning EU law.

Effectiveness and equivalence

'Effectiveness' dictates that national procedural rules must not render the exercise of EU law rights impossible or excessively difficult. 'Equivalence' requires national procedural rules and remedies in EU law actions to be no less favourable than those applying to similar domestic law actions. Unsurprisingly, the application of these principles has frequently proved difficult. Initially, the Court of Justice adopted an interventionist approach, holding that particular national rules did not comply. More recently, it has taken a more cautious, case-by-case approach, acknowledging that national courts alone have intimate knowledge of national procedural rules.

Application of the principles

The 'effectiveness' and 'equivalence' tests have been applied, in particular, to limitation periods and the level of damages awards. The Court of Justice has held that national time limits for bringing actions are 'reasonable' and compatible with EU law only if they do not make it excessively difficult or impossible for individuals to rely on EU rights.

· ·

Emmott v Minister for Social Welfare (Case C-208/90) [1991] ECR I-4269

The claim, based upon Ireland's failure correctly to implement **Directive 79/7** on equal treatment in social security, was brought outside the national three-month time limit. The Court of Justice held that a defaulting Member State may not rely on an individual's delay in bringing proceedings to protect rights conferred by a directive. Moreover, the time limit could not begin to run until the directive had been properly implemented.

· ·

Following *Emmott*, the Court of Justice has looked for evidence that the particular circumstances of the case will lead to an unjust result. For instance, in *Levez v Jennings* (Case C-326/96) the Court did not criticize the national two-year limitation applied in sex discrimination cases. However, it held that it would be incompatible with the principle of effectiveness to permit an employer to rely on the rule in the particular circumstances of that case. Unfortunately, this case-by-case approach is not conducive to legal certainty.

Factortame III makes clear that the principle of effectiveness must also be applied to damages awards. The reparation must be 'commensurate with the loss or damage sustained so as to ensure the effective protection of [individuals'] rights'. Applying this principle in *Marshall*, the Court of Justice had held that the statutory ceiling for damages under the **Sex Discrimination Act 1975** prevented full and effective compensation for Mrs Marshall's loss and was incompatible with [EU] law.

Case	Facts	Principle
Van Gend en Loos v Nederlandse Administratie der Belastingen (Case 26/62) [1963] ECR 1	Challenge to an increased customs duty as breaching an EC Treaty provision concerning the free movement of goods (now 30 TFEU).	'The Community constitutes a new legal order in international law, for whose benefits the states have limited their sovereign rights, albeit within limited fields'.
Costa v ENEL (Case 6/64) [1964] ECR 585	Challenge to Italian legislation.	EU law takes precedence over post-dating national legislation that conflicts with it.
Internationale Handelsgesellschaft GmbH (Case 11/70) [1970] ECR 1125	[EU] levies claimed to be contrary to the German constitution.	EU law takes precedence over all national law, including national constitutional law.
Amministrazione delle Finanze dello Stato v Simmenthal (Case 106/77) [1978] ECR 629	Should a national court disapply national provisions that violate [EU] law?	Any conflicting national law must be set aside, whether prior or subsequent to the EU rule.
R v Secretary of State for Transport, ex parte Factortame Ltd (II) (Case 213/89) [1990] ECR 1–2433	Application for an interim injunction.	The effectiveness of EU law would be impaired if a national rule could prevent the grant of interim relief in relation to EU law rights. The rule must be set aside.
Van Gend en Loos v Administratie der Belastingen (Case 26/62) [1963] ECR 1	Challenge to an increased customs duty as a breach of an EC Treaty provision concerning the free movement of goods (now 30 TFEU).	Principle of direct effect established. A Treaty article is directly effective if clear, precise, and unconditional and its implementation requires no legislative intervention by Member States. Treaty articles are capable of vertical direct effect.

Key cases

✶✶✶✶✶✶✶✶✶✶✶✶✶

Case	Facts	Principle
Defrenne v Sabena (Case 43/75) [1976] ECR 455	Defrenne sought to invoke a Treaty Article (now 157 TFEU) in an equal pay claim.	Treaty articles are also capable of horizontal direct effect. Conditions for direct effect loosened: a Treaty article must be sufficiently clear, precise, and unconditional.
Van Duyn v Home Office (Case 41/74) [1974] 1337	Van Duyn challenged the UK's decision to refuse her entry, seeking to rely on Directive 64/221.	Directives are capable of direct effect. Van Gend conditions applied: the provision must be clear, precise, and unconditional.
Pubblico Ministerio v Ratti (Case 148/78) [1979] ECR 1269	Claim concerning two directives relating to product labelling.	A directive cannot be directly effective until its implementation deadline has passed.
Marshall v Southampton & South West Hampshire Area Health Authority (Case 152/84) [1986] ECR 723	Marshall sought to rely on Directive 76/207 in a sex discrimination claim.	Directives can only be invoked vertically, against the state, or a public body.
Foster v British Gas (Case C-188/89) [1990] ECR I-3133	Foster sought to rely on Directive 76/207 in a sex discrimination claim.	'Public body' includes a body made responsible by the state for providing a public service, under state control, and with special powers for that purpose, beyond those normally applicable between individuals.
Von Colson and Kamman v Land Nordrhein-Westfalen (Case 14/83) [1984] ECR 1891	Von Colson sought to rely on Article 6 of Directive 76/207.	The provision was not sufficiently clear and precise to have direct effect. The German court must interpret the relevant national provision in line with Article 6. Principle of indirect effect created.
Marleasing SA v La Comercial Internacional de Alimentación SA (Case C-106/89) [1990] ECR I-4135	Horizontal claim concerning the Company Law Directive 68/151.	If no direct effect: national courts must, as far as possible, interpret national law, whether adopted before or after a directive, in the light of the wording and purpose of the directive.
Francovich and Bonifaci v Republic of Italy (Cases C-6/90 & C-9/90) [1991] ECR I-5357	Damages claim against Italy: non-implementation of a directive.	Right to damages, provided the conditions are satisfied.

Case	Facts	Principle
Brasserie du Pêcheur v Germany and *R v Secretary of State for Transport, ex parte Factortame Ltd and Others* (Joined Cases C-46 & 48/93) [1996] ECR I-1029	Damages claim: other kinds of breach of [EU] law by Member States.	Right to damages, provided the conditions are satisfied.
R v HM Treasury, ex parte British Telecommunications (Case C-392/93) [1996] ECR I-1631	The UK had implemented a directive incorrectly.	State liability can arise in respect of incorrect implementation of a directive.
R v Ministry of Agriculture, Fisheries and Food, ex parte Hedley Lomas (Ireland) Ltd (Case C-5/94) [1996] ECR I-2553	Refusal of licences for export of live animals to Spain.	State liability can arise in respect of administrative acts.
Köbler v Austria (Case C-224/01) [2003] ECR I-1039	Damages claim: national court's interpretation of [EU] law.	An erroneous interpretation of EU law by a court of last instance can give rise to state liability.

 ? Exam questions

Problem question

Fred is a laboratory technician employed by the Home Office in London. He has encountered problems at work and is considering bringing proceedings against his employer.

(Fictitious) Directive 2003/555 ('the Directive') provides that all overtime worked by laboratory technicians must be paid at no less than three times the normal hourly rate. The Directive also provides that laboratory technicians must receive health and safety training. An annex to the Directive sets out the details of the required training, which must include sessions covering all new handling techniques relating to toxic substances. The deadline for implementation of the Directive was 31 December 2005.

The (fictitious) Laboratory Technicians Act 1950 ('the Act') provides that all overtime worked by laboratory technicians must be paid at no less than twice the normal hourly rate. The Act also

Exam questions

provides that all laboratory technicians must receive health and safety training but does not specify the content of the training.

Fred occasionally works overtime and, under his contract of employment, receives twice his normal hourly rate of pay. He is dissatisfied with this but when he complained, his employer pointed out that this overtime rate complies with the Act.

Last month, Fred came into contact with a toxic substance at work and, as a result, suffered respiratory problems. Whilst Fred has received health and safety training, he has not received training in recently developed handling techniques for toxic substances. He believes that, had he received such training, he would not have been exposed to the associated health risk.

(a) Advise Fred as to whether he has any cause of action against his employer under EU law.

(b) How would your answer differ (if at all) if Fred was employed not by the Home Office but by Fyso (UK) plc ('Fyso').

[For the purposes of this question, you are NOT required to consider any possible action for damages against the UK Government.]

Essay question

Trace the development of the principles of direct effect, indirect effect, and state liability by the Court of Justice, evaluating their significance for individual claimants.

Outline answers are available at the end of the book.

Scan here

Scan this QR code image with your mobile device to see a full answer to these questions or log onto www.oxfordtextbooks.oc.uk/orc/concentrate/

#3
Preliminary rulings: Article 267 TFEU

The examination

Expect essay or problem questions in this area. Favourite essay topics include the purpose of **Article 267 TFEU** and the separation of functions between national courts and the Court of Justice; the coherence and effectiveness of the scheme of discretionary and obligatory references within the EU legal order; abuse of the procedure and the Court's refusal of references. Problem scenarios typically focus on disputes progressing through national courts and the application of **Article 267** at the various levels of the national system.

Chapter overview

Article 267 TFEU preliminary rulings

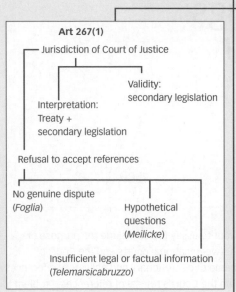

Art 267(1)

Jurisdiction of Court of Justice

Interpretation:
Treaty +
secondary legislation

Validity:
secondary legislation

Refusal to accept references

No genuine dispute
(*Foglia*)

Hypothetical
questions
(*Meilicke*)

Insufficient legal or factual information
(*Telemarsicabruzzo*)

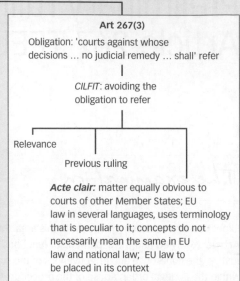

Art 267(3)

Obligation: 'courts against whose
decisions ... no judicial remedy ... shall' refer

CILFIT: avoiding the
obligation to refer

Relevance

Previous ruling

Acte clair: matter equally obvious to
courts of other Member States; EU
law in several languages, uses terminology
that is peculiar to it; concepts do not
necessarily mean the same in EU
law and national law; EU law to
be placed in its context

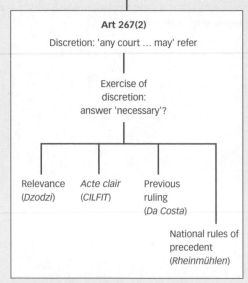

Art 267(2)

Discretion: 'any court ... may' refer

Exercise of
discretion:
answer 'necessary'?

Relevance
(*Dzodzi*)

Acte clair
(*CILFIT*)

Previous
ruling
(*Da Costa*)

National rules of
precedent
(*Rheinmühlen*)

Key facts

- **Article 267 TFEU** (ex **Article 234 EC**) gives the Court of Justice jurisdiction to deliver **preliminary rulings** on the validity and interpretation of EU law.

- The primary purpose of **Article 267** is to ensure that EU law has the same meaning and effect in all the Member States.

- Where it considers a decision on a question of EU law is necessary to enable it to give judgment, any court may refer that question to the Court of Justice (the discretion to refer).

- Where a question of EU law is raised before a national court of last resort, that court must refer it to the Court of Justice (the obligation to refer).

- However, in *CILFIT* the Court of Justice set out circumstances in which a national court of last resort is not obliged to refer.

- On occasions, the Court of Justice has declined to accept a reference, on the grounds that the question referred was irrelevant or hypothetical or that there was no genuine dispute between the parties.

Treaty of Lisbon

The **Treaty of Lisbon** amended the **EC Treaty** and renamed it the **Treaty on the Functioning of the European Union (TFEU)**, replaced all references to 'European Community' and 'Community law' with 'EU' and 'EU law' respectively, and changed the numbering of Treaty articles. Note that pre-Lisbon case law uses the previous terminology and Treaty numbering. This chapter uses the term 'EU' and the new Treaty numbering throughout, placed in brackets where they appear in the case summaries.

Article 267 TFEU

Article 267 provides:

> The Court of Justice of the European Union shall have jurisdiction to give preliminary rulings concerning:
>
> (a) the interpretation of the Treaties;
> (b) the validity and interpretation of acts of the institutions, bodies, offices or agencies of the Union
>
> Where such a question is raised before any court or tribunal of a Member State, that court or tribunal may, if it considers that a decision on the question is necessary to enable it to give judgment, request the Court to give a ruling thereon.
>
> Where any such question is raised in a case pending before a court or tribunal of a Member State against whose decisions there is no judicial remedy under national law, that court or tribunal shall bring the matter before the Court.
>
> If such a question is raised in a case pending before a court or tribunal of a Member State with regard to a person in custody, the Court of Justice of the European Union will act with the minimum of delay.

Outline of the procedure and timing of the reference

When a national court is discharging its duty to apply EU law, it may be uncertain as to its meaning. Sometimes, questions concerning the validity of EU secondary legislation may be raised in national proceedings. In such situations a national court may, and in certain circumstances must, refer the matter to the Court of Justice. The **preliminary reference** comprises a question or questions about EU law, together with an indication of the factual and legal context of the case. The Court delivers its judgment on the correct interpretation or on validity and refers this back to the national court, which must decide the case before it on the basis of the Court's response. It is important to note that the parties to an action have no right to a reference. **Article 267** does not set out an appeals procedure. Rather, it provides a mechanism enabling national courts to obtain authoritative rulings on the interpretation or validity of EU law.

The Court of Justice has recognized that it is for the national court to determine the timing of the reference. Nevertheless, the Court has emphasized that it can provide a useful response only if the facts and relevant legal issues have been established (*Irish Creamery Milk Suppliers Association v Ireland* (Cases 36 & 71/80)). Indeed, as will be noted later, the Court has sometimes refused to accept references when it has been provided with insufficient information.

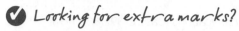 *Looking for extra marks?*

Whilst the core rationale for the preliminary rulings procedure is the uniform and consistent interpretation of EU law, **Article 267** has even broader significance. The role it has played in the development of EU law is hugely important. **Article 267** embodies the mechanism through which the Court of Justice has developed major legal principles such as **direct effect** and **indirect effect**. For instance, it was on an **Article 267** reference from the Dutch court that the Court established the principle of direct effect, in *Van Gend* (Case 26/62). Many of the cases referred to in this book began in national courts and were decided in the context of preliminary rulings. Currently, around half the cases heard by the Court of Justice reach it by this means. Although it does not provide an appeal procedure, **Article 267** is also important for individuals. Through the national court, it provides them with a means of access to the Court of Justice.

Binding effect of preliminary rulings

For some time, uncertainty persisted as to whether preliminary rulings bind only the parties to the dispute giving rise to the reference, or whether they should be applied in subsequent cases. *International Chemical Corporation v Amministrazione Finanze* (Case 66/80) established that all national courts and tribunals are bound by rulings on validity. Further, in *Kühne & Heitz v Productschap voor Pluimvee en Eieren* (Case C-453/00), concerning the decision of a Dutch administrative body, the Court of Justice confirmed that its rulings on interpretation bind all national courts and administrative authorities across the EU.

However, the binding effect of a preliminary ruling does not preclude national courts from seeking further guidance from the Court of Justice on interpretation or validity. The Court retains the right to depart from its previous rulings and may do so, for instance when a different conclusion is warranted by different facts.

The Court's jurisdiction under Article 267

The Court of Justice has jurisdiction to rule on the interpretation or validity of EU law (save in certain areas expressly excluded by the Treaties, such as the common foreign and security policy). It has no jurisdiction to rule on the application of EU law, on the interpretation of national law, or on the compatibility of national law with EU law. Where such questions are raised, the Court is likely to reformulate them in terms that raise general points of EU law. Nonetheless, in practice the distinction between interpretation and application may not be easily drawn. Indeed, the Court does sometimes express an opinion as to the application of its ruling.

R v HM Treasury, ex parte British Telecommunications (Case C-392/93) [1996] ECR I-1631

The UK had implemented **Directive 90/531**, but incorrectly. BT, which claimed it had suffered loss as a result, sought damages from the UK Government.

The Court of Justice held that liability to damages would arise in a case of incorrect implementation of a directive, provided the three *Factortame III* conditions were met: the directive was intended to confer rights on individuals, the breach was sufficiently serious, and there was a direct causal link between the breach and the loss. Apparently assuming that the first and third conditions were met, the Court went on to declare that the Directive was unclear. It was capable of more than one reasonable interpretation and the Commission had never challenged the UK's interpretation. Consequently, the UK's error was excusable and the breach was not sufficiently serious.

Such 'interference' by the Court of Justice in the application of EU law may cause difficulties. In *Reed*, the English High Court considered that the Court had exceeded its jurisdiction in this respect.

Arsenal Football Club v Reed (Case C-206/01) [2002] ECR I-10273

Arsenal had tried to prevent Reed from selling football souvenirs carrying the Arsenal name and logos. The reference to the Court of Justice concerned the interpretation of the **Trade Mark Directive**. The Court found that there was an infringement of the Directive and, rather than expressing its judgment in general terms, referred directly to the parties and the particular circumstances of the case.

The High Court took the view that the Court of Justice had made findings of fact that conflicted with the facts which it had itself already established. Accordingly, it refused to accept the Court's conclusion that there was an infringement by Reed and gave judgment for him, declaring that it had no power to cede to the Court of Justice a jurisdiction it did not have. Subsequently, the Court of Appeal overruled the High Court's decision, holding that the difference between the conclusions of the Court of Justice and the trial judge arose not from any inconsistency in findings of fact, but rather from a variance in legal reasoning.

Revision tip

Think about the rationale for **Article 267** and the separation of functions between the Court of Justice and national courts.

'Court or tribunal'

Article 267 refers to a 'court or tribunal of a Member State'. The meaning of these terms is a matter of EU law (*Politi v Italy* (Case 43/71)). *Broeckmeulen* provided some indication of the scope of 'court or tribunal'.

Broeckmeulen v Huisarts Registratie Commissie (Case 246/80) [1981] ECR 2311

Broeckmeulen was refused registration as a medical general practitioner in the Netherlands, despite holding a Belgian medical qualification. He sought to rely on [EU] rules on the free movement of professionals before the Appeals Committee of the Dutch medical professional body. On a preliminary reference from that committee, the first question for the Court of Justice was whether the committee was a 'court or tribunal'.

The Court responded that, in the absence of a right of appeal to the ordinary courts, the Appeals Committee was a 'court or tribunal' since it operated with the consent and cooperation of the public authorities and delivered final decisions following an adversarial procedure.

Dorsch Consult Ingenieurgesellschaft v Bundesbaugesellschaft Berlin (Case C-54/96) provided further guidance on the scope of 'court or tribunal'. Various factors are taken to be taken into account, such as whether the body is established by law and is permanent, whether its procedure is *inter partes*, whether it applies rules of law and is independent, and whether its jurisdiction is compulsory. Over the years, the Court has accepted references from a wide range of bodies, including administrative tribunals, professional disciplinary bodies, tax adjudicators, and insurance officers.

Refusal to accept references

Pursuant to the primary purpose of **Article 267**, to ensure that EU law has the same meaning and effect in all Member States, the Court of Justice has generally encouraged national courts to refer. Initially, the Court adopted an open approach, taking the view that it was for the national court alone to assess whether a decision on a question of EU law was necessary to enable it to give judgment. The Court later moved on from this position, indicating that its receptiveness to references is not without limits and that it will exert control over admissibility. From time to time, the Court has declined to accept references, most notably where they amounted to an abuse or misuse of the procedure. It has refused jurisdiction where there is no genuine dispute between the parties, where the questions referred are irrelevant or hypothetical, and where the national court has failed to provide sufficient legal or factual information.

No genuine dispute

Foglia v Novello (No 1) (Case 104/79) [1980] ECR 745 and *Foglia v Novello (No 2)* (Case 244/80) [1981] ECR 3045

Foglia had agreed to sell Italian liqueur wine to Novello in France. Under the contract Novello would reimburse any taxes incurred by Foglia, unless they infringed [EU] law. Foglia's separate contract with Danzas, the carrier, stipulated that Foglia would not be liable for any charges that violated [EU] law. French taxes were levied and paid by Foglia, who sought to recover the relevant amount from Novello in the Italian court, claiming that the French taxes breached [EU] law. A reference was made to the Court of Justice.

The Court refused the reference, finding that there was no genuine dispute and that the parties had engineered the situation to challenge the French tax in the Italian court (*Foglia (No 1)*).

Dissatisfied with this outcome, the Italian court made a further reference. The Court again refused jurisdiction, stating that it did not deliver advisory opinions on general or hypothetical questions (*Foglia (No 2)*).

✅ Looking for extra marks?

In referring for the second time the Italian judge was clearly perturbed that the Court's initial response departed from its previously open approach to receiving references. *Foglia (No 2)* confirmed that the Court intended to assert control over the admissibility of references. It declared that, whilst having regard to the national court's assessment of the need for a reference, it would check its jurisdiction by making its own assessment.

It was suggested that the Court's refusal of the *Foglia* reference was motivated partly by its recognition of national sensitivities about challenges to domestic legislation in the courts of other Member States. Later cases indicate that the Court will be prepared to accept references in such circumstances (see for instance *Eau de Cologne v Provide* (Case C-130/88)). However, the Court has reiterated its statement in Foglia that it will apply 'special vigilance' to ensure that the information provided by the national court establishes the need for a reference. That need was not established, for instance, in *Bacardi-Martini SAS v Newcastle United Football Club* (Case C-318/00). Here, the Court declined to accept a reference from the English High Court concerning French legislation on alcohol advertising and [EU] rules on the free movement of services.

Hypothetical or irrelevant questions

Despite the Court's declared intentions in *Foglia (No 2)*, it was some years before it adopted a similar stance again. One notable case in which it did so is *Meilicke*.

Meilicke v ADV/ORGA AG (Case C-83/91) [1992] ECR I-4871

A German academic, who had propounded views about the Second Banking Directive, challenged the theory of non-cash contributions of capital developed by the German courts, claiming that it was incompatible with the Directive. There was no evidence that the issue of non-cash contributions was relevant to the case. Citing *Foglia (No 2)* and reiterating that it had no jurisdiction to give advisory opinions on hypothetical questions, the Court of Justice declined to give a ruling.

Insufficient legal or factual information

A number of cases decided since *Foglia* demonstrate that the Court of Justice will be prepared to respond to a reference only if the facts and the legal issues are made clear in the order for reference. For example, in *Telemarsicabruzzo SpA v Circostel* (Cases C-320–322/90) the Court refused jurisdiction because the national court had supplied insufficient information on the facts and the relevant national provisions.

Revision tip

Be familiar with the cases demonstrating the limits to the Court's receptiveness to references from national courts.

Jurisdiction of the national courts to refer

Article 267 draws a distinction between the obligation to refer (**Article 267(3)**) and the discretion to refer (**Article 267(2)**).

Obligation to refer

Article 267(3) provides that where a question of interpretation or validity is raised before a court or tribunal of a Member State 'against whose decisions there is no judicial remedy under national law' that court or tribunal 'shall bring the matter before the Court'.

Courts 'against whose decisions there is no judicial remedy under national law'

Put simply, these are courts of last resort or final appeal. **Article 267(3)** clearly applies, for instance, to the English Supreme Court. However, the precise scope of 'courts . . . against whose decision there is no judicial remedy under national law' is a matter of debate. There are two different views as to the kinds of bodies that **Article 267(3)** covers. According to the 'concrete theory', the obligation to refer applies to courts whose decisions are not subject to appeal in the particular case in which the question of EU law arises. The 'abstract theory' embodies the notion that 'courts . . . against whose decisions there is no judicial remedy under national law' comprise exclusively those courts which occupy the highest position in the national system and whose decisions are therefore never subject to appeal. *Costa* suggested that the Court of Justice inclines to the former view, the 'concrete theory'.

....

Costa v ENEL (Case 6/64) [1964] ECR 585

The case before the Italian magistrates' court concerned a claim for such a small sum of money that there was no right of appeal to a higher national court. The Court of Justice declared that '. . .

national courts against whose decisions, as in the present case, there is no judicial remedy, must refer the matter to the Court of Justice'.

Particular problems have arisen in the UK concerning the position of the Court of Appeal, since an appeal from that court can only be brought with leave of the Court of Appeal or the Supreme Court. If leave is refused, does the Court of Appeal become a court 'against whose decisions there is no judicial remedy under national law'? This question was raised in the English court in *Chiron Corporation*.

Chiron Corporation v Murex Diagnostics [1995] All ER (EC) 88

The Court of Appeal considered that it was not a court of last resort where it had refused leave to appeal. It took the view that the possibility of an application to the House of Lords (now the Supreme Court) for leave to appeal constituted a 'judicial remedy'. Before refusing leave to appeal, the House of Lords should consider whether the case raised an issue of [EU] law. If it did, that court could either refer the question immediately or grant leave to appeal, with a view to referring the question in the course of the appeal proceedings.

Although the Court of Appeal concluded that it was not a court of last resort, it reasoned that if it transpired that a ruling on [EU] law was necessary, and provided the House of Lords adopted one of the proposed alternative courses of action, a reference would ultimately be made. Subsequently, *Lyckeskog* endorsed this approach.

Lyckeskog (Case C-99/00) [2002] ECR I-4839

Here, the decision of the Court of Appeal for Western Sweden was subject to appeal to the Swedish Supreme Court, but only with leave from the latter court. On a reference from the Court of Appeal, the Court of Justice held that the fact that the merits of the appeal were subject to a prior declaration of admissibility by the Supreme Court did not deprive the parties of a judicial remedy. If a question of [EU] law arose, the Supreme Court would be under an obligation, under **Article [267(3)]**, to refer the matter to the Court of Justice either at the stage of considering admissibility or at a later stage.

CILFIT: avoiding the obligation to refer

The central purpose of **Article 267** is to prevent the creation, in any Member State, of a body of national case law that is out of line with EU law. It would therefore be reasonable to conclude that the obligation on courts of last resort to refer questions of EU law to the Court of Justice should be absolute and unqualified. Indeed, the wording of **Article 267(3)** is apparently unequivocal – courts of last resort '. . . shall bring the matter before the Court of Justice . . .'. However, in *CILFIT*, the Court of Justice acknowledged that there are exceptions to this obligation. The starting point for the national court must be whether a decision on the question of EU law is necessary to enable it to give judgment.

CILFIT Srl v Ministero della Sanita (Case 283/81) [1982] ECR 3415

In the context of a challenge to an Italian levy on imported wool under **Regulation 827/68**, the Italian Supreme Court referred to the Court of Justice a question concerning its obligation to refer. The Ministry of Health argued that the interpretation of the Regulation was so obvious as to rule out any doubt as to its meaning and that this obviated the need for a reference. The claimant importers maintained that since a question of [EU] law had arisen, the Supreme Court could not, as a court of last resort, escape its obligation to refer.

Affirming the relationship between [**Article 267(2) and (3)**] the Court declared that a national court of last resort has the same discretion as any other national court to ascertain whether a decision on a question of [EU] law is necessary to enable it to give judgment. Accordingly, a national court of last resort has no obligation to refer where a question of [EU] law is not relevant. Further, a national court of last resort is not obliged to refer if the Court of Justice has previously ruled on the point or where the correct interpretation of [EU] law is so obvious as to leave no scope for reasonable doubt as to its meaning. Nonetheless, in all these circumstances, national courts of last resort are free to bring the matter before the Court of Justice if they consider this to be appropriate.

Development of precedent

In setting out the 'previous ruling' exception in *CILFIT*, the Court of Justice was reiterating its earlier conclusion in *Da Costa*.

Da Costa en Schaake NV v Nederlandse Belastingadministratie (Cases 28–30/62) [1963] ECR 31

A chemical importer challenged Dutch import duties in the Dutch court. The facts and issues of interpretation were materially identical to those raised previously in *Van Gend*.

The Court began by pointing out that [**Article 267(3)**] 'unreservedly' requires national courts of last resort to refer every question of interpretation raised before them. However, despite that requirement, the Court concluded that 'the authority of an interpretation . . . already given by the Court may deprive the obligation of its purpose and thus empty it of its substance. Such is the case when the question raised is materially identical with a question which has already been the subject of a preliminary ruling in a similar case'.

Nonetheless, the Court emphasized that [**Article 267**] allows any national court to refer questions of interpretation again. In response to the question raised, the Court restated its judgment in *Van Gend*. Then, declaring that the questions of interpretation were identical and that no new factor had been presented, the Court referred the national court directly to the *Van Gend* judgment.

Thus, *Da Costa* established that a previous ruling removes the obligation to refer where the facts and questions of interpretation are identical. The Court went further in *CILFIT*, holding that the same principle applies 'where previous decisions . . . have already dealt with the point of law in question, irrespective of the nature of the proceedings which led to those decisions, even if the questions at issue are not strictly identical'.

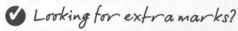 **Looking for extra marks?**

Da Costa and *CILFIT* indicate the development of a system of precedent. The Court of Justice permits, indeed encourages, national courts to rely on its previous rulings, not only when the facts and questions of interpretation are identical but also when the nature of the proceedings is different and the questions are not identical.

Moreover, as has been seen, preliminary rulings on validity and interpretation are binding, not only on the parties to the dispute but also in subsequent cases.

Nevertheless, the binding effect of a preliminary ruling does not preclude national courts from seeking further guidance from the Court of Justice. The Court retains the right to depart from its previous rulings and may do so, for instance, when a different conclusion is warranted by different facts.

Looking for extra marks?

The development of precedent, together with the binding effect of preliminary rulings, has brought a subtle change to the relationship between the Court of Justice and national courts. Whereas that relationship was originally perceived as horizontal, its roots firmly grounded in cooperation, it is increasingly becoming vertical in nature, with the Court of Justice occupying a position of superiority to national courts.

Doctrine of acte clair

The term '*acte clair*', which translated literally means 'clear act', is applied to a provision of EU law whose interpretation is clear or, as enunciated in *CILFIT*, is 'so obvious as to leave no scope for reasonable doubt as to its meaning'. According to *CILFIT*, when the meaning is clear, there is no need to refer. Whilst this exception appears to allow national courts ample opportunity to avoid making references, *CILFIT* narrowed its scope to a considerable degree. The national court must be convinced that the matter is equally obvious to the courts of the other Member States. *CILFIT* emphasized that [EU] law is drafted in several languages, uses terminology that is peculiar to it, and must be placed in its context; legal concepts do not necessarily have the same meaning in [EU] law and the law of the various Member States.

It would be surprising to encounter many national courts with sufficient linguistic ability to be able adequately to bear all these matters in mind. The *CILFIT* criteria are difficult to satisfy and, in practice, national courts have tended to interpret *acte clair* more loosely.

It is now apparent, however, that too broad an approach to the application of *acte clair* carries risks, for instance where a national court of last resort avoided a reference in reliance on *acte clair* and one party was deprived of EU law rights as a result. In *Köbler v Austria* (Case C 224/01) the Court of Justice held that state liability in damages would arise if it was manifestly apparent that a national court had failed to meet its obligations under [**Article 267(3)**], for instance by misapplying the *acte clair* doctrine. More recently in ***Traghetti del Mediterraneo SpA v Italy*** (Case C-173/03) the Court declared that it could not rule out liability for damage caused by 'manifest errors' of interpretation of [EU] law by a court of last instance.

Revision tip

Think about the circumstances in which a national court of last resort can legitimately decline to refer. Be familiar with the authorities.

Discretion to refer

Article 267(2) sets out the power, or discretion, of every national court to refer questions of interpretation or validity of EU law. It provides that 'any court or tribunal may, if it considers that a decision on the question is necessary to enable it to give judgment, request the Court to give a ruling thereon'. Importantly, however, the power to refer does not deprive a lower national court of the right to reach its own conclusions on the meaning of EU law and to decline to make a reference. That is so even if, in the terms of **Article 267(2)**, a decision on the question is 'necessary' to enable it to give judgment. **Article 267** is designed to ensure that any 'necessary' questions of EU law will ultimately be referred at final appeal stage.

References on validity

National courts have no power to declare EU law invalid (***Foto-Frost v Hauptzollamt Lübeck-Ost*** (Case 314/85)). Consequently, if a national court's decision depends upon the validity of an EU measure, it must make a reference. Here, a national court may grant interim relief by temporarily suspending a national measure which is being challenged on the grounds of the validity of the EU measure on which it is based (***Zückerfabrik Süderdithmarschen v Hauptzollamt Itzehoe*** (Case C-143/88)).

Guidance on the exercise of the discretion

The Court of Justice has provided guidance on the exercise of the **Article 267(2)** discretion. The English courts have also made declarations on this matter. Lord Denning's statements in the Court of Appeal in ***Bulmer Ltd and another v Bollinger SA and Others*** [1974] tended to discourage references and in the early cases the English judges would frequently take their lead from this, showing reluctance to exercise their discretion to refer. Later, the advantages of the Court of Justice in interpreting [EU] law were emphasized by the English courts, demonstrating a more positive approach to exercising the discretion.

Whilst guidance from the Court of Justice clearly carries more authority than any statements of national courts, neither can fetter the **Article 267(2)** discretion. Lower courts remain free to refuse to make a reference. How, then, is the discretion to be exercised?

Jurisdiction of the national courts to refer
✳✳✳✳✳✳✳✳✳✳✳✳

Relevance

Dzodzi v Belgium (Cases C-297/88 & C-197/89), concerning an interpretation of [EU] law which bore directly on the interpretation of Belgian national law, established that it is for the national court to determine the relevance of the questions referred. As noted later, the Court of Justice has rejected references seeking an interpretation bearing no relation to the main action, though such cases are rare.

Acte clair

Having established relevance, the next consideration for the national court is likely to be whether the provision of EU law is clear. If it is, a reference will not be necessary. In this respect, the *CILFIT* criteria for *acte clair* provide useful guidance. As already noted in relation to the obligation to refer, because these criteria demand a significant level of language expertise on the part of the national court, as well as an overview of EU law, in reality they are not easily satisfied. Moreover, as Bingham J (as he then was) pointed out in the English High Court in *Commissioners of Customs and Excise v Samex* [1983], the Court of Justice has distinct advantages that are not necessarily enjoyed by a national court. It has the ability to make comparisons between [EU] texts in different language versions, has a panoramic view of the [EU] and its institutions and possesses detailed knowledge of [EU] legislation. Later, Sir Thomas Bingham MR (as he later became) in *R v Stock Exchange, ex parte Else (1982) Ltd* [1993] again referred to the advantages of the Court of Justice in interpreting [EU] law, declaring that 'if the national court has any real doubt, it should ordinarily refer'.

A previous ruling does not preclude a reference

A previous ruling by the Court of Justice on a similar question does not preclude a reference (*Da Costa*). As noted earlier, in *Da Costa* the question referred was substantially the same as that referred in *Van Gend*. Nonetheless, the Court affirmed that [**Article 267(2)**] allows a national court, if it considers it desirable, to 'refer questions of interpretation to the Court again'. Thus a reference was not ruled out, although in responding to the question in *Da Costa*, the Court simply repeated its judgment in *Van Gend*.

National rules of precedent

National rules of precedent have no impact on the discretion to refer (*Rheinmühlen-Düsseldorf v Einfuhr- und Vorratsstelle für Getreide und Futtermittel* (Case 146/73)). This means that the ruling of a higher national court on an interpretation of EU law does not prevent a lower court in the national system from requesting a ruling on the same provisions from the Court of Justice.

Revision tip

Be prepared to discuss national courts' discretion to refer and the Court of Justice's guidance on the exercise of that discretion.

Reform

The Court of Justice's workload has risen significantly over the years and currently references for preliminary rulings can take around 20 months. Modifications to the Court's Rules of Procedure have helped to alleviate the difficulties, for instance the provision for expedited hearings in urgent cases and the power to give preliminary rulings by reasoned order where an identical question has been dealt with previously. Other means of reducing the Court's case load have been canvassed and discussed, notably in the paper 'The Future of the Judicial System of the European Union' (1999, produced by members of the Court of Justice and the Court of First Instance) and the Due Report (2000). These include restricting the power to make references to courts of last resort, removing the obligation to refer save for questions that are 'sufficiently important', and the creation of decentralized regional courts. The **Treaty of Nice** gave the Court of First Instance the power to give preliminary rulings, as specified by the **Statute of the Court of Justice**, though currently the Statute does not confer **Article 267** jurisdiction on the General Court (formerly the Court of First Instance).

 **Key cases**

Case	Facts	Principle
Foglia v Novello (No 1) (Case 104/79) [1980] ECR 745 and *Foglia v Novello (No 2)* (Case 244/80) [1981] ECR 3045	Challenge in the Italian court to French taxes levied on imported liqueur wine.	No genuine dispute: reference refused.
Meilicke v ADV/ORGA AG (Case C-83/91) [1992] ECR I-4871	Reference concerning the Second Banking Directive.	Questions were hypothetical: reference refused.
Telemarsicabruzzo SpA v Circostel (Cases C-320–322/90) [1993] ECR I-393	No information provided on the facts and legal background.	National court had supplied insufficient information: reference refused.
Costa v ENEL (Case 6/64) [1964] ECR 585	Claim before Italian magistrates: no right of appeal as the sum of money concerned was so small.	'. . . national courts against whose decisions, as in the present case, there is no judicial remedy, must refer the matter to the Court of Justice'.

Case	Facts	Principle
Lyckeskog (Case C-99/00) [2002] ECR I-4839	The decision of the Court of Appeal for Western Sweden was subject to appeal to the Swedish Supreme Court, but only with leave from the latter court.	The need for leave to appeal did not preclude a judicial remedy. If a question of EU law arose, the Supreme Court would be obliged to refer, either when considering admissibility or at a later stage.
CILFIT Srl v Ministero della Sanità (Case 283/81) [1982] ECR 3415	Challenge to an Italian levy on imported wool.	No obligation to refer if the question is not relevant; there is a previous ruling by the Court of Justice; or the correct interpretation of EU law is *acte clair*.
Köbler v Austria (Case C-224/01) [2003] ECR I-10239	Köbler claimed that failure to refer deprived him of his [EU] law rights.	State liability in damages would arise if the national court of last resort had failed in its obligations, for instance by misapplying *acte clair*.
Dzodzi v Belgium (Cases C-297/88 & C-197/89) [1990] ECR I-3763	Interpretation of [EU] law bore directly on the interpretation of Belgian law.	It is for the national court to determine the relevance of the questions referred.
Da Costa en Schaake NV v Nederlandse Belastingadministratie (Cases 28–30/62) [1963] ECR 31	The facts and questions of interpretation were materially identical to those raised previously in *Van Gend*.	A previous ruling by the Court of Justice does not preclude a reference.
Rheinmühlen-Düsseldorf v Einfuhr- und Vorratsstelle für Getreide und Futtermittel (Case 146/73) [1974] ECR 139	A German lower court sought a reference despite a ruling by a higher national court involving questions of [EU] law.	National rules of precedent have no impact on the discretion to refer: the ruling of a higher national court on an interpretation of EU law does not preclude a reference from a lower court.

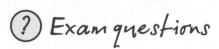

Problem question

Maxisports SA, a French manufacturer of fitness equipment, agreed to supply rowing machines to Ben, a UK retailer. Under the contract, Ben reserved the right to reject the goods if they failed to comply with any relevant provisions of EU law. (Fictitious) Council Regulation 27/89 ('the Regulation') requires fitness equipment to be fitted with safety notices in a 'permanent form'.

The machines arrived at Ben's store in London. They carried safety notices attached to the machines with plastic tabs. Ben refused to take delivery, claiming that the machines did not comply with the Regulation because the notices were not in a 'permanent form'. Ben brought proceedings in the High Court for return of the purchase price. Maxisports rejected this claim on the grounds that the rowing machines complied with the Regulation.

In the High Court it was established that the rowing machines had a working life of up to six years and that the safety notices were sufficiently secure to remain intact for between three and four years. The court was referred to an earlier House of Lords' decision in which the words 'permanent form' in the Regulation had been interpreted to include any method of attachment that could reasonably be expected to endure throughout the period of the manufacturer's guarantee. Their Lordships had reasoned that equipment became obsolete once a guarantee had expired, because repairs were so expensive. Counsel for Maxisports argued that, since Maxisports' machines were guaranteed for three years, the safety notices were in a 'permanent form' and that therefore the machines complied with the Regulation. The High Court took the view that it was bound by the House of Lords' interpretation and declined to make a reference to the Court of Justice. It gave judgment for Maxisports.

On appeal, the Court of Appeal disagreed with the House of Lords' interpretation of 'permanent form' stating that these words clearly meant that the notices must be attached to fitness equipment in such as way as to remain intact throughout its working life. Nonetheless, taking the view that it was bound by the House of Lords' interpretation, the court refused to make a reference to the Court of Justice, gave judgment for Maxisports, and refused leave to appeal to the Supreme Court.

Consider the application of Article 267 TFEU to this situation.

Essay question

Article 267 TFEU embodies a method of cooperation between national courts and the Court of Justice which ensures that EU law has the same meaning in all the Member States

How far do you consider this to be an accurate evaluation of the Article 267 preliminary reference procedure?

Outline answers are available at the end of the book.

Scan here

Scan this QR code image with your mobile device to see a full answer to these questions or log onto www.oxfordtextbooks.oc.uk/orc/concentrate/

#4

Direct actions in the Court of Justice of the European Union: Articles 258–260, 263, 265, 277, and 340 TFEU

The examination

The coverage of **direct actions** varies greatly from course to course and the wide variety of potential questions reflects this. You may be tested on your knowledge of procedure and your ability to evaluate this, for instance in relation to enforcement actions under **Article 258 TFEU**. You may be asked to analyse developing case law, for instance concerning the difficulties for individuals in establishing standing under **Articles 263 and 265 TFEU** or the right to damages against the EU under **Article 340 TFEU**. In compiling problem questions, examiners often draw inspiration from the facts of cases, so be familiar with these.

Overview: Article 263 TFEU

Overview: Article 263 TFEU

Challenging EU law: non-privileged applicants

Court of Justice has jurisdiction to review the legality of acts of the institutions

Any natural or legal person ('non-privileged applicant') may challenge:
- an act addressed to the applicant
- an act addressed to another person which is of direct and individual concern to the applicant
- a regulatory act which is of direct concern to the applicant and which does not entail implementing measures

Locus standi: non-privileged applicants

An act addressed to another person
Applicant must show both direct and individual concern

A regulatory act which is of direct concern to the applicant and which does not entail implementing measures

Direct concern

A direct link or an unbroken chain of causation between the EU measure and the damage suffered: Member State has no discretion in implementation (*Municipality of Differdange*)

Individual concern

The decision affects the applicant 'by reason of certain attributes which are peculiar to them or by reason of circumstances in which they are differentiated from all other persons' (*Plaumann*)

'Closed class' test:
an applicant is individually concerned if it was a member of class of persons that was fixed and ascertainable at the date the measure was passed (*Paraiki-Patraiki*)

Reform:
Court of Justice rejects less restrictive test (*UPA*, *Jégo-Quéré*)

Grounds for annulment
- Lack of competence (eg *Germany v European Parliament and Council (Tobacco Advertising)*)
- Infringement of an essential procedural requirement (eg *Roquette Frères*)
- Infringement of the Treaty or of any rule of law relating to its application (eg *Transocean Marine Paint*)
- Misuse of powers (eg *UK v Council*)

Key facts

- As well as actions brought indirectly to the Court of Justice through preliminary references from national courts under **Article 267**, the **TFEU** also provides for actions that are brought directly before the Court.

- Under **Articles 258 and 259 TFEU** (ex **Articles 226 and 227 EC**), respectively, the European Commission and Member States may bring enforcement proceedings against a Member State in breach of Treaty obligations. **Article 260 TFEU** (ex **Article 228 EC**) requires compliance with the Court's judgment.

- **Article 263 TFEU** (ex **Article 230 EC**) concerns judicial review of EU acts. The outcome of a successful action is annulment.

- **Article 265 TFEU** (ex **Article 232 EC**) provides for actions against the EU institutions for failure to act.

- **Article 277 TFEU** (ex **Article 241 EC**) may be invoked in the course of other proceedings, for instance in an action under **Article 263**, to challenge the underlying regulation on which a contested act is based.

- Under **Article 340 TFEU** (ex **Article 288 EC**) individuals who have suffered loss as a result of EU action can recover damages.

Treaty of Lisbon

The **Treaty of Lisbon** amended the **EC Treaty** and renamed it the **Treaty on the Functioning of the European Union (TFEU)**, replaced all references to 'European Community' and 'Community law' with 'EU' and 'EU law' respectively, and changed the numbering of Treaty articles. Note that pre-Lisbon case law uses the previous terminology and Treaty numbering. This chapter uses the term 'EU' and the new Treaty numbering throughout, placed in brackets where they appear in the case summaries.

Enforcement actions against Member States (Articles 258–260 TFEU)

Member States have a duty, under **Article 4 TEU**, to fulfil their EU obligations. **Articles 258–260** provide enforcement mechanisms comprising proceedings against Member States in breach of EU law, brought by the European Commission (**Article 258**) or another Member State (**Article 259**) directly in the Court of Justice. **Article 260** complements these provisions by requiring Member States to comply with the Court's judgment.

Originally, **Article 258** was intended to be the principal mechanism for enforcement of EU law. However, since the development of the doctrines of **direct effect**, **indirect effect**, and **state liability**, providing for the enforcement of EU law in the national court at the suit of individuals, direct actions in the Court of Justice form only part of the system of 'dual enforcement' of EU law.

Enforcement actions by the Commission (Article 258 TFEU)

What constitutes a breach?

Whilst the Treaty provides no definition, the Court of Justice has held that breaches include not only acts but also failures to act. Commonly, infringements comprise failure to implement directives or to implement them correctly, or direct breaches of the Treaty.

Commission v Belgium (Case 1/86) [1987] ECR 2797

In proceedings brought by the Commission under [**Article 258 TFEU**], the Court of Justice found that Belgium had not met its Treaty obligations by failing to implement, by the deadline, a directive concerning water pollution.

Spanish Strawberries concerned a failure to act.

Commission v France (Spanish Strawberries) (Case C-265/95) [1997] ECR I-6959

For over a decade, the French authorities had failed to prevent violent protests by French farmers directed against agricultural products being imported from other Member States. In [**Article 258**] proceedings, the Court of Justice held that, in failing to take adequate preventative action, France had breached its obligations under **Article 10 EC** (now **Article 4 TEU**).

Identifying breaches

The Commission discovers suspected breaches through its own investigations, complaints from private parties, or reports from Member States. Individual citizens or companies affected by a breach cannot compel the Commission to take action.

....

Star Fruit Company v Commission (Case 247/87) [1989] ECR 291

Star Fruit had complained to the Commission about breaches of [EU] law by France relating to the organization of the French banana market and now brought proceedings against the Commission under [**Article 265 TFEU**] (considered later) for failure to act. The Court of Justice held that the Commission has a discretion, not a duty, to commence proceedings. Individuals cannot require the Commission to take action.

....

✅ *Looking for extra marks?*

The discretion may be criticized as diluting the effectiveness of EU law enforcement.

The Commission is not obliged to keep the complainant informed of the progress of any action that it may be taking, though in a 2002 Communication, it undertook to keep complainants more closely informed.

Member States as defendants

Although national governments are the defendants in **Article 258** proceedings, an action may be brought in respect of the failure of any state agency, whether executive, legislative, or judicial.

....

Commission v Belgium (Case 77/69) [1970] ECR 237

Belgium maintained that it was not responsible for its Parliament's failure, through lack of time, to amend national tax legislation, which violated [EU] law. The Court of Justice held that Member States are responsible 'whatever the agency of the State whose action or inaction is the cause of the failure to fulfil its obligations, even in the case of a constitutionally independent institution'.

....

Procedure

Administrative stage

Article 258 provides that 'If the Commission considers that a Member State has failed to fulfil an obligation under the Treaties, it shall deliver a reasoned opinion on the matter after giving the state concerned the opportunity to submit its observations'. The administrative phase incorporates the required elements: the Member State concerned must be given the opportunity to submit its observations; if the Commission is not satisfied, it delivers a reasoned opinion.

The Commission's practice is first to raise the matter informally with the Member State. If not satisfied with the response, it commences the formal procedure.

Formal proceedings begin with the 'letter of notice' to the Member State setting out the Commission's reasons for suspecting an infringement. The Member State must be given a reasonable period of time to respond. Typically, there follow discussions between the Commission and the Member State, with a view to negotiating a settlement. If this proves impossible, the Commission moves to the next phase, the reasoned opinion.

The **reasoned opinion** sets out precisely the grounds of complaint and specifies a time limit within which the Member State is required to take action to end the infringement. In determining whether the deadline is reasonable, the Court of Justice takes account of all the circumstances.

. . . .

Commission v France (Case C-1/00) [2001] ECR I-9989

France had continued to ban beef imports from the UK, despite the relaxation of the export restrictions imposed on the UK by the EU during the BSE ('mad cow disease') crisis. The Commission took action under [**Article 258**]. France complained that it had been given insufficient time to respond to the Commission's opinion. The Court of Justice held that a very short period would be justified where, as here, the Member State is already fully aware of the Commission's views.

. . . .

Measures taken by the Commission during the administrative stage, including the letter of notice and reasoned opinion, have no binding force. They cannot be challenged under **Article 263 TFEU** (considered later).

Judicial stage

Once the time limit for a response to the reasoned opinion has passed, if the matter is not settled the Commission may commence proceedings in the Court of Justice. Here, the Commission cannot rely on matters not raised in the reasoned opinion. Interested Member States, but not individuals, may intervene in the proceedings.

Revision tip

Questions may require consideration of the procedure – be familiar with this.

Defences

The Court of Justice has generally been dismissive of defences raised by Member States, save for those based on a denial of the alleged facts or of the obligation.

Enforcement actions by the Commission (Article 258 TFEU)

✶✶✶✶✶✶✶✶✶✶

Force majeure

Force majeure was defined in *McNicholl v Ministry of Agriculture* (Case 296/86) as abnormal and unforeseeable circumstances, beyond the control of the person committing the breach, the consequences of which could not have been avoided through the exercise of all due care. *Force majeure* may provide a defence.

> #### Commission v Italy (Re Transport Statistics) (Case 101/84) [1985] ECR 2629
>
> The Court of Justice accepted that the bombing of the data-processing centre involved in the implementation of a directive could amount to *force majeure* and would provide a defence to non-implementation. However, a delay of over four years in implementing was too long and inexcusable.

Political or economic difficulties

This defence is unlikely to succeed.

> #### Commission v UK (Tachographs) (Case 128/78) [1979] ECR 419
>
> The Court of Justice rejected the UK's defence to its non-implementation of [an EU] measure requiring the fitting of tachographs in lorries on the basis that this would be costly and cause difficulties with trade unions.

Reciprocity

The Court of Justice has rejected the defence of **reciprocity** – that non-compliance is justified because other Member States have not complied or an EU institution has failed to act.

> #### Commission v Belgium and Luxembourg (Cases 90–91/63) [1964] ECR 625
>
> The Court rejected the argument of the two governments that their actions, allegedly breaching **Article 25 EC** (now **Article 30 TFEU**), would have been lawful had the Council adopted measures which it had power to enact.

> #### Commission v France (Case 232/78) [1979] ECR 2729
>
> It was no defence that another Member State had failed to fulfil a similar obligation or that the Commission had not brought proceedings against that state.

Actual compliance

Where a national provision conflicts with EU law, it is no defence that the provision is not applied in practice or that there is administrative compliance with EU law.

Commission v France (Case 167/73) [1974] ECR 359

French provisions on employment in the merchant fleet were discriminatory and violated [EU] law. The Court rejected France's argument that the provisions were not enforced in practice.

Revision tip

Get to grips with the cases on defences – you may need to apply these to facts (problem questions) or discuss them (essay questions).

Interim measures

It can take many months to reach a resolution, during which there may be continuing harm to affected individuals. **Articles 278 and 279 TFEU** (ex **Articles 242 and 243 EC**), respectively, provide for suspension orders and orders for interim measures.

Commission v UK (Case C-246/89R) [1989] ECR 3125

The Court of Justice ordered the suspension of provisions of the UK **Merchant Shipping Act 1988**, which the Commission claimed infringed [EU] law, pending judgment in the main [**Article 258**] enforcement proceedings.

Effect of a judgment (Article 260 TFEU)

Article 260 requires Member States to comply with the Court's judgment. If the Commission considers that the state has not complied it may bring the case before the Court, after giving that state the opportunity to submit its observations. The **Treaty on European Union** amended **Article 228 EC** (now **Article 260 TFEU**) to allow the Commission to recommend an appropriate lump sum or penalty payment. The Court of Justice is not bound to follow this recommendation. It can set any level of penalty it wishes, with no upper limit, including a dual financial penalty, incorporating both a penalty payment levied in respect of each day (or other time period) of delay in complying with the judgment and a lump sum penalty (*Commission v France* (Case C-304/02)). Where, at the date of the judgment, a Member State has complied with its obligations, the imposition of a penalty payment will not be necessary, though the Court of Justice may order a lump sum payment where the breach was serious and has persisted for a considerable period of time (*Commission v France* (Case C-121/07)).

    Article 260(3) TFEU, introduced by the **Treaty of Lisbon**, provides that when the Commission brings a case before the Court pursuant to **Article 258** on the grounds that a Member State has failed to fulfil its obligation to notify measures transposing a directive, it may specify the amount of lump sum or penalty payment to be paid by the Member State concerned which it considers appropriate in the circumstances. If the Court finds that there is an infringement it may impose a lump sum or penalty payment not exceeding the specified amount, taking effect on a date specified by the Court.

Enforcement actions brought by Member States (Article 259 TFEU)

A Member State may bring an action against another Member State which it considers has failed to fulfil EU obligations. First, the complaint must be brought before the Commission which, before any Court action is taken, asks for submissions from both states, delivers a reasoned opinion, and seeks a settlement. Sometimes, the Commission takes over the action, as it did in *Commission v France* (Case 1/00). **Article 259** actions are rare, as Member States generally prefer, for political reasons, to ask the Commission to act under **Article 258**.

Action for annulment: Article 263 TFEU

Whereas **Articles 258 and 259** concern proceedings against Member States for alleged breaches of EU law, **Article 263** provides for judicial review of acts adopted by the EU institutions, through direct actions in the Court of Justice. Actions brought by individuals are heard, at first instance, in the General Court (formerly the Court of First Instance). Applicants may challenge acts of the institutions on grounds of 'lack of competence, infringement of an essential procedural requirement, infringement of the Treaties or of any rule of law relating to their application, or misuse of powers'. If the challenge is successful, the act is annulled.

Annulment actions may be brought by Member States, the EU institutions (against other EU institutions), and individuals. Member States, the European Parliament, the Council, and the Commission have automatic right of access to the Court in such cases. By contrast, individuals' right of access – their 'standing' or '*locus standi*' to bring **Article 263** proceedings – is limited. These limitations have given rise to widespread criticism and to calls for reform of this area of EU law.

Revision tip

Locus standi (standing) is the most contentious element of **Article 263**. Questions frequently focus on this aspect.

Acts that may be challenged

Article 263 allows the Court of Justice to review the legality of acts of the EU institutions, other than recommendations or opinions, which are 'intended to produce legal effects vis-à-vis third parties'. The **Treaty of Lisbon** extended the category of reviewable acts in **Article 263** to include the acts of 'bodies, offices or agencies of the Union intended to produce legal effects vis-à-vis third parties'. Whilst reviewable acts clearly include legally binding acts, namely regulations, directives, and decisions, other kinds of act may also be susceptible to judicial review. For instance, the Court of Justice held that a Council resolution concerning the European Road Transport Agreement could be challenged (*Commission v Council (ERTA)* (Case 22/70)).

In *IBM v Commission* (Case 60/81) the Court defined a reviewable act as 'any measure the legal effects of which are binding on, and capable of affecting the interests of, the applicant by bringing about a distinct change in his legal position'.

Unfortunately, whether a particular act results in such a change is not always easily ascertained. The Court's conclusions have sometimes been controversial, as may be illustrated by *IBM* and *SFEI*. In *IBM*, the Court refused to allow IBM to challenge a letter from the Commission setting out its intention to institute competition proceedings and the basis of its case. By contrast, a letter from the Commission stating that it intended to close its file on a complaint alleging breaches of competition law was held to be susceptible to judicial review (*SFEI v Commission* (Case C-39/93P)).

Time limit

Actions must be brought within two months of publication of the measure or its notification to the applicant or, in the absence of either, the date on which it came to the applicant's knowledge.

Why seek judicial review?

Judicial review provides applicants with the means to challenge EU acts which they believe have impacted on them adversely. For instance, in *Commission v Council (ERTA)* the Commission challenged the Council's power to participate in negotiation and conclusion of the European Road Transport Agreement, claiming that it, and not the Council, held the necessary powers. Typically, individuals seek to challenge EU acts which affect their business interests. The fishing company Jégo-Quéré, for instance, sought to challenge a regulation on the preservation of hake stocks which prohibited the use of small-meshed fishing nets (*Commission v Jégo-Quéré* (Case C-263/02P)). Other challenges have concerned the withdrawal of subsidies or import licences or the imposition of import quotas.

Revision tip

Consider the cases carefully, thinking about the kinds of situations in which individuals have sought to challenge EU acts.

Standing: who may bring Article 263 proceedings?

Standing or *locus standi*, meaning the right to bring a legal challenge before the Court, depends upon the prospective applicant's status. There are three classes of applicants – privileged, semi-privileged, and non-privileged.

Action for annulment: Article 263 TFEU
✱✱✱✱✱✱✱✱✱✱

Privileged and semi-privileged applicants

Privileged applicants, comprising Member States, the Council, Commission, and Parliament, do not need to establish any particular interest in the legality of EU acts. They have an unlimited, automatic right to bring **Article 263** proceedings. Semi-privileged applicants, comprising the Court of Auditors, the European Central Bank, and the Committee of the Regions, have standing under **Article 263** 'for the purpose of protecting their prerogatives', in other words when their interests are affected.

Non-privileged applicants

These comprise all other applicants, be they natural persons (including individuals in business), or legal persons (companies). Challenges by non-privileged applicants begin in the General Court, with appeal lying to the Court of Justice. Unlike privileged and semi-privileged applicants, non-privileged applicants' right of access to the Court is severely limited.

Revision tip

Non-privileged applicants figure prominently in questions. Make sure you are confident about the principles applying to them.

Standing: non-privileged applicants

The **Lisbon Treaty** amended the provisions of **Article 230 EC** relating to the standing of non-privileged applicants.

Article 263 TFEU provides that:

Any natural or legal person may . . . institute proceedings against an act addressed to that person or which is of direct and individual concern to them, and against a regulatory act which is of direct concern to them and does not entail implementing measures.

In other words a non-privileged applicant may challenge:

- an act addressed to the applicant;
- an act addressed to another person which is of direct and individual concern to the applicant;
- a regulatory act which is of direct concern to the applicant, and which does not entail implementing measures.

'An act addressed to that person'

With respect to acts addressed directly to the applicant, such as Commission decisions on competition law breaches addressed directly to companies, admissibility is unproblematic. Such measures may be challenged without restriction, provided they are brought within the two-month time limit. Whilst the similar provision in **Article 230 EC** referred to a 'decision' addressed to the applicant, the position under the amended provision remains substantially unchanged, since acts addressed to individuals typically take the form of decisions.

'An act addressed to another person'

'An act addressed to another person' clearly includes a decision addressed to another person (typically to a Member State or Member States). To challenge such a measure, the applicant must establish both direct and individual concern.

By contrast, the position regarding regulations is less clear. Previously, under **Article 230 EC**, in order to establish standing to challenge a regulation (in addition to the requirements for direct and individual concern), an applicant had to show that the measure was 'a decision in the form of a regulation'. Although the Court of Justice addressed this provision in a number of cases, the precise scope of the 'decision in disguise' requirement remained uncertain. With the **Lisbon Treaty** amendments, this provision has been abandoned in its entirety. However, fresh uncertainty has been introduced by the new provision in **Article 263 TFEU** concerning 'regulatory acts'.

'A regulatory act which is of direct concern to the applicant, and which does not entail implementing measures'

Article 263 affords standing to a non-privileged applicant in respect of 'a regulatory act which is of direct concern to the applicant, and which does not entail implementing measures'. Unfortunately, the Treaties do not define 'regulatory act', though the **TFEU** makes a distinction between 'legislative acts' (adopted by the Council and the European Parliament under legislative procedures) and 'non-legislative acts' (adopted by the Commission under delegated powers) (**Articles 289–290 TFEU**). If defined broadly, 'regulatory act' could include both legislative regulations and non-legislative regulations. Conversely, if defined narrowly, 'regulatory act' could well be confined to non-legislative regulations.

The broad definition of 'regulatory act' would result in a more liberal approach to standing for non-privileged applicants, since only direct concern would need to be established in relation to both legislative and non-legislative regulations, provided the regulation in question did not entail implementing measures. On the other hand, if the narrow definition were to be adopted, legislative regulations would presumably fall within the scope of 'acts addressed to another person' and applicants would need to establish both direct and individual concern.

It will be for the European Court of Justice to decide the meaning of 'regulatory act' and the Court's conclusion on this point will no doubt be awaited with great interest. Whatever the outcome, 'direct concern' (in relation to all acts, save those addressed to the applicant) and 'individual concern' (in relation to 'acts addressed to another person') will continue to be key concepts in EU judicial review.

Direct concern

To establish direct concern the applicant must show a direct link or unbroken chain of causation between the act and the damage sustained. A link is not established if the measure eaves

Action for annulment: Article 263 TFEU

****

a Member State discretion in implementation, for here the applicant is affected not by the act itself but by its implementation.

Municipality of Differdange v Commission (Case 222/83) [1984] ECR 2889

A Commission decision addressed to Luxembourg authorized it to grant aid to steel producers, provided they reduced production capacity. The applicant sought annulment of the decision, claiming that reduced production would result in the loss of local tax revenue. The Court of Justice held that the decision left the national authorities and producers discretion in implementation, particularly regarding the choice of factories for closure. It was the exercise of that discretion that affected the applicant, which was therefore not directly concerned by the Commission decision.

Identification of direct concern can entail fine distinctions.

Paraiki-Patraiki v Commission (Case 11/82) [1985] ECR 207

The applicant companies sought to challenge a Commission decision authorizing France to impose quotas on cotton yarn imports from Greece. The French authorities had discretion, since they could choose whether or not to use the authorization. Despite this, the Court of Justice held that the possibility that the authorities would not impose quotas was 'purely theoretical', since France already restricted Greek yarn imports and had requested permission to impose even stricter quotas. The applicants were therefore directly concerned by the decision.

With respect to 'regulatory acts', the distinction (if any) between direct concern and 'entailing implementing measures' remains to be determined.

Individual concern

This requirement is applied very restrictively and has proved a significant hurdle for applicants. The **Plaumann** formula is the classic test.

Plaumann v Commission (Case 25/62) [1963] ECR 95

Plaumann, a clementine importer, sought to challenge a Commission decision addressed to Germany refusing it authorization to reduce customs duties on clementines imported into the [EU]. The Court of Justice declared that persons other than those to whom a decision is addressed are individually concerned only if the decision affects them 'by reason of certain attributes which are peculiar to them or by reason of circumstances in which they are differentiated from all other persons'. The decision must distinguish them individually in the same way that it distinguished the original addressee. Plaumann was affected because of a commercial activity that in future could be taken up by any other person. The company could not claim to be singled out by the decision and so was not individually concerned.

✅ Looking for extra marks?

The **Plaumann** test has been criticized as commercially unrealistic and, in practice, virtually impossible to satisfy. Whilst theoretically anyone in the EU can set up business in a particular sector, for instance as a clementine importer, this may not be possible where, as is often the case, the sector is dominated by a small number of operators. Against that commercial reality, it can be argued that anyone might, in theory, enter the market or, more generally, that the distinguishing characteristics claimed by the applicant may in the future be acquired by any other person. Consequently, it is difficult to establish individual concern.

Despite the difficulties, non-privileged applicants are sometimes able to establish individual concern. They have done so, in particular, when they were a member of a class of persons that was fixed and ascertainable (a 'closed class') at the date the measure was passed and, consequently, the measure had only retrospective impact on a specific group of persons.

....

Paraiki-Patraiki v Commission (Case 11/82) [1985] ECR 207

It will be recalled that the applicants sought annulment of a Commission decision authorizing France to impose quotas on cotton yarn imports from Greece. Considering individual concern, the Court of Justice declared that the mere fact that the applicants exported the product to France was not sufficient to distinguish them from any other current or future exporter. However, they were distinguished by the fact that, before the adoption of the decision, they had entered into contracts for sale of the products. They were held to be individually concerned.

....

Because the applicants had entered into contracts before the decision was adopted, they were part of a closed class of applicants, a class that was fixed and ascertainable at the date the measure was passed.

✅ Looking for extra marks?

The Court of Justice has held steadfastly to the restrictive interpretation of 'individual concern', doubtless fearful of opening the floodgates to challenges to EU law and of hindering the institutions' ability to adopt legislation in the general interest. In defence of this stance, the Court referred to the other possible routes open to applicants, in particular indirect challenge through **Article 267** and damages claims against the EU under **Article 340**. The continuing criticism of the Court's unswerving approach, denying access to judicial review to large numbers of non-privileged applicants, culminated in pressure for reform in **UPA** and **Jégo-Quéré**. Both concerned challenges to regulations.

....

Union de Pequeños Agricultores v Council (UPA) (Case 50/00P) [2002] ECR I-6677

UPA's challenge to a regulation withdrawing aid for olive oil producers had been held inadmissible by the Court of First Instance (CFI). UPA had failed to establish individual concern. The CFI ejected

UPA's argument that the current test for individual concern denied individuals effective legal protection, declaring that UPA could have brought proceedings in the national court and sought an **Article 267** reference on the legality of the regulation.

On appeal to the Court of Justice, Advocate-General Jacobs articulated the difficulties of the **Article 267** route. In particular, there may be no national implementing measure on which national action could be based, a national court has no power to annul EU law, an applicant cannot insist on a reference, and the preliminary reference procedure entails delay and cost. He proposed a new test for individual concern: 'the measure has, or is liable to have, a substantial adverse effect on [the applicant's] interests'.

The Court of Justice rejected these arguments and reaffirmed the existing case law on individual concern.

Before the judgment in *UPA*, and in the light of Advocate-General Jacobs's opinion in that case, in *Jégo-Quéré v Commission* (Case T-177/01), the CFI called for review of the test for individual concern. It proposed that an individual should be regarded as individually concerned by a regulation if it 'affects his legal position in a manner which is both definite and immediate, by restricting his rights or by imposing obligations on him'. The Court of Justice subsequently upheld the Commission's appeal against the CFI's decision in *Jégo-Quéré*, again reaffirming the *Plaumann* test for individual concern (*Commission v Jégo-Quéré* (Case C-263/02P)).

Revision tip

Be familiar with the key points on standing for non-privileged applicants – direct concern, individual concern, and the new provision on 'regulatory acts'.

Grounds for annulment

The grounds for annulment, which may well overlap in individual cases, are set out in **Article 263(2)**.

Lack of competence

Here, the institution adopting the measure does not have the necessary power. For instance, in *Germany v European Parliament and Council (Tobacco Advertising)* (Case C-376/98) a directive banning tobacco advertising, identified as a public health measure, was annulled because it was adopted under a Treaty article concerning the internal market. Lack of competence is similar to *ultra vires* in English law.

Infringement of an essential procedural requirement

This arose, for instance, in *Roquette Frères v Council* (Case 138/79), concerning a failure to consult Parliament before the adoption of a measure, as required by the Treaty.

Infringement of the Treaty or of any rule of law relating to its application

This broad ground covers any infringement of EU law, including the general principles of non-discrimination, proportionality, and fundamental human rights. **Transocean Marine Paint v Commission** (Case 17/74) provides an example of annulment on the basis of a breach of the principle of natural justice.

Misuse of powers

This entails the adoption of a measure for a purpose other than that intended by the Treaty provision constituting its **legal base**. In **UK v Council** (Case C-84/94), for instance, the UK argued, unsuccessfully, that the **Working Time Directive** was wrongly based on **Article 118a EC** (now **Article 153 TFEU**) concerning health and safety at work.

Effect of annulment

If the grounds are established, the measure is declared void and the institution concerned must take measures to comply with the judgment.

Action for failure to act: Article 265 TFEU

Article 265 allows privileged and non-privileged applicants to challenge inaction by the EU institutions, the European Central Bank and the bodies, offices, or agencies of the EU, where they have a duty to act. That duty must be sufficiently well defined.

European Parliament v Council (Case 13/83) [1985] ECR 1513

Parliament challenged the Council's failure to implement a common transport policy, as required by **Article 74 EC** (now **Article 90 TFEU**), and to ensure freedom to provide transport services, as required by various other Treaty provisions. Parliament succeeded on the second allegation, as the relevant obligation was clear, but not on the first, as the obligation was not sufficiently precise.

Originally, strict *locus standi* requirements were imposed on non-privileged applicants.

Bethell v Commission (Case 246/81) [1982] ECR 2277

Lord Bethell sought to challenge the Commission's failure to act on breaches of the competition rules by airlines. Declaring the action to be inadmissible, the Court of Justice held that to bring a challenge under [**Article 265**], the applicant must show that it would be an addressee of the potential act.

Subsequently, the standing requirements have been relaxed.

T Port v Bundesanstalt für Landeswirtschaft und Ernährung (Case C-68/95) [1996] ECR I-6065

The Court of Justice applied *locus standi* requirements analogous to those under [**Article 263 TFEU**], holding that the applicant must show that it would be directly and individually concerned by the potential act.

An action will be admissible only if the institution concerned has first been called upon to act and has failed to define its position within two months. Following a declaration of failure to act, the institution must take the necessary measures to comply with the Court's judgment (**Article 266**).

Relationship between Articles 263 and 265

Articles 263 and 265 complement each other by covering, respectively, illegal action and illegal inaction. They have been described by the Court of Justice as prescribing 'one and the same method of recourse' (*Chevally v Commission* (Case 15/70)). They can be pleaded in the alternative but both cannot be applied to the same circumstance.

Eridania v Commission (Cases 10 & 18/68) [1969] ECR 459

The Court of Justice held that the Commission's refusal to revoke certain decisions on the grant of aid to sugar producers amounted to an act, not a failure to act. Accordingly, only [**Article 263**] could be applied. [**Article 265**] should not be used to bypass the limitations of [**Article 263**], notably the two-month time limit for bringing proceedings. The annulment action was held inadmissible for lack of direct and individual concern.

Plea of illegality: Article 277 TFEU

Under **Article 277** 'any party', including privileged and non-privileged applicants, may challenge an 'act of general application' indirectly, even where the two-month time limit laid down by **Article 263** has elapsed. **Article 277** does not provide an independent cause of action but may be invoked during other proceedings. For instance, in an action for annulment of a decision under **Article 263**, the applicant may seek to challenge the underlying regulation on which that decision is based. The grounds for review are identical to the **Article 263** grounds. The outcome of a successful challenge is a declaration of inapplicability.

Overview: Article 340 TFEU

EU liability in damages

Non-contractual liability: 'The Union shall, in accordance with the general principles common to the laws of the Member States, make good any damage caused by its institutions or by its servants in the performance of their duties' (Article 340 TFEU)

General principles common to the laws of the Member States – applicant must establish:

- wrongful act
- actual damage
- causation
  (Lütticke)

Wrongful act

Schöppenstedt

(General legislative measures involving choices of economic policy)

The applicant must show:

- **a sufficiently serious breach** *(HNL)*
  (institution has 'manifestly and gravely disregarded the limits on its discretion' with regard to the effect of the measure *(HNL)*; or Court of Justice may require the conduct to be 'verging on the arbitrary' *(Amylum)*
- **of a superior rule of law for the protection of individuals**
  (eg general principles of law, such as non-discrimination *(HNL)*

Bergaderm

Infringement of a rule of law intended to confer rights on individuals

Test for a sufficiently serious breach: the degree of discretion accorded to the institution, not the arbitrariness of the act or the seriousness of the damage caused

Damage

Must be quantifiable and exceed the loss arising from the normal economic risks inherent in business (eg *HNL*)

Causation

The damage must be a sufficiently direct consequence of the institution's breach *(Dumortier)*

Plea of illegality: Article 277 TFEU
****

Article 340 provides a mechanism for recovery of damages by individuals who have suffered loss as a result of EU action:

> In the case of non-contractual liability, the Union shall, in accordance with the principles common to the laws of the Member States, make good any damage caused by its institutions or by its servants in the performance of their duties.

This is an independent form of action, so an applicant need not first secure annulment under **Article 263**.

In cases of damage caused by EU officials, the Court of Justice will apply the test in *Sayag v Leduc* (Case 9/69): the EU 'is only liable for acts of its servants which, by virtue of an internal and direct relationship, are the necessary extension of the tasks entrusted to [it]'. Where, more commonly, the claim concerns an act of an EU institution, three elements must be established: a wrongful or illegal act, damage, and causation (*Lütticke v Commission* (Case 4/69)).

Wrongful act: the original approach in *Schöppenstedt*

Under the so-called *Schöppenstedt* formula, a distinction was drawn between legislative and administrative acts (*Schöppenstedt Aktien-Zuckerfabrik v Council* (Case 5/71)). With regard to administrative breaches, liability could be established on the basis of illegality alone.

Administrative breaches

Adams provides an example.

....

Adams v Commission (Case 145/83) [1985] ECR 3539

Adams had alerted the Commission to alleged competition law breaches by his employer, the Swiss pharmaceutical company Hoffmann-La Roche. The Commission disclosed documents to the company from which the latter identified Adams as the informant. Subsequently Adams was convicted of economic espionage in Switzerland. In [**Article 340**] proceedings brought by Adams, the Court of Justice found that the Commission's negligence in disclosing the documents to La Roche and its failure to warn Adams, who had moved to Italy, that he would be prosecuted if he returned to Switzerland, gave rise to liability in damages.

....

General legislative measures involving choices of economic policy

In *Schöppenstedt* the Court applied a more rigorous test to general legislative measures involving choices of economic policy. For these measures, liability arose only where there was a 'sufficiently flagrant violation of a superior rule of law for the protection of the individual'.

A sufficiently flagrant violation of a superior rule of law

Applying *Schöppenstedt* subsequently, the Court of Justice included within the scope of 'superior rule of law' Treaty articles and general principles of law, such as equality, proportionality, legal certainty, and legitimate expectation. According to *Schöppenstedt*, not only must the applicant establish a breach, but that breach must be a sufficiently flagrant violation of superior rule of law for the protection of individuals. Where the institution concerned acted with a wide discretion, the applicant must show that the institution manifestly and gravely disregarded the limits on its powers. In *HNL*, the Court's assessment was based upon the effect of the measure.

· ·

Bayerische HNL Vermehrungsbetriebe GmbH v Council and Commission
(Cases 83 & 94/76, 4, 15 & 40/77) [1978] ECR 1209

In order to reduce surplus stocks of skimmed milk powder, a regulation was passed requiring its purchase for use in poultry feed. Previously, the Court of Justice had held the regulation void, as discriminatory and disproportionate. Here, the applicant claimed an adverse effect on its business because the measure increased the cost of feed. The Court found that the regulation affected wide categories of traders, reducing its effect on individual businesses. Further, the regulation had only limited impact on the price of feed, by comparison with the impact of world market price variations. Consequently, the breach was not manifest and grave.

· ·

In other cases the Court focused on the nature of the breach. In *Amylum* it applied an even more rigorous test, requiring the institution's conduct to be 'verging on the arbitrary'.

· ·

Amylum NV v Council and Commission (Isoglucose) (Cases 116 & 124/77)
[1979] ECR 3497

A small group of isoglucose producers sought damages in respect of a regulation imposing production levies, which had previously been held invalid for discrimination because no levies were imposed on sugar, a competing product. Despite the serious impact of the measure, including the liquidation of one of the companies, the action failed. The Court of Justice held that the institution's conduct could not be regarded as 'verging on the arbitrary'.

· ·

✅ *Looking for extra marks?*

In applying these restrictive tests the Court of Justice sought to ensure that the risk of successful damages claims by individuals did not hinder the legislative function. The strictness of the tests meant that such actions rarely succeeded.

Bergaderm: a different approach

The development of state liability caused the Court of Justice to reconsider its approach to EU liability. In *Bergaderm* it aligned the principles relating to state and EU liability, reiterating its previous declarations in *Brasserie du Pêcheur and Factortame III* (Cases C-46 & 48/93).

Plea of illegality: Article 277 TFEU
****

....

Laboratoires Pharmaceutiques Bergaderm SA and Goupil v Commission
(Case C-352/98P) [2000] ECR I-5291

This was an appeal against a Court of First Instance decision rejecting Bergaderm's damages claim in respect of loss suffered as a result of a directive restricting the permissible ingredients of cosmetics, on health grounds.

The Court of Justice affirmed that the same conditions apply to state liability and EU liability. Liability arises where the rule infringed confers rights on individuals, the breach is sufficiently serious and there is a direct causal link between the breach and the damage. A sufficiently serious breach is established when there is a manifest and grave disregard of discretion by the EU or the Member State. Where that discretion is considerably reduced or there is no discretion, a mere infringement may be sufficient. The general or individual nature of a measure is not decisive in identifying the limits of the institution's discretion.

....

This represents a significant departure from *Schöppenstedt*. The rule infringed need no longer be a 'superior rule of law', but merely intended to confer rights on individuals. The decisive test for a sufficiently serious breach is the degree of discretion accorded to the institution, rather than the arbitrariness of the act or the seriousness of the damage. It is likely that the additional factors set out in *Brasserie du Pêcheur* will be applied, namely the clarity of the rule, whether the error of law was excusable or inexcusable, and whether the breach was intentional or voluntary. Finally, a distinction is no longer drawn between administrative and legislative acts.

Revision tip

Be ready to discuss the developing test for a 'wrongful act' under **Article 340** and the closer alignment of state and EU liability.

Damage

The applicant must prove the loss, which must be quantifiable and exceed the loss arising from the normal economic risks inherent in business. In **HNL**, for instance, the loss did not satisfy this requirement. Damage to person or property and economic loss are recoverable, but the Court will not compensate speculative loss. Steps must be taken to mitigate the loss. Damages will be reduced if the applicant has in some way contributed to its loss.

Causation

To establish the necessary causal link, the applicant must show that the damage is a sufficiently direct consequence of the institution's breach. Compensation is not available for every harmful consequence, however remote.

Dumortier Frères v Council (Cases 64 & 113/76, 167 & 239/78, 27, 28 & 45/79) [1979] ECR 3091

In relation to an unlawful withdrawal of production subsidies, the Court of Justice rejected claims based on reduced sales, financial problems, and factory closures. Even if the Council's actions had exacerbated the applicants' difficulties, those difficulties were not a sufficiently direct consequence of the unlawful conduct to give rise to liability.

Concurrent liability

Frequently, EU legislation requires implementation by national authorities. Where loss results wholly or partly from implementation, the question arises as to whether the applicant should bring proceedings against the national authorities in the national court, against the relevant EU institution in the Court of Justice, or both. Only national courts have jurisdiction to award damages against national authorities and, conversely, claims in respect of damage caused by EU institutions must be brought in the EU General Court. The Court of Justice has held that any national cause of action must be exhausted before proceedings are brought before the Court of Justice, provided the national action can result in compensation (***Krohn v Commission*** (Case 175/84)).

Time limit

Article 340 proceedings must be brought within five years of the materialization of the damage (**Statute of the Court, Article 46**).

 **(✱) Key cases**

Case	Facts	Principle
Article 258 cases		
Commission v Belgium (Case 1/86) [1987] ECR 2797	Failure to implement a directive.	Breaches include acts and failures to act.
Star Fruit Company v Commission (Case 247/87) [1989] ECR 291	Star Fruit complained to the Commission about breaches of [EU] law by France.	The Commission has a discretion, not a duty, to commence proceedings.

Key cases

****

Case	Facts	Principle
Commission v Italy (Re Transport Statistics) (Case 101/84) [1985] ECR 2629	Failure to implement a directive due to the bombing of a data-processing centre.	This could amount to force majeure and provide a defence to non-implementation but a delay of four years was inexcusable.
Commission v UK (Tachographs) (Case 128/78) [1979] ECR 419	Failure to implement a directive on fitting tachographs to lorries due to cost and political difficulties.	Defence based on economic and political difficulties rejected.
Commission v France (Case 232/78) [1979] ECR 2729	France argued in its defence that another Member State had failed to fulfil a similar obligation and that the Commission had not brought proceedings.	Defence based on reciprocity rejected.
Commission v France (Case 167/73) [1974] ECR 359	Discriminatory French provisions on employment in the merchant fleet were not enforced in practice.	Actual or administrative compliance is no defence.
Article 263 cases		
IBM v Commission (Case 60/81) [1981] ECR 2639	IBM sought to challenge a letter from the Commission setting out its intention to institute competition proceedings.	'Reviewable act': 'any measure the legal effects of which are binding on, and capable of affecting the interests of, the applicant by bringing about a distinct change in his legal position'.
Municipality of Differdange v Commission (Case 222/83) [1984] ECR 2889	A Commission decision addressed to Luxembourg authorized it to grant aid to steel producers, provided they reduced production capacity.	The decision left the national authorities, and the companies, discretion in implementation in the choice of factories to be closed. The exercise of that discretion affected the applicant, which was not therefore directly concerned.
Paraiki-Patraiki v Commission (Case 11/82) [1985] ECR 207	The applicants sought to annul a Commission decision authorizing France to impose quotas on cotton yarn imports from Greece.	The possibility that France would not use its discretion was 'purely theoretical'; it had already restricted Greek yarn imports and requested permission to impose even stricter quotas. The applicants were therefore directly concerned by the decision.

Case	Facts	Principle
Plaumann v Commission (Case 25/62) [1963] ECR 95	Plaumann, a clementine importer, sought to challenge a Commission decision addressed to Germany, refusing it authorization to reduce customs duties on clementines.	Persons other than those to whom a decision is addressed are individually concerned only if the decision affects them 'by reason of certain attributes which are peculiar to them or by reason of circumstances in which they are differentiated from all other persons'.
Jégo-Quéré v Commission (Case T-177/01) [2002] ECR II-2365	The applicant sought to challenge a regulation concerning fishing-net mesh sizes.	The Court of First Instance proposed that an individual should be considered individually concerned by a regulation if it 'affects his legal position, in a manner which is both definite and immediate, by restricting his rights or by imposing obligations on him'.
Union de Pequeños Agricultores v Council (UPA) (Case 50/00P) [2002] ECR I-6677	UPA's challenge to a regulation withdrawing aid for olive oil producers had been held inadmissible by the Court of First Instance. UPA had failed to establish individual concern.	On appeal to the Court of Justice, the A-G proposed a new test for individual concern: 'the measure has, or is liable to have, a substantial adverse effect on his interests'. The Court of Justice rejected this test, reaffirming the existing case law.
Commission v Jégo-Quéré (Case C-263/02P) [2004] ECR I-3425)	The applicant sought to challenge a regulation concerning fishing-net mesh sizes.	The Court of Justice reaffirmed the Plaumann test for individual concern.
Article 340 cases		
Lütticke v Commission (Case 4/69) [1971] 325	Action concerning the Commission's refusal to bring enforcement proceedings against Germany.	The applicant must establish a wrongful or illegal act, damage, and causation.
Schöppenstedt Aktien-Zuckerfabrik v Council (Case 5/71) [1971] 975	Action concerning a regulation on sugar prices.	The breach must be a sufficiently flagrant violation (sufficiently serious breach (HNL)) of a superior rule of law for the protection of individuals.

Case	Facts	Principle
Bayerische HNL Vermehrungsbetriebe GmbH v Council and Commission (Cases 83 & 94/76, 4, 15 & 40/77) [1978] ECR 1209	The applicant claimed damages in respect of a regulation requiring the purchase of skimmed milk powder for use in poultry feed.	Where the institution concerned acted with a wide discretion, the applicant must show that the institution manifestly and gravely disregarded the limits on its powers.
Amylum NV v Council and Commission (Isoglucose) (Cases 116 & 124/77) [1979] ECR 3497	The applicants sought damages in respect of a regulation imposing production levies.	The institution's conduct must be 'verging on the arbitrary'.
Laboratoires Pharmaceutiques Bergaderm SA and Goupil v Commission (Case C-352/98P) [2000] ECR I-5291	Appeal against a Court of First Instance decision rejecting Bergaderm's damages claim relating to a directive on cosmetics ingredients.	The same conditions apply to state liability and EU liability. The right to reparation arises where the rule infringed confers rights on individuals, the breach is sufficiently serious, and there is a direct causal link between the breach and the damage.
Dumortier Frères v Council (Cases 64 & 113/76, 167 & 239/78, 27, 28 & 45/79) [1979] ECR 3091	Damages claim concerning withdrawal of production subsidies.	The damage caused must be a sufficiently direct consequence of the institution's breach.

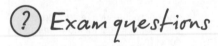 (?) Exam questions

Problem question

In 2007 the European Commission adopted (fictitious) Regulation 364/2007, which requires Member States to issue wine import licences each month to importers from outside the EU who submit licence applications during the previous month. On 1 February 2010 the European Commission issued a (fictitious) decision addressed to France allowing it to restrict licences for Argentinian wine imports for February 2010 so as to limit the amount that could be imported into France by an applicant to 10,000 litres during that month.

Argenco SA ('Argenco') imports Argentinian wine into the EU. In January 2010 it applied to import 15,000 litres of wine into France in February. A licence was granted on 2 February but was limited to 10,000 litres. The French authorities claimed to be acting pursuant to the Commission decision of 1 February.

Argenco now seeks your advice on instituting annulment proceedings in the General Court in respect of the Commission decision. Advise Argenco as to whether such an action would be admissible.

How, if at all, would your answer differ if in December 2009 the French authorities had informed Argenco that they had sought permission from the Commission to restrict import licences for Argentinian wine to 10,000 litres for the month of February 2010?

Essay question

In the case of non-contractual liability, Article 340 TFEU requires the EU to make good any damage caused by its institutions. Unfortunately, this provision has been interpreted so restrictively that individual applicants face almost insurmountable difficulties in establishing EU liability.

In the light of this statement, critically discuss the interpretation and application of Article 340 (and its predecessor, Article 288 EC) by the Court of Justice.

Outline answers are available at the end of the book.

Scan here

Scan this QR code image with your mobile device to see a full answer to these questions or log onto www.oxfordtextbooks.oc.uk/orc/concentrate/

#5
Free movement of goods

The examination

Free movement of goods is a key area of EU law and a favourite exam topic. Problem questions frequently concern national legislation that hinders trade between Member States. You may be asked, for instance, to advise a trader who is being prevented from importing goods from one Member State to another by legislation of the state of importation imposing requirements that are difficult or expensive to satisfy. Essay questions may ask you to discuss the range of free movement rules, the scope and development of derogation, and the approach of the Court of Justice in support of free trade, through liberal interpretation of the Treaty prohibitions and restrictive interpretation of the derogation provisions.

Key facts

- Free movement of goods is one of the four 'freedoms' of the internal market.

- Obstacles to free movement comprise tariff barriers to trade (customs duties and charges having equivalent effect), non-tariff barriers to trade (quantitative restrictions and measures having equivalent effect), and discriminatory national taxation.

- Where Member States set up such obstacles, they frequently do so to protect domestic products from competition from imports.

- The **TFEU** prohibits all kinds of restrictions on trade between Member States. **Article 30** (ex **Article 25 EC**) prohibits customs duties and charges having equivalent effect; **Article 34** (ex **Article 28 EC**) prohibits quantitative restrictions and all measures having equivalent effect; and **Article 110** (ex **Article 90 EC**) prohibits discriminatory national taxation.

- In *Cassis de Dijon* the Court of Justice held that measures satisfying certain 'mandatory requirements', which would otherwise be classified as measures having equivalent effect, do not breach **Article 34**, provided they are proportionate to their objective.

- In *Keck*, the Court declared that certain 'selling arrangements' fall outside the scope of **Article 34**.

- **Article 36** (ex **Article 30 EC**) allows derogation from the free movement of goods principle, setting out the grounds on which Member States may justify particular restrictions.

Treaty of Lisbon

The **Treaty of Lisbon** amended the **EC Treaty** and renamed it the **Treaty on the Functioning of the European Union (TFEU)**, replaced all references to 'European Community' and 'Community law' with 'EU' and 'EU law' respectively, and changed the numbering of Treaty articles. Note that pre-Lisbon case law uses the previous terminology and Treaty numbering. This chapter uses the term 'EU' and the new Treaty numbering throughout, placed in brackets where they appear in the case summaries.

Chapter overview

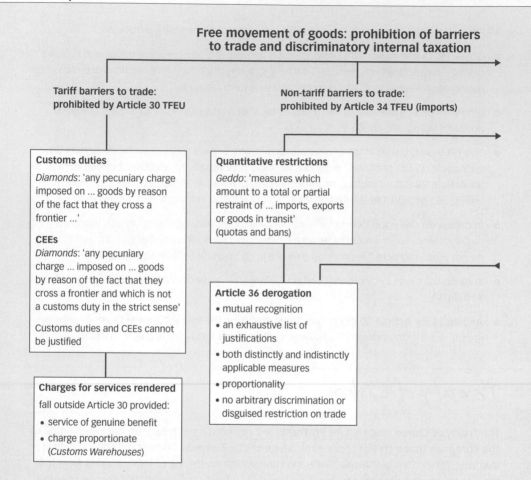

Free movement of goods: prohibition of barriers to trade and discriminatory internal taxation

Tariff barriers to trade: prohibited by Article 30 TFEU

Non-tariff barriers to trade: prohibited by Article 34 TFEU (imports)

Customs duties

Diamonds: 'any pecuniary charge imposed on ... goods by reason of the fact that they cross a frontier ...'

CEEs

Diamonds: 'any pecuniary charge ... imposed on ... goods by reason of the fact that they cross a frontier and which is not a customs duty in the strict sense'

Customs duties and CEEs cannot be justified

Quantitative restrictions

Geddo: 'measures which amount to a total or partial restraint of ... imports, exports or goods in transit' (quotas and bans)

Article 36 derogation
- mutual recognition
- an exhaustive list of justifications
- both distinctly and indistinctly applicable measures
- proportionality
- no arbitrary discrimination or disguised restriction on trade

Charges for services rendered

fall outside Article 30 provided:
- service of genuine benefit
- charge proportionate (*Customs Warehouses*)

Chapter overview

Free movement of goods: prohibition of barriers to trade and discriminatory internal taxation

Discriminatory internal taxation: prohibited by Article 110 TFEU

Measures having equivalent effect (MEQRs)

Dassonville: 'All trading rules enacted by Member States which are capable of hindering, directly or indirectly, actually or potentially, intra-Community trade'

Directive 70/50: measures hindering imports that do not apply equally (distinctly applicable) and measures governing marketing that do apply equally (indistinctly applicable)

Article 110(1)

Taxation of similar products must be equal

Article 110(2)

Where products are in competition, taxation must not give advantage to the domestic product

---

Measures falling outside Article 34

Cassis:

- mutual recognition
- rule of reason: mandatory requirements
- indistinctly applicable measures only
- proportionality
- extension of mandatory requirements in later cases

Keck:

- 'selling arrangements'
- applying to all affected traders
- having no greater impact on imports than on the domestic product

---

Objective justification

Possible in relation to indirect discrimination (*Chemial Farmaceutici*)

Introduction

The establishment of an **internal market**, in which goods, persons, services, and capital move freely without restriction, is fundamental to the goal of economic integration within the EU. Before turning to the EU rules supporting free trade in the internal market, it is useful briefly to consider the relationship between the EU internal market and the customs union.

Customs union

The EU **customs union** is based upon provisions concerning the movement of goods both into and within the EU. It has an external aspect, incorporating the **common customs tariff** (a common level of duty charged by all Member States on goods imported from third countries) and an internal aspect (a **free trade area** where customs duties and other trade restrictions between Member States are prohibited). The internal aspect of the customs union is an element of the EU internal market.

Internal market

Article 26 TFEU (ex **Article 14 EC**) defines the internal market as 'an area without internal frontiers in which the free movement of goods, persons, services and capital is ensured'. This definition identifies the **four freedoms** and underlines the free movement of goods as a core EU principle.

Restrictions on the free movement of goods

To achieve free movement of goods within the internal market, the **TFEU** prohibits import and export restrictions between Member States. Such restrictions, commonly referred to as 'barriers to trade', are frequently imposed by Member States for **protectionist motives**, to protect domestic products from competition from imports. Barriers to trade can be tariff or non-tariff. Both are prohibited. The **TFEU** also prohibits national taxation that discriminates between imported and domestic products.

Tariff barriers to trade

Tariff barriers to trade are import (or export) restrictions involving direct payments of money. They comprise customs duties and charges having equivalent effect to customs duties (CEEs). They are prohibited by **Article 30 TFEU**.

Customs duties and CEEs

A **customs duty** has two defining elements, referred to in numerous cases, such as *Diamonds* (*Sociaal Fonds voor de Diamantarbeiders v Chougol Diamond Co* (Cases 2 & 3/69)). First, it is a pecuniary charge (payment of money) and, secondly, it is imposed on goods by reason of the fact that they cross a frontier. The Court of Justice defined '**CEE**' in *Diamonds* as 'any pecuniary charge . . . imposed on . . . goods by reason of the fact that they cross a frontier and which is not a customs duty in the strict sense'. The charge need not be protectionist to constitute a breach.

Once identified as a customs duty or CEE, a charge cannot be justified and infringes **Article 30**. However, a charge may fall outside **Article 30** altogether, for instance if it is for services rendered to the importer.

Revision tip

Because they are easily identified, customs duties are unlikely to occur in practice. Consequently, they rarely feature in examination questions, but watch out for CEEs.

Charges for services rendered

Sometimes, Member States have argued that charges imposed on imports (or exports) fall outside **Article 30** because they are levied for services rendered, such as health inspection services (see for instance *Commission v Germany (Health Inspection Service)* (Case 314/82)).

Commission v Italy (Statistical Levy) (Case 24/68) [1969] ECR 193

Italy relied on this argument in relation to a charge it imposed on imports and exports, used to fund a statistical service for importers and exporters. The Court of Justice rejected this claim, holding that any benefit was so general and difficult to assess that the charge could not constitute a charge for services rendered. It was a breach of [**Article 30**].

For the charge to escape **Article 30**, not only must the service be of direct benefit to the importer (or exporter) but the charge must be **proportionate** to the value of the service.

Commission v Belgium (Customs Warehouses) (Case 132/82) [1983] ECR 1649

Belgium levied charges for storage of imported goods at public warehouses irrespective of whether the importer was depositing the goods to await customs clearance or simply presenting the goods for customs clearance. The Court of Justice held that a charge is a CEE unless it is the 'consideration for a service actually rendered'. Further, the charge must not exceed the value of the service.

Fees for health inspections required by EU law fall outside **Article 30**, provided they are proportionate, in the EU interest, and promote the free movement of goods (*Commission v Germany (Animal Inspection Fees)* (Case 18/87)).

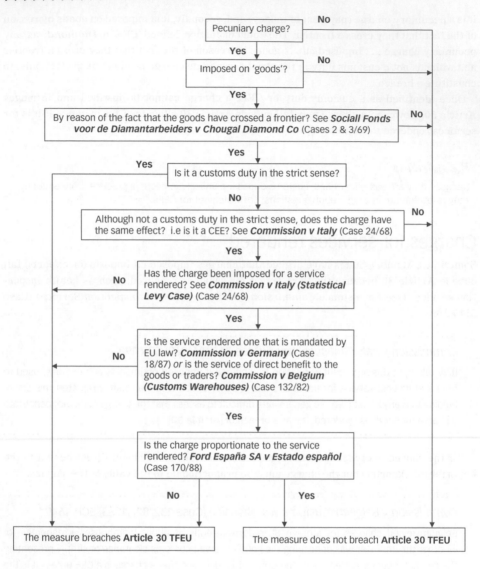

Figure 5.1 Article 30 TFEU

Prohibition of discriminatory taxation: Article 110 TFEU

Article 110 relates to national taxation systems operating internally. *Denkavit v France* (Case 132/78) defined internal taxation as 'a general system of internal dues applied systematically and in accordance with the same criteria to domestic products and imported products alike'. Internal taxation is distinguished from customs duties and CEEs. A charge is a tax if it is part of an internal system of taxation, as indicated by **Denkavit**. Customs duties and CEEs are charges levied on goods by reason of importation. **Articles 110 and 30** are complementary yet mutually exclusive (**Deutschmann v Germany** (Case 10/65)), so a charge on goods cannot be both a tax and a customs duty/CEE. The distinction is important because if classed as a customs duty or CEE it is unlawful under **Article 30 TFEU**. If classed as a tax, it is permissible provided it complies with **Article 110 TFEU**.

It is important to recognize that EU law does not prohibit national taxation but it does prohibit taxation that discriminates between imported and domestically produced goods. **Article 110(1)** prohibits taxes on imported products exceeding those applied to similar domestic products. **Article 110(2)** prohibits taxes on imported products giving indirect protection to other products. The Court of Justice has interpreted this to mean that where imported and domestic products are in competition, national taxation must not give advantage to domestic products. The approach of the Court of Justice used to be to treat the concepts of similar and competing as interchangeable. However, it should be noted that if **Article 110(1)** is breached, the Member State must equalize taxation. If **Article 110(2)** is breached, the Member State only has to remove the competitive effect of the tax regulation. Before turning to these provisions in more detail, the concepts of **direct** and **indirect discrimination** are considered, since both kinds of discrimination can infringe **Article 110**.

Direct and indirect discrimination

Measures that openly tax imported and domestic goods at different rates are directly discriminatory. Direct discrimination is rarely applied, as it is easily identified. However, it has occasionally occurred, for example in **Lütticke (Alfons) GmbH v Hauptzollamt Saarlouis** (Case 57/65) concerning a German tax on imported, but not domestically produced, powdered milk.

Indirectly discriminatory taxation is more difficult to identify. This is taxation that appears not to discriminate between imported and domestically produced goods but nevertheless has a discriminatory effect.

· ·

Humblot v Directeur des Services Fiscaux (Case 112/84) [1985] ECR 1367

A French system of annual vehicle taxation subjected lower power-rated cars to a lower tax than higher power-rated cars. As France did not produce the latter, the effect was to place imported cars at a competitive disadvantage, amounting to indirect discrimination and a breach of [**Article 110**].

· ·

Methods of tax collection and the basis of assessment

Discrimination may arise from the way in which tax is collected or the basis of assessment.

Commission v Ireland (Excise Payments) (Case 55/79) [1980] ECR 481

Ireland allowed domestic producers of spirits, beer, and wine deferment of tax payments until the products were marketed, whilst importers had to pay on importation. The tax rate was equal but the system of collection was discriminatory and breached [**Article 110**].

Outokumpu Oy (Case C-213/96) [1998] ECR I-1777

Finnish tax on domestically produced electricity varied according to the method of production, whereas imported electricity was taxed at a flat rate that was higher than the lowest rate charged on the domestic product. The Court of Justice held that there is a breach of [**Article 110**] where a different method of calculation leads, if only in certain cases, to a higher tax on the imported product.

Objective justification

Directly discriminatory taxation can never be justified and always breaches **Article 110**. By contrast, indirectly discriminatory taxation may be **objectively justified**.

Chemial Farmaceutici SpA v DAF SpA (Case 140/79) [1981] ECR 1

Italy imposed a higher tax on synthetic alcohol than on alcohol produced by fermentation, even though the products had identical uses. Italy produced very little synthetic alcohol. It argued that the system was based on a 'legitimate choice of economic policy' aimed to encourage production by fermentation rather than from ethylene, which, it maintained, should be reserved for more important economic uses. Although, on the facts, the Court of Justice found no discriminatory effect on the imported product, it accepted that legitimate policy objectives would justify differential taxation.

'Similar' products

Since **Article 110(1)** prohibits the differential taxation of 'similar' products, the 'similarity' of the imported and domestic products is clearly important. In a number of cases concerning alcoholic drinks, the Court of Justice has interpreted 'similar' broadly, to mean similar characteristics and comparable use, for instance in considering the similarity of Scotch whisky and liqueur fruit wine (*John Walker v Ministeriet for Skatter* (Case 243/84) and non-fruit spirits and fruit spirits (*Commission v France (French Taxation of Spirits)* (Case 168/78)).

'Indirect protection to other products'

Under **Article 110(2)**, where imported and domestic goods are not 'similar', but simply in competition with each other, national taxation must not give advantage to the domestic product.

Prohibition of discriminatory taxation: Article 110 TFEU

✳✳✳✳✳✳✳✳✳✳✳✳

Commission v United Kingdom (Excise Duties on Wine) (Case 170/78) [1980] ECR 417, [1983] ECR 2265

The UK taxed wine at a higher rate than beer. Comparing beer with the cheaper varieties of wine, the Court of Justice found that there was a degree of substitution between them and that the two products were in competition. Since the taxation system favoured the domestic product, it breached [**Article 110(2)**].

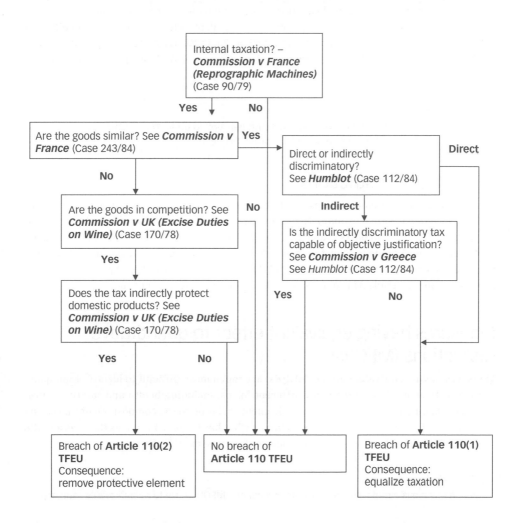

Figure 5.2 Article 110 TFEU

Harmonization of taxation

Harmonization of taxation within the EU could solve the problems arising from discriminatory taxation. However, whilst progress has been made on the approximation of VAT, excise duty, and corporation tax, Member States remain resistant to further transfer of control to the EU in this area.

Non-tariff barriers to trade

These are barriers to trade that do not involve direct payments of money, comprising quantitative restrictions and all measures having equivalent effect. Both are prohibited by **Article 34 TFEU** (relating to imports) and **Article 35 TFEU** (relating to exports). Most of the case law on **non-tariff barriers** concerns imports and so **Article 34** is the focus of this section.

Revision tip

Be able to distinguish 'tariff barriers' from 'non-tariff barriers' to trade. This will help you to correctly categorize restrictions presented in a problem question.

Quantitative restrictions

Like customs duties, **quantitative restrictions** are generally easily recognized. They were defined in *Geddo v Ente Nazionale Risi* (Case 2/73) as 'measures which amount to a total or partial restraint of . . . imports, exports or goods in transit', in other words import (or export) quotas and bans. A **quota** is a 'partial restraint' as it places a limit on the quantity of particular goods that can be imported. A **ban** is a 'total restraint' as it blocks the import of particular goods altogether. **Article 34** prohibits quantitative restrictions on imports.

Measures having equivalent effect to quantitative restrictions (MEQRs)

Measures having equivalent effect (MEQRs) are much more difficult to identify than quantitative restrictions. They take many different forms, including health and safety requirements, packaging requirements, and requirements relating to the composition or marketing of goods. 'MEQR' was defined in *Dassonville*, in what has become known as the '*Dassonville* formula'. **Directive 70/50** provides guidance on the scope of 'MEQR'.

Revision tip

Problem questions almost invariably feature at least one MEQR. Learn to recognize this category of restriction by studying the cases carefully.

Definition of 'MEQR': Dassonville

· ·

Procureur du Roi v Dassonville (Case 8/74) [1974] ECR 837

Traders who had imported Scotch whisky from France into Belgium were prosecuted in Belgium for infringement of national legislation requiring imported goods bearing a designation of origin to be accompanied by a certificate of origin issued by the state of origin. In their defence, the traders claimed that the requirement was an MEQR. The Court of Justice defined 'MEQRs' as: 'All trading rules enacted by Member States which are capable of hindering, directly or indirectly, actually or potentially, intra-Community trade . . .'. Applying this definition, the Court held that the Belgian requirement was an MEQR and a breach of [**Article 34**].

· ·

This definition is wide in scope, covering measures that are capable of hindering interstate trade actually and directly and also potentially and indirectly. Nonetheless, in *Dassonville* the Court accepted that 'reasonable' restraints may not be caught by Article 34, signalling an approach which, as will be seen later, it developed further in the *Cassis* 'rule of reason'.

Scope of MEQR: Directive 70/50

Directive 70/50 was a transitional measure, now expired, but it still gives useful guidance on the scope of 'MEQR'. The Directive identifies two categories of MEQR. First, it refers to measures that do not apply equally to domestic and imported products (**Article 2**), commonly called '**distinctly applicable measures**' because they make a distinction between domestic and imported products. Secondly, the Directive refers to measures that do apply equally to domestic and imported products (**Article 3**), commonly called '**indistinctly applicable measures**' because they make no distinction between domestic and imported products.

The Directive provides examples within each category, for instance distinctly applicable measures that restrict the advertising of imported products or lay down less favourable prices for imported products, and indistinctly applicable measures that deal with the 'shape, size, weight, composition, presentation, identification, or putting up' of products.

Revision tip

Problem questions: be confident about the *Dassonville* formula and **Directive 70/50** and always apply both to determine whether a measure is an MEQR.

Distinctly applicable MEQRs: examples from the cases

Typically, distinctly applicable measures treat imported and domestic products unequally by applying only to the imported product, placing it at a competitive disadvantage as against the domestic product.

Non-tariff barriers to trade

****

Rewe-Zentralfinanz v Landwirtschaftskammer Bonn (San Jose Scale) (Case 4/75) [1975] ECR 843

German inspection of imported (but not domestic) plant products, such as apples, to prevent the spread of a pest known as San Jose Scale was held to be an MEQR.

Procureur du Roi v Dassonville (Case 8/74) [1974] ECR 837

The Belgian rule requiring certificates of origin applied only to imports. The measure was an MEQR.

Sometimes, distinctly applicable measures treat imported and domestic products unequally by applying only to the domestic product, giving it a competitive advantage over the imported product.

Commission v Ireland ('Buy Irish' Campaign) (Case 249/81) [1982] ECR 4005

An Irish Government campaign to help promote Irish products, including widespread advertising of domestic (but not imported) products and use of the 'Guaranteed Irish' symbol constituted an MEQR.

Commission v Germany (Case C-325/00) [2002] ECR 1-9977

A 'quality label' awarded by a German public body to German products of a certain quality which indicated their German origin and was likely to encourage consumers to buy these, rather than imported products, was an MEQR, even though its use was optional.

All these cases concerned national provisions constituting a hindrance or disincentive to the importer, either because they imposed conditions which were difficult or costly to satisfy and/or because they gave advantage to the domestic product.

Indistinctly applicable MEQRs: examples from the cases

Indistinctly applicable measures apply equally to imported and domestic products.

Whilst indistinctly applicable MEQRs appear not to discriminate, their effect is to disadvantage imported products, creating a disincentive to importation and a hindrance to interstate trade.

Commission v United Kingdom (Origin Marking of Goods) (Case 207/83) [1985] ECR 1202

A UK requirement that certain goods (clothing and textiles, domestic electrical appliances, footwear, and cutlery) for retail sale in the UK be marked with their country of origin was an MEQR because, although it applied equally to imports and domestic products, it enabled consumers to distinguish between domestic and imported products, allowing them to assert any prejudices they may have against foreign products.

Walter Rau Lebensmittelwerke v de Smedt PvbA (Case 261/81) [1982] ECR 3961

Belgium required all margarine for retail sale to be cube-shaped.

There was no distinction between imports and the domestic product, but the effect was to increase the costs of non-Belgian producers, who would need to adapt their packaging to comply with a requirement that was not imposed by their own national legislation. The measure was an MEQR.

Revision tip

In order to apply *Cassis de Dijon* and **Article 36** (see later) correctly, you must be able to distinguish between distinctly and indistinctly applicable MEQRs.

Obligation to ensure the free movement of goods

Not only must Member States refrain from imposing measures that restrict the free movement of goods, they must also take steps to ensure the free movement of goods.

Commission v France (Case C-265/95) [1997] ECR I-6959

The French authorities had failed to prevent violent protests by French farmers against agricultural products being imported from other Member States, such as interception of lorries, violence against lorry drivers, and damage to goods displayed in French shops. The Court of Justice held that France was in breach of **Article 10 EC** (now **Article 4 TEU**), which requires Member States to take all appropriate measures to fulfil Treaty obligations.

Schmidberger v Austria (Case C-112/00) [2003] ECR I-5659

Austria's decision to allow a demonstration by environmental protesters, which caused a 30-hour motorway closure and impeded the free movement of goods, was a breach of **Article 34**, though the decision was justified on the grounds of the rights to freedom of expression and assembly.

Cassis de Dijon: measures falling outside Article 34

The notion that 'reasonable' restraints may fall outside **Article 34**, introduced in *Dassonville*, was developed in *Cassis de Dijon*.

Rewe-Zentral AG v Bundesmonopolverwaltung für Branntwein (Case 120/78) [1979] ECR 649 *(Cassis de Dijon)*

The applicant was refused permission to import Cassis de Dijon (blackcurrant liqueur) into Germany from France because the product did not comply with a German requirement that fruit liqueurs, to be marketed lawfully in Germany, must have a minimum alcohol content of 25%. The alcohol content of the French cassis was between 15 and 20%. The applicant challenged the legislation, claiming that it was an MEQR.

Germany argued that the measure was justified on grounds of public health and the fairness of commercial transactions, asserting that low-alcohol spirits create a tolerance to alcohol and cause alcoholism and that the high rate of national tax on high-alcohol drinks gave low-alcohol drinks a competitive advantage. The Court of Justice applied two principles that have become known as the 'principle of mutual recognition' and the 'rule of reason'.

Principle of mutual recognition

Mutual recognition is the fundamental principle underlying free movement of goods, articulated in *Cassis de Dijon*: provided goods have been lawfully produced and marketed in one Member State, there is no reason why they should not be introduced into another without restriction. *Prantl* illustrates this principle.

Criminal proceedings against Karl Prantl (Case 16/83) [1984] ECR 1299

German legislation restricted the use of bulbous 'Bocksbeutel' bottles to wine produced in certain German regions, where the bottles were traditional. These bottles were also traditional in parts of Italy. Prantl was prosecuted for importing into Germany Italian wine in 'Bocksbeutel' bottles. Applying the principle of mutual recognition, the Court of Justice held that national legislation may not prevent wine imports by reserving the use of a particular shape of bottle to its own national product, where similar shaped bottles were also used traditionally in the state of origin.

The *Cassis* rule of reason

According to the principle of mutual recognition, free trade between Member States is based upon the assumption that goods lawfully produced and marketed in one Member State are acceptable in another. However, this assumption will be set aside if the *Cassis* **'rule of reason'** applies. Restrictive measures falling within the rule of reason, which would otherwise be classified as MEQRs under *Dassonville*, are outside the scope of **Article 34**.

Cassis de Dijon contd

Unsurprisingly, the Court was unimpressed by Germany's arguments relating to alcohol tolerance and the competitive advantage afforded to low-alcohol drinks by German taxation. However, the Court held that certain kinds of restriction would be permissible on particular grounds, the 'mandatory requirements':

> obstacles to movement within the [EU] resulting from disparities between the national laws relating to the marketing of the products in question must be accepted in so far as those provisions may be recognised as being necessary in order to satisfy mandatory requirements relating in particular to the effectiveness of fiscal supervision, the protection of public health, the fairness of commercial transactions and the defence of the consumer.

This is known as the **Cassis** 'rule of reason'.

Put another way, the rule of reason provides that restrictions on trade resulting from national provisions on product marketing, which differ from those applying in other Member States, are permissible if they are necessary to satisfy one of the **mandatory requirements**. The mandatory requirements are the justifications that allow restrictions of this kind to escape the scope of **Article 34**.

No harmonizing rules

The **Cassis** rule of reason applies only in the absence of EU rules governing the interest concerned. If there is EU **harmonizing legislation** in a particular area, Member States may not impose additional requirements, unless that legislation expressly permits it.

Only indistinctly applicable measures

The rule of reason applies only to indistinctly applicable measures. Distinctly applicable measures cannot be justified by **Cassis** mandatory requirements. This limitation was not contained in the **Cassis** judgment itself but has been applied by the Court of Justice subsequently, for example in **Commission v Ireland**.

Commission v Ireland (Restrictions on Importation of Souvenirs) (Case 113/80) [1981] ECR 1625

The Court of Justice refused to apply the rule of reason to a distinctly applicable Irish measure, adopted allegedly in the interests of consumers and fair trading, requiring imported souvenirs depicting Irish motifs (such as shamrocks) to be marked 'foreign' or with their country of origin.

Extension of the mandatory requirements

It will be recalled that the *Cassis* rule of reason incorporates four mandatory requirements: the effectiveness of fiscal supervision, the protection of public health, the fairness of commercial transactions, and the defence of the consumer. This list is not exhaustive and, in later cases, the Court of Justice has added further mandatory requirements, including environmental protection (*Danish Bottles*), legitimate interests of economic and social policy (*Oebel*), and national and regional socio-cultural characteristics (*Torfaen Borough Council*).

Commission v Denmark (Danish Bottles) (Case 302/86) [1988] ECR 4607

Danish legislation for the protection of the environment limited the use of beer and soft drinks containers that had not been approved by the National Agency for the Protection of the Environment and required all containers to be reusable and subject to a deposit-and-return system. The Court of Justice held that the protection of the environment, as 'one of the [EU's] essential objectives', may justify restrictions on the free movement of goods.

Oebel (Case 155/80) [1981] ECR 1993

The Court of Justice found that German legislation prohibiting night working in bakeries and night deliveries of bakery products which, it was claimed, restricted deliveries into neighbouring Member States in time for breakfast, was compatible with **Article 34** because 'trade within the [EU] remained possible at all times'. Whilst it was not necessary for the German Government to justify the legislation, the Court recognized that legitimate interests of economic and social policy, designed to improve working conditions, could constitute a mandatory requirement.

Torfaen Borough Council v B&Q plc (Case 145/88) [1989] ECR 3851

With limited exceptions, the **Shops Act 1950** prohibited Sunday trading in the UK. B&Q argued that this provision was an MEQR because its consequence was to reduce sales and hence the volume of imports from other Member States. The Court of Justice found that the Sunday trading rules were justified because they were in accord with national or regional socio-cultural characteristics.

Proportionality

By permitting only 'necessary' restrictions, the rule of reason embodies a **proportionality** requirement. Restrictions must go no further than is necessary to achieve their objective, namely the effectiveness of fiscal supervision, the protection of public health, the fairness of commercial transactions, the defence of the consumer, or any other mandatory requirement. Proportionality has frequently proved an insurmountable hurdle for Member States, as demonstrated by *Cassis*, *Walter Rau*, and *Beer Purity*.

Cassis de Dijon contd

Germany's justifications for its legislation on the alcohol content of fruit liqueurs, the protection of public health, and the fairness of commercial transactions, fell within the 'mandatory requirements'. However, the provision was not necessary to satisfy those requirements. The same objectives could have been achieved by means that were less of a hindrance to trade, such as a requirement to label the products with their alcohol content.

Walter Rau contd

Belgium maintained that national legislation requiring margarine to be retailed in cube shapes was necessary to protect the consumer from the risk of confusing butter and margarine. The Court held that, whilst, in principle, legislation designed to prevent consumer confusion is justified, legislation prescribing a particular form of packaging goes further than is necessary to achieve that objective. Consumer protection could be achieved by measures which were less of a hindrance to interstate trade, such as a labelling requirement.

Commission v Germany (Beer Purity Laws) (Case 178/84) [1987] ECR 1227

Germany sought to justify a rule requiring all drinks marketed as 'bier' to contain only specified ingredients on grounds of consumer protection, claiming that German consumers associated 'bier' with products containing only these ingredients. The Court of Justice declared that consumer protection could be achieved by measures that were less of a hindrance to imports, namely a requirement for beer to be labelled with an indication of its ingredients.

Revision tip

Understand the meaning of proportionality and be familiar with its application in the cases. Typical problem questions will require you to apply this principle.

Keck and Mithouard: selling arrangements
Dual burden and equal burden rules

A number of cases following *Cassis* exposed a distinction between two categories of indistinctly applicable measures. First, there are rules relating to goods themselves, referred to as '**dual burden**' rules. These impose requirements that are additional to requirements that may be applied in the state of origin, creating an extra burden for producers. The 'cubeshaped margarine' requirement in *Walter Rau* is an example. Secondly, there are rules that concern the marketing of goods, described as '**equal burden**' because they impose an equal burden on domestic and imported products. They have an impact on the overall volume of sales, and therefore on imports, but they have no greater impact on imported products than on domestic products. *Keck* articulated this distinction.

The *Keck* judgment

. . . .

Keck and Mithouard (Cases C-267 & 268/91) [1993] ECR I-6097

Keck and Mithouard were prosecuted for reselling goods at a loss, breaching French competition law. Relying on **Article [34]** as a defence, they argued that the French legislation violated the free movement of goods principle. The Court of Justice acknowledged that the legislation restricted the overall volume of sales and hence the volume of sales of products from other Member States. However, the Court held, national measures prohibiting certain 'selling arrangements' do not fall within the *Dassonville* formula 'provided that those provisions apply to all affected traders operating within the national territory and provided that they affect in the same manner, in law and in fact, the marketing of domestic products and of those from other Member States'. Such provisions do not impede market access for imported products any more than for domestic products and fall outside [**Article 34**].

. . . .

✅ *Looking for extra marks?*

In *Keck*, the Court of Justice indicated that its judgment was aimed at traders who invoke [**Article 34**] to challenge national rules restricting their commercial freedom. Challenges of this kind had been made in the UK 'Sunday trading' cases, for instance in *B&Q*, referred to earlier.

Application of *Keck*

Keck applies only to rules concerning 'selling arrangements' and not to rules relating to the goods themselves, such as packaging, content, and labelling. In practice, this distinction may prove difficult to make, though later decisions have provided guidance on the scope of 'selling arrangement'. This term includes restrictions on shop opening hours (*Tankstation 't Heukske vof and JBE Boermans* (Joined Cases C-401/92 & C-402/92)), on the kinds of retail outlets from which certain goods can be sold (*Commission v Greece* (Case C-391/92)), and on product advertising (*Konsumentombudsmannen (KO) v De Agostini (Svenska) Förlag AB and Konsumentombudsmannen (KO) v TV Shop i Sverige AB* (Cases C-34–36/95)).

Even where a restriction is characterized as a selling arrangement, *Keck* stipulates that it will only escape **Article 34** if it applies to all affected traders in the national territory and affects in the same manner, in law and in fact, the marketing of domestic products and imported products. Any restriction with a discriminatory effect on imports constitutes an MEQR.

....

Schutzverband gegen unlauteren Wettbewerb v TK-Heimdienst Sass GmbH
(Case-254/98) [2000] ECR I-151

Austrian legislation prohibited butchers, bakers, and grocers from selling their goods on rounds from door to door unless they also conducted business from permanent establishments in the district. Whilst the legislation concerned selling arrangements applying to all traders, the Court of Justice found that traders from other Member States, to have the same access to the Austrian market as local traders, would need to incur the additional cost of setting up permanent establishments. The legislation impeded access to the Austrian market for imports and infringed [**Article 34**].

....

Revision Tip

Keck applies to 'selling arrangements', but only where they have no greater impact on imports than on domestic products. Remember that both elements of the rule must be satisfied. Where a measure fails to satisfy the **Keck** requirements, potential justification should be considered under the **Cassis** rule of reason or the **Article 36** derogation (see the following section).

Article 36 TFEU: derogation

Article 36, sets out the grounds on which Member States may justify restrictions on interstate trade, allowing **derogation** from the free movement of goods principle. Because of the fundamental importance of free movement to the internal market, the Court of Justice interprets these grounds very restrictively.

Article 36

Article 36 provides:

> **Articles 34 and 35** shall not preclude prohibitions or restrictions on imports, exports and goods in transit justified on grounds of public morality, public policy or public security; the protection of health and life of humans, animals or plants; the protection of national treasures possessing artistic, historic or archaeological value; or the protection of industrial and commercial property. Such prohibitions or restrictions shall not, however, constitute a means of arbitrary discrimination or a disguised restriction on trade between Member States.

An exhaustive list

Unlike the *Cassis* list of mandatory requirements, which has been extended by the Court of Justice, the **Article 36** list of justifications is exhaustive, as was made clear in *Commission v Ireland*.

. . . .

Commission v Ireland (Restrictions on Importation of Souvenirs) (Case 113/80) [1981]
ECR 1625

The Court of Justice refused to apply the *Cassis* rule of reason to a distinctly applicable Irish
measure requiring imported souvenirs depicting Irish motifs to be marked 'foreign' or with their
country of origin. The Court also refused to accept a justification based on consumer protection,
since this justification is not listed in [**Article 36**].

. . . .

Distinctly and indistinctly applicable measures

However, **Article 36** is broader than *Cassis* in that the justifications can apply to both distinctly and indistinctly applicable measures.

Proportionality

Like the *Cassis* rule of reason, **Article 36** requires measures to be 'justified' on one of the specified grounds. They must be no more than is necessary to achieve the desired aim, in other words they must be proportionate to their objective.

No arbitrary discrimination or disguised restriction on trade

For derogation to apply, a measure must not constitute 'a means of arbitrary discrimination or a disguised restriction on trade between Member States'. This precludes protectionist measures.

. . . .

Commission v United Kingdom (Imports of Poultry Meat) (Case 40/82)
[1982] ECR 2793

A UK licence requirement, introduced purportedly to prevent the spread of Newcastle disease,
effectively imposed a ban on turkey meat imports. The Court found that, in reality, the measure was designed to protect domestic producers, just as the Christmas season was beginning.
The measure amounted to arbitrary discrimination and a disguised restriction on trade.

. . . .

Mutual recognition

As under *Cassis*, the principle of mutual recognition applies. Unless restrictions are justified and proportionate, there is no reason why goods that have been lawfully produced and marketed in one Member State should not be introduced into another.

Article 36 grounds

Public morality

This ground was considered in two cases concerning restrictions on imports of pornography.

R v Henn and Darby (Case 34/79) [1979] ECR 3795

English customs legislation prohibited imports of pornographic films and magazines, despite there being no absolute ban on trade in similar material in the UK. Declaring that it was for Member States to determine the requirements of public morality nationally, the Court of Justice accepted the UK's argument that the legislation was justified on public morality grounds.

Conegate Ltd v Customs and Excise Commissioners (Case 121/85) [1986] ECR 1007

The UK customs authorities had seized a consignment of inflatable dolls and other erotic articles imported from Germany. The Court took a stricter view than in **Henn** and **Darby**. Although there were restrictions on similar domestic goods, these did not prohibit manufacture and sale. The UK could not rely on the public morality ground, though it would not be precluded from applying the same restrictions to the imported goods once they had entered the UK.

Public policy

Potentially wide in scope, 'public policy' has been interpreted narrowly by the Court of Justice. This ground cannot be used as a general justification embracing more specific defences, such as consumer protection, but must be given its own independent meaning (**Commission v Italy (Re Ban in Pork Imports)** (Case 7/61)). The public policy ground has rarely been invoked. **R v Thompson** provides one example.

R v Thompson (Case 7/78) [1978] ECR 2247

Recognizing a state's need to protect its right to mint coinage and to protect coinage from destruction, the Court of Justice held that a prohibition on import and export of gold collectors' coins was justified on public policy grounds.

Public security

This ground was successfully invoked in **Campus Oil**.

Campus Oil Ltd v Minister for Industry and Energy (Case 72/83) [1983] ECR 2727

Irish legislation required importers to purchase a percentage of their requirements from a state-owned oil refinery. The Court of Justice found that the measure was justified on public security grounds, since it ensured the maintenance of Irish refining capacity for products that were fundamental to the provision of essential services. An interruption of supplies could seriously threaten public security.

Protection of health and life of humans, animals, or plants

Two contrasting decisions, referred to earlier, elucidate the scope of this ground. German inspections of imported (but not domestically produced), apples were held to be justified on health grounds, as the imported fruit presented a risk not present in domestic apples. There must be a genuine health risk (*San Jose Scale*). By contrast, the Court of Justice rejected health justifications for UK restrictions on poultry meat imports. The measures were not part of a seriously considered health policy and constituted a disguised restriction on trade (*Imports of Poultry Meat*). The health risk was assessed in *DocMorris*.

Deutsche Apothekerverband v 0800 DocMorris NV (Case C-322/01) [2003] ECR I-14887

Germany banned the sale of medicines by mail order and over the internet. The measure related to 'selling arrangements', but fell outside **Keck** because it had a greater impact on imports than on domestic products. Thus, the ban infringed [**Article 34**]. The Court of Justice held that the measure could be justified on health grounds in relation to prescription medicines because consumers needed to receive individual advice and the authenticity of prescriptions must be checked. By contrast, non-prescription medicines did not present a risk, because the 'virtual pharmacy' could provide an equal or better level of advice than traditional pharmacies. Here, the prohibition was not justified.

One difficult area is the use of additives in foodstuffs, since there may be scientific uncertainty as to the extent of any risk.

Officier van Justitie v Sandoz BV (Case 174/82) [1983] ECR 2445

Holland prohibited the sale of muesli bars with added vitamins, maintaining that the vitamins were harmful to health. The bars were freely available in Germany and Belgium. The vitamins themselves presented no health risk, and were in fact necessary to human health, but their over consumption across a range of foodstuffs would constitute a risk. As scientific research had been unable to determine the critical amount or the precise effects, the Court of Justice declared that it was for Member States to decide the appropriate degree of public health protection, whilst observing the principle of proportionality. Member States must authorize marketing when the addition of vitamins to foodstuffs meets a technical or nutritional need.

In *Beer Purity*, a German ban on additives was held to be to be disproportionate.

Commission v Germany (Beer Purity Laws) (Case 178/84) [1987] ECR 1227

In addition to the rule on beer ingredients, noted earlier, German legislation also banned the use of all additives in beer. Seeking to rely on the [**Article 36**] public health derogation, the

German Government argued that because the German population drank large quantities of beer, the use of additives presented a greater public health risk in Germany than elsewhere in the [EU]. Noting that Germany permitted additives in virtually all other drinks, the Court of Justice decided that high beer consumption did not justify banning all additives in this particular product.

Protection of national treasures possessing artistic, historic, or archaeological value

The scope of this justification remains uncertain. In *Commission v Italy (Export Tax on Art Treasures, No 1)* (Case 7/68) the Court indicated that quantitative restrictions (but not charges) would be justified where the object of those restrictions was to prevent art treasures from being exported from a Member State.

Protection of industrial and commercial property

EU law protects the ownership of industrial and commercial property rights, such as patents, copyright, trade marks, and design rights. However, any improper use of these rights, constituting an obstacle to trade, will be condemned by the Court of Justice.

No harmonizing rules

Article 36 applies only in the absence of EU rules governing the interest concerned. If there is harmonizing legislation in a particular area, Member States may not impose additional requirements, unless the legislation expressly permits it.

✅ *Looking for extra marks?*

The account of **Cassis** and **Article 36** presented earlier sets out the established position that the **Article 36** list of justifications cannot be extended in the way that the **Cassis** list of mandatory requirements has been extended and that the **Cassis** rule of reason can apply only to indistinctly applicable measures. These principles, perfectly encapsulated, for instance, in **Commission v Ireland (Restrictions on Importation of Souvenirs)**, together with the principles of mutual recognition and proportionality, still hold good. You should discuss and apply them in answers.

At the same time, be aware that the Court of Justice has sometimes blurred the distinction between **Cassis** and **Article 36**, particularly regarding national measures for the protection of the environment. This point is illustrated by **PreussenElektra AG v Schleswag AG** (Case C-379/98), concerning German legislation requiring German electricity suppliers to purchase the electricity produced from renewable sources in their area of supply. Here, the Court avoided any discussion of the distinction between [**Article 36**] and **Cassis**, finding that this distinctly applicable measure was justified on environmental grounds.

Note that there is some overlap between the **Cassis** mandatory requirements and the **Article 36** justifications, notably the public health ground. Where this ground is invoked to justify an indistinctly applicable measure, the case may be presented under either **Cassis** or **Article 36**.

Article 36 TFEU: derogation
✱✱✱✱✱✱✱✱✱✱✱✱

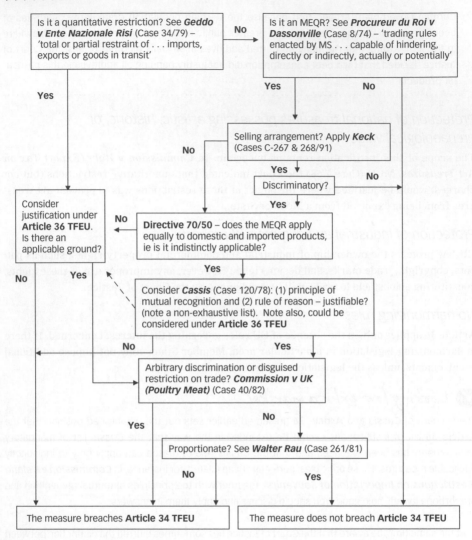

Figure 5.3 Article 34 TFEU

Harmonization

Harmonization aims to eliminate disparities between national product standards that hinder interstate trade, by establishing EU-wide standards. Once a measure harmonizing an area comprehensively is adopted, Member States have no recourse to derogation in that area. **Article 115 TFEU** (ex **Article 94 EC**) provides for the adoption of harmonizing directives for this purpose. Early progress on harmonization was slow, as the adoption of measures under **Article 115** required unanimity in the Council of Ministers. Consensus on comprehensive, detailed rules was difficult to achieve.

In 1985 a new approach focused on a minimum level of EU regulation in relation to technical harmonization and standards, rather than on comprehensive rules. A Council Resolution of 7 May 1985 states that directives are to be based upon the essential requirements with which products must conform. The detailed technical specifications are not a matter for EU legislation but for competent organizations, such as research and standards institutes.

Harmonization was progressed further with **Article 114 TFEU** (ex **Article 95 EC**), introduced by the **Single European Act 1986**, providing for the adoption of measures concerning the establishment and functioning of the internal market, by qualified majority vote. Member States wishing to apply stricter standards than those contained in EU harmonizing measures may seek approval from the Commission on the basis of 'major needs' or in relation to the environment or the working environment. Similarly, after the adoption of a harmonizing measure, approval may be sought under **Article 115** for the introduction of new national provisions based on new scientific evidence relating to the protection of the environment or the working environment.

✅ Looking for extra marks?

Taking an overview of this area of EU law, two distinct but complementary approaches to achieving the free movement of goods can be identified. The first is deregulatory and negative, entailing the prohibition of national rules that frustrate the internal market objective. The second is based upon positive integration. This approach seeks to eliminate barriers to interstate trade through the application of the principle of mutual recognition and through harmonization in areas such as technical requirements and health and safety.

✳ Key cases

Case	Facts	Principle
Diamonds (Sociaal Fonds voor de Diamantarbeiders v Chougol Diamond Co (Cases 2 & 3/69)) [1969] ECR 211	Belgian charge on imported diamonds.	'CEE': '. . . any pecuniary charge . . . imposed on . . . goods by reason of the fact that they cross a frontier and which is not a customs duty in the strict sense'. The charge need not be protectionist to constitute a breach.

Key cases

✳✳✳✳✳✳✳✳✳✳✳✳

Case	Facts	Principle
Commission v Belgium (Customs Warehouses) (Case 132/82) [1983] ECR 1649	Belgium charged importers for storage facilities.	For a charge to escape Article 30, the service must be of direct benefit to the importer (or exporter) and the charge must be proportionate to the value of the service.
Denkavit v France (Case 132/78) [1979] ECR 1923	French charge on meat products.	Internal taxation: '. . . a general system of internal dues applied systematically and in accordance with the same criteria to domestic products and imported products alike'.
Humblot v Directeur des Services Fiscaux (Case 112/84) [1985] ECR 1367	French two-tier system of car taxation based on power-rating.	Indirect discrimination: does not openly discriminate on the basis of product origin but its effect is to disadvantage imports.
Chemial Farmaceutici SpA v DAF SpA (Case 140/79) [1981] ECR 1	Italy taxed synthetic alcohol at a higher rate than alcohol produced by fermentation.	Indirectly discriminatory taxation can be objectively justified.
Geddo v Ente Nazionale Risi (Case 2/73) [1973] ECR 865	Italian levy on rice.	Quantitative restrictions: '. . . measures which amount to a total or partial restraint of . . . imports, exports or goods in transit'.
Procureur du Roi v Dassonville (Case 8/74) [1974] ECR 837	Belgian legislation requiring certificates of origin.	MEQRs: 'All trading rules enacted by Member States which are capable of hindering, directly or indirectly, actually or potentially, intra-Community trade are to be considered as measures having an effect equivalent to quantitative restrictions'.
Rewe-Zentralfinanz v Landwirtschaftskammer Bonn (San Jose Scale) (Case 4/75) [1975] ECR 843	Germany inspected imported (but not domestic) apples.	A distinctly applicable measure: the measure did not apply equally to imports and the domestic product.
Walter Rau Lebensmittelwerke v de Smedt PvbA (Case 261/81) [1982] ECR 3961	Belgium required margarine for retail sale to be cube-shaped.	An indistinctly applicable measure: the measure applied equally to imports and the domestic product.

Case	Facts	Principle
Rewe-Zentral AG v Bundesmonopolverwaltung für Branntwein (Case 120/78) [1979] ECR 649 (*Cassis de Dijon*)	German requirement: fruit liqueurs sold in Germany must have a minimum alcohol content of 25%.	Principle of mutual recognition: provided goods have been lawfully produced and marketed in one Member State, there is no reason why they should not be introduced into another without restriction. Rule of reason: restrictions must be accepted in so far as they are necessary to satisfy 'mandatory requirements'; the measure must be proportionate.
Commission v Ireland (Restrictions on Importation of Souvenirs) (Case 113/80) [1981] ECR 1625	Ireland required imported souvenirs depicting Irish motifs to be marked 'foreign' or with their country of origin.	The *Cassis* rule of reason applies only to indistinctly applicable measures. The Article 36 list of justifications is exhaustive.
Commission v Denmark (Danish Bottles) (Case 302/86) [1988] ECR 4607	Danish legislation for the protection of the environment concerning drinks containers.	The *Cassis* list of mandatory requirements extended by the Court of Justice to the protection of the environment.
Keck and Mithouard (Cases C-267 & 268/91) [1993] ECR I-6097	French competition rules prohibiting resale of goods at a loss.	National measures prohibiting 'selling arrangements' fall outside *Dassonville* 'provided that those provisions apply to all affected traders operating within the national territory and provided that they affect in the same manner, in law and in fact, the marketing of domestic products and of those from other Member States'.

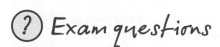

Problem question

Consider the following fictitious situation:

Freddie is a UK manufacturer of widget-grinding machines ('WGMs'), which he has supplied to widget manufacturers in the UK and France for the past ten years. Freddie now plans to import his machines into Portugal.

Freddie has learned that under Portuguese legislation a licence is required for the import of WGMs. Licence applications are considered by the Portuguese authorities in January and July

Exam questions

each year. Freddie has been told that Portugal places an annual limit on the number of WGMs that may be imported and has regulations stipulating that manufacturing machinery, including WGMs, can only be sold through government sales outlets.

Portugal also has health and safety legislation requiring all WGMs to be fitted with an external 'vacuum filtration' unit to collect particles emitted by the grinding process. This legislation has recently been introduced following the publication of a research study conducted in Portuguese heavy industry. The study suggests that, over the past six months, the number of new cases of industrial lung disease has been significantly lower amongst widget-grinding operatives working on Portuguese-manufactured machines (most of which already comply with the new legislation) than amongst operatives working on imported machines (none of which currently complies). Freddie's machines do not comply with the Portuguese legislation. They are fitted with internal 'vacuum filtration' units which, in Freddie's view, operate much more efficiently than the externally fitted filtration units required by the legislation.

Advise Freddie as to the application, if any, of EU law on the free movement of goods to all aspects of this situation.

Essay question

The free movement of goods is an essential element of the internal market and both EU legislation and the decisions of the Court of Justice support the achievement of this aspect of economic integration. However, the EU internal market is imperfect, so far as goods are concerned. There remain impediments to free movement which are not only embedded in the legislation but also arise from the case law of the Court of Justice.

In the light of this statement, critically discuss the extent to which EU legislation and the case law of the Court of Justice ensure the free movement of goods in the internal market.

Outline answers are available at the end of the book.

 Scan here

Scan this QR code image with your mobile device to see a full answer to these questions or log onto www.oxfordtextbooks.oc.uk/orc/concentrate/

#6
Free movement of persons

The examination

Free movement of persons is a popular examination topic. A topical issue for essay questions is the development of Union citizenship rights, associated case law, and **Directive 2004/38**. Other favourites are the rights of the self-employed and the developing alignment of the principles applying to persons exercising the right of establishment and persons providing services in another Member State. Some courses concentrate on free movement of workers, frequently the basis of problem questions. Look out for situations involving Union citizens seeking to exercise worker rights in another Member State and family members wishing to move with them. EU law on the free movement of persons is a combination of Treaty provisions, secondary legislation, and case law. All must be addressed, whether the question concerns workers or the self-employed.

Overview: legislation

TFEU

Article 21 TFEU: Union citizens

'Every citizen of the Union shall have the right to move and reside freely within the territory of the Member States, subject to the limitations and conditions laid down in this Treaty and by the measures adopted to give it effect'

Article 45 TFEU: Workers

Article 45(1): principle of free movement for workers
Article 45(2): no discrimination on grounds of nationality
Article 45(3): subject to limitations on grounds of public policy, public security, or public health, free movement entails the right to:

- accept offers of employment
- move freely within the territory of the Member States for this purpose
- stay in a Member State for the purposes of employment
- remain after employment has ceased
- Article 45(4): 'the provisions of this Article shall not apply to employment in the public service'

Article 18 TFEU: general principle of non-discrimination

'Within the scope of application of this Treaty ... any discrimination on grounds of nationality shall be prohibited'

Secondary legislation

Regulation 492/2011: workers – no discrimination on grounds of nationality regarding:

- access to employment
- conditions of employment

Directive 2004/38: Union citizens

Rights of entry and residence for up to three months (Articles 5-6):
- all Union citizens
- their family members

Rights of entry and residence for more than three months (Article 7):
Union citizens who are:
- workers
- self-employed
- persons who have sufficient resources and sickness insurance students (must make a declaration of sufficient resources and have sickness insurance)
and
- their family members

Jobseekers (Art 14): if seeking employment + have chance of being engaged

Overview: legislation

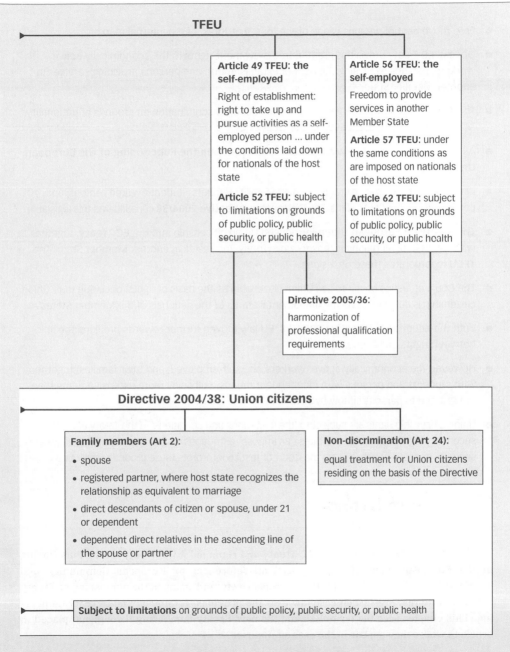

TFEU

Article 49 TFEU: the self-employed

Right of establishment: right to take up and pursue activities as a self-employed person ... under the conditions laid down for nationals of the host state

Article 52 TFEU: subject to limitations on grounds of public policy, public security, or public health

Article 56 TFEU: the self-employed

Freedom to provide services in another Member State

Article 57 TFEU: under the same conditions as are imposed on nationals of the host state

Article 62 TFEU: subject to limitations on grounds of public policy, public security, or public health

Directive 2005/36:

harmonization of professional qualification requirements

Directive 2004/38: Union citizens

Family members (Art 2):

- spouse
- registered partner, where host state recognizes the relationship as equivalent to marriage
- direct descendants of citizen or spouse, under 21 or dependent
- dependent direct relatives in the ascending line of the spouse or partner

Non-discrimination (Art 24):

equal treatment for Union citizens residing on the basis of the Directive

Subject to limitations on grounds of public policy, public security, or public health

Key facts

- Free movement of persons is one of the four 'freedoms' of the internal market.

- Original EC Treaty provisions granted free movement rights to the economically active – workers, persons exercising the right of establishment, and persons providing services in another Member State.

- The Treaty also set out the general principle of non-discrimination on grounds of nationality, 'within the scope of application of the Treaty'.

- All these provisions are now contained in the **Treaty on the Functioning of the European Union (TFEU)**.

- Early secondary legislation granted rights to family members, students, retired persons, and persons of independent means. The **Citizenship Directive 2004/38** consolidated this legislation.

- The **Treaty on European Union** introduced Union citizenship into the **EC Treaty**, together with the right of all Union citizens to move freely and reside in another Member State. The **TFEU** incorporates these provisions.

- The Court of Justice began to use Union citizenship as the basis of rights, declaring that 'Union citizenship is destined to be the fundamental status of the nationals of the Member States'.

- With the adoption of **Directive 2004/38**, EU law moved further towards breaking the link between rights and economic status.

- However, the economically active (workers, the self-employed, and their families) together with students and persons with independent means, still enjoy more extensive rights than are granted to persons simply by virtue of Union citizenship.

- Union citizenship rights are subject to 'the limitations and conditions' in the Treaty and secondary legislation. Member States can impose restrictions on grounds of public policy, public security, or public health, though the Court of Justice interprets these grounds restrictively.

Treaty of Lisbon

The **Treaty of Lisbon** amended the **EC Treaty** and renamed it the **Treaty on the Functioning of the European Union (TFEU)**, replaced all references to 'European Community' and 'Community law' with 'EU' and 'EU law' respectively, and changed the numbering of Treaty articles. Note that pre-Lisbon case law uses the previous terminology and Treaty numbering. This chapter uses the term 'EU' and the new Treaty numbering throughout, placed in brackets where they appear in the case summaries.

Free movement rights

Original Treaty provisions reflected the EU's economic origins, allowing the economically active – workers, the self-employed, and persons providing services – to move around the EU to take up employment or business activity and establishing the principle of non-discrimination on grounds of nationality. The **TFEU** now incorporates these rights in **Articles 45** (workers), **49** (the self-employed), **56** (persons providing services), and **18** (non-discrimination) (ex **Articles 39, 43, 49, 12 EC**). Later provisions, introduced by the **Treaty on European Union**, created Union citizenship and granted free movement rights to all Union citizens (**Articles 20, 21 TFEU** (ex **Articles 17, 18 EC**)).

These provisions were supplemented by secondary legislation according free movement rights to family members, students, retired persons, and persons of independent means (respectively **Directives 68/360, 90/366, 90/365, 90/364**). These directives have been repealed and their provisions consolidated into the **Citizenship Directive 2004/38**.

Limitations

Rights of free movement are not unlimited. **Article 21 TFEU** makes them subject to the 'conditions and limitations laid down in this Treaty and by the measures adopted to give it effect'. Member States can limit free movement and residence rights on grounds of public policy, public security, and public health. These grounds, set out in the Treaty, are defined and elaborated in **Directive 2004/38**.

Revision tip

It is essential to get to grips with this legislation. As you work through this chapter, use the Legislation overview chart to help you.

Citizens of the European Union

Article 20 TFEU provides that 'Citizenship of the Union is hereby established' and that every national of a Member State is a Union citizen. Article 21 grants free movement rights to all Union citizens, subject to 'the limitations and conditions' in the Treaty and secondary legislation. Clarification of the scope of Union citizens' free movement rights is found in case law and in **Directive 2004/38**.

Overview: case law

Union citizens
(Art 21 TFEU)

- *Grzelczyk*: 'Union citizenship is destined to be the fundamental status of the nationals of the Member States'
- Court of Justice based non-discrimination rights on citizenship
- *Baumbast*: the Court of Justice based residency rights on citizenship status, while recognizing that the Art 21 TFEU rights remain 'subject to the limitations and conditions laid down in this Treaty and by the measures adopted to give it effect'

Workers
(Art 45 TFEU, Directive 2004/30, Regulation 492/2011)

Who is a 'worker'? (no Treaty definition):

- *Lawrie-Blum*: '[the] essential feature of an employment relationship... is that for a certain period of time a person performs services for and under the direction of another person in return for which he receives remuneration'
- *Levin, Kempf*: part-time work
- *Ninni-Orasche*: fixed-term contracts
- *Steymann*: unpaid work
- *Bettray, Trojani*: is rehabilitation 'work'?

Equal access to employment (Regulation 492/2011):

- *French Merchant Seamen*: a breach of Article 4 (no limits by number or percentage)
- *Groener*: no breach of Art 3 (linguistic knowledge)

Access to public service posts (Art 45(4) TFEU):

- *Commission v Belgium*: 'public service' involves 'the exercise of power conferred by public law' where there is a 'responsibility for safeguarding the general interests of the State'

Equality of treatment in employment (Regulation 492/2011):

- *Cristini*: 'social and tax advantages' need not form part of the contract of employment

Jobseekers
(Directive 2004/38 (Art 14))

- *Royer*: right to enter to seek work
- *Antonissen*: right to remain if making genuine efforts to find work, with a real chance of being employed

Overview: case law

Self-employed persons
(Art 49 TFEU – right of establishment, Art 56 TFEU – freedom to provide services, Directive 2004/38 – right to enter and remain)

Establishment

Rules of professional conduct:

- *Gebhard*: 'measures liable to hinder or make less attractive the exercise of fundamental freedoms guaranteed by the Treaty' must be applied in a non-discriminatory manner, justified in the general interest and suitable for and proportionate to their objective

Professional qualifications:

- *Thieffry*: qualifications recognized as equivalent must be accepted

Provision of services

- *Van Binsbergen*: professional requirements are compatible with EU law provided they are equally applicable to host state nationals, objectively justified in the public interest, and proportionate

- *Säger*: Art 56 not only requires the abolition of discrimination but also restrictions that are 'liable to prohibit or otherwise impede' the provision of services. Restrictions are acceptable only where justified by imperative reasons in the public interest, equally applicable to national and non-national providers insofar as the interest is not protected by rules applying in the state of origin, and proportionate

---

Recipients of services
(Directive 2004/38)

- *Cowan*: recipients of (tourist) services entitled to equal treatment under Art 18 TFEU

Rights attached to Union citizenship: the Court of Justice

Originally, free movement and non-discrimination rights were largely confined to the economically active and their families, though the Court of Justice consistently stressed the importance of free movement as a matter of social justice, as the means for individuals to pursue enhanced life quality through increased mobility. Significantly, after Union citizenship was created, the Court began to use citizenship as the basis for rights, declaring that 'Union citizenship is destined to be the fundamental status of the nationals of the Member States' (*Grzelczyk v Centre Public d'Aide Sociale d'Ottignies-Louvain-la-Neuve* (Case C-184/99)). In *Sala*, the Court based non-discrimination rights on citizenship.

Sala v Freistaat Bayern (Case C-85/96) [1998] ECR I-2691

Sala, a Spanish national living in Germany, had been allowed to remain despite having no [EU] residency rights, her economic status being unclear. She challenged the authorities' refusal to grant her welfare benefits on the same basis as German nationals. The Court of Justice held that, as a Union citizen lawfully resident in another Member State, Sala could rely on the non-discrimination provisions of [**Article 18**] to claim entitlement to equal treatment with nationals.

The same principles have been applied subsequently, for instance in *Grzelczyk*. Later, the Court based residency rights on citizenship status, while recognizing that such rights remain 'subject to the limitations and conditions laid down in this Treaty and by the measures adopted to give it effect'.

Baumbast v Secretary of State for the Home Department (Case C-413/99) [2002] ECR I-7091

Baumbast, a German national who had been employed and then self-employed in the UK, challenged the refusal to renew his residence permit on the grounds that he was no longer economically active in the UK. The Court of Justice declared that Union citizenship formed the basis for residency rights, albeit subject to the conditions imposed by the relevant secondary legislation (**Directive 90/364**) granting residency rights to financially independent persons, provided they had sufficient financial means and sickness insurance. Baumbast had sufficient means not to become a financial burden on the UK and, whilst his sickness insurance fell short of what was required, it would be disproportionate to refuse him residency rights. He had a continued right of residence in the UK, arising by direct application of [**Article 21**].

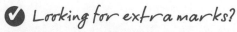 Looking for extra marks?

Even before Union citizenship was established, **Directives 90/364**, **90/365**, and **90/366** concerning students, retired persons, and persons with independent means had extended free movement rights to **economically inactive** persons. The economic link was further weakened as the Court of Justice granted rights of non-discrimination and residence on the basis of Union citizenship. **Directive 2004/38** reiterates that Union citizenship is the fundamental status upon which free movement rights are based (**recital 3**).

Revision tip

Be familiar with these cases. You will need to discuss them in an answer concerning the significance of Union citizenship and its development as the basis for free movement rights.

Rights attached to Union citizenship: Directive 2004/38

Directive 2004/38 lays down the conditions governing the exercise of free movement and residence rights by Union citizens and their families in the EU, their rights of permanent residence, and the limitations on grounds of public policy, public security, or public health.

All Union citizens and their families

The Directive allows all Union citizens, and their family members irrespective of nationality, to leave their home state and move to and reside in another Member State for up to three months, without conditions or formalities, other than the requirement to hold a valid identity card or passport (Union citizens) or a passport (non-EU family members). Non-EU nationals may also be required to hold an entry visa (**Articles 4–6**). For economically inactive Union citizens and their family members, the rights apply provided individuals do not become an unreasonable burden on the host state's social security system. However, expulsion must not be an automatic consequence of recourse to welfare (**Article 14(3)**). Member States are not obliged to grant welfare benefits during this three-month period, save to workers, self-employed persons, and their families (**Article 24(2)**).

Workers, the self-employed, and their families

The **TFEU** enshrines the primary free movement rights of economically active Union citizens in **Articles 45** (workers) and **49** (the self-employed). Under **Directive 2004/38** these persons have the right to reside in the host state for more than three months (**Article 7(1)(a)**). That right extends to family members who are Union citizens (**Article 7(1)(d)**) and to those who are not (**Article 7(2)**). The Directive also confirms the right of Union citizens to enter and remain in another Member State to seek work (**Article 14(4)(b)**), a right originally established by the Court of Justice (*Procureur du Roi v Royer* (Case 48/75)). All these rights are considered in more detail presently.

Persons with independent means, students, and their families

The Directive sets out a right of residence of more than three months for three other groups: persons with independent means (**Article 7(1)(b)**), students (**Article 7(1)(c)**), and their family members (**Article 7(1(d)**). Persons with independent means and students must have sufficient resources for themselves and their families not to become a burden on the host state's social welfare system and have sickness insurance. Member States must not lay down a fixed amount which they regard as 'sufficient resources' but take account of an individual's personal situation (**Article 8(4)**). Students must simply make a declaration of sufficient resources (**Article 7(1)(c)**).

As to financial support for studies, the non-discrimination right covers tuition fees (*Gravier v City of Liege* (Case 293/83)). According to **Directive 2004/38**, Member States are not obliged to provide maintenance grants and student loans to persons other than workers, the self-employed, and their families (**Article 24(2)**). This provision draws on the decisions in *Lair v Universität Hannover* (Case 39/86) and *Brown v Secretary for State for Scotland* (Case 197/86). Here, the Court of Justice restricted access to a maintenance grant to workers, the self-employed, persons who retain such status, and their families. However, the later *Bidar* judgment, handed down before **Directive 2004/38** came into effect, indicates that economically inactive persons are entitled to student grants and loans provided they are lawfully resident and sufficiently integrated into the host state.

....

R v London Borough of Ealing & Secretary of State for Education, ex parte Bidar (Case C-209/03) [2005] ECR I-2119

Bidar, a French national, had come to the UK with his mother (who died soon after their arrival), completed his secondary education (whilst living with his grandmother), and started a course at University College, London. His student loan application was rejected on the ground that he was not settled in the UK. The Court of Justice held that, in view of developments since *Lair* and *Brown*, notably the creation of Union citizenship, the Treaty right in [**Article 18**] granted equality with nationals regarding student grants and loans, though a Member State would be justified in requiring a certain degree of integration into the state's society.

....

Subsequently, the Court of Justice found that a five-year residency condition imposed by the Dutch authorities was not excessive for the purposes of guaranteeing integration in these circumstances (*Förster v Hoofddirectie van de Informatie Beheer Groep* (Cases C-158–157)).

Family members

Directive 2004/38 grants entry and residence rights to the families of Union citizens exercising free movement rights as workers, self-employed persons, jobseekers, students, or persons with independent means (**Articles 5–7**). Family member rights are sometimes described as 'parasitic' because they are not independent rights but derived from the Union citizen's primary rights. Family members who are Union citizens may themselves acquire independent EU rights.

'Family member'

'Family member' means, irrespective of nationality, the Union citizen's spouse and registered partner; direct descendants under 21 or who are dependent, and those of the spouse or registered partner; and dependent direct relatives in the ascending line and those of the spouse or registered partner (**Article 2**). According to case law, dependency results from a factual situation in which the Union citizen is actually providing support (*Centre Public d'Aide Sociale de Courcelles v Lebon* (Case 316/85)).

Member States must also facilitate entry and residence for other specified individuals, irrespective of nationality: persons who in the state of origin were dependants or members of the Union citizen's household or need his/her personal care for serious health reasons and the partner with whom the Union citizen has a durable relationship (**Article 3**).

'Family member' is defined more narrowly for students, being confined to the spouse or registered partner and dependent children, though in relation to students, dependent direct relatives in the ascending line are added to the list of persons whose entry Member States must facilitate (**Article 7(4)**).

Spouses and partners

The legislation pre-dating **Directive 2004/38** made no reference to 'partner', but only to 'spouse'. The Court of Justice stated in *Netherlands State v Reed* (Case 59/85) that 'spouse' was restricted to persons married to each other. Now, under **Directive 2004/38** 'family member' also includes:

> the partner with whom the Union citizen has contracted a registered partnership, on the basis of the legislation of a Member State, if the legislation of the host Member State treats registered partnerships as equivalent to marriage and in accordance with the conditions laid down in the relevant legislation of the host Member State. (**Article 2(2)(b)**)

✅ Looking for extra marks?

Since Member States retain competence in the legal regulation of non-marital relationships, this provision will inevitably give rise to differences of treatment across the EU.

Marriages of convenience

Directive 2004/38 consolidates previous case law on marriages of convenience (*Secretary of State for the Home Department v Akrich* (Case C-109/01)). **Article 35** allows Member States to refuse, terminate, or withdraw rights in cases of abuse or fraud, such as marriages of convenience, provided such action is **proportionate**.

Death or departure of the Union citizen

Should the Union citizen die or leave the host state, the rights of family members hold-ing Union citizenship are unaffected, though before acquiring permanent residency rights they must meet the **Article 7(1)** conditions (be workers, self-employed, students, have independent means, or be family members of a Union citizen holding such status) (**Article 12(1)**).

The position of non-EU family members is more precarious. If the Union citizen dies they can stay, provided they have lived with him/her in the host state for at least a year. Before acquiring a permanent residency right, their right remains subject to them being workers or self-employed; or having sufficient resources for themselves and their families and sick-ness insurance; or being family members of a person satisfying one of these requirements (**Article 12(2)**).

Non-EU family members have no right to stay if the Union citizen leaves the host state, unless they can rely on **Article 12(3)**. This provision consolidates previous case law (*Eternach and Moritz v Minister van Onderwijs en Wetenschappen* (Cases 389/87 & 390/87); *Baumbast, R v Secretary of State for the Home Department* (Case C-413/99)). It provides that, following the Union citizen's death or departure, his/her children in education in the host state, and the parent who has actual custody, irrespective of nationality, retain residency rights until the children's studies are completed (**Article 12(3)**).

Divorce

Separation has no effect on rights (*Diatta v Land Berlin* (Case 267/83)). Divorce, annul-ment of marriage, or termination of a registered partnership can have a significant impact. Again, the position of family members who hold Union citizenship is stronger than that of non-EU family members. The rights of the former are unaffected, though before acquiring permanent residency rights, they must meet the **Article 7(1)** conditions (**Article 13(1)**).

Non-EU family members can remain only in limited circumstances: the marriage/partner-ship has lasted at least three years, with one year in the host state; or the spouse/partner has custody of a Union citizen's children; or there are particularly difficult circumstances, such as being the victim of domestic violence; or where the spouse/partner has access rights to a child in the host state. Before acquiring a permanent residency right, their right to reside remains subject to them being workers or self-employed; or having sufficient resources for themselves and their families and sickness insurance; or being family members of a person satisfying one of these requirements (**Article 13(2)**).

✔ Looking for extra marks?

Although family members have rights 'irrespective of nationality', **Directive 2004/838** makes signifi-cant distinctions between EU and non-EU family members. Whilst the substance of their respective rights is generally the same, there are notable differences relating, in particular, to the right to remain following divorce or if the Union citizen dies or leaves the host state.

Right to take up employment

Irrespective of nationality, family members may take up employment or self-employment (**Article 23**).

Equal treatment

The right to equal treatment applies without limitation to family members of the economically active. For family members of other Union citizens (persons of independent means and students) their right to equal treatment is limited, as there is no entitlement to social assistance during the first three months of residence and no right to student grants or loans (**Article 24**).

Regulation 492/2011, Article 10 provides that workers' children have a right of access, under the same conditions as nationals of the host state, to the general educational, apprenticeship, and vocational training courses. This includes 'general measures intended to facilitate educational attendance', including grants (*Casagrande v Landeshauptstadt München* (Case 9/74)). As already noted, children still in education in the host state may remain until their studies are completed.

Administrative formalities

Member States are entitled to track population movements through administrative formalities and apply proportionate and non-discriminatory sanctions for non-compliance. This would include a requirement to report to the authorities within a reasonable period of time following arrival (*Criminal Proceedings against Lynne Watson and Alessandro Belmann* (Case 118/75); *Messner* (Case C-265/88); **Article 5, Directive 2004/38**). For residence periods over three months, Union citizens may be required to register with the authorities (**Article 8**). Non-EU family members must apply for and be issued with a residence card (**Article 9**). Proportionate and non-discriminatory sanctions may be imposed for non-compliance. Deportation would be a disproportionate sanction in these circumstances (*Procureur du Roi v Royer* (Case 48/75)).

Right of permanent residence

Union citizens who have resided in the host state legally and continuously for five years and non-EU family members who have resided with them in the host state for at least five years, acquire permanent residency rights. The right is unaffected by temporary absences of up to six months. Once acquired, the right is not subject to economic status and sufficient resources and can be lost only through absences exceeding two years (**Article 16**).

Limitations

Union citizens' free movement rights are 'subject to the conditions and limitations' in the Treaty (**Article 21 TFEU**). Member States may limit the rights of economically active EU migrants on grounds of public policy, public security, or public health (**Articles 45(3), 52 TFEU**). **Directive 2004/38** defines the scope of the limitations, which it applies to all persons exercising rights of free movement under the Directive. The limitations are considered in detail later in this chapter.

Revision tip

Who has rights under **Directive 2004/38**? What are the rights? Are you confident about the detailed provisions? Briefly, how might the rights be limited?

EU rights in the state of origin

The Court of Justice has held that EU free movement rights cannot be claimed against a home state unless the individual has already exercised free movement rights (*Morson and Jhanjan v Netherlands* (Cases 35 & 36/82)).

The necessary EU element may be established where an individual returns to the home state following a period of economic activity in another Member State (*R v Immigration Appeal Tribunal and Singh, ex parte Secretary of State for the Home Department* (Case C-370/90)).

To benefit from rights of re-entry, a spouse must originally have been lawfully resident in the state of re-entry. However, when assessing a claim, the authorities must have regard to the right to respect for human life under **Article 8 of the European Convention on Human Rights** (*Secretary of State for the Home Department v Akrich* (Case C-109/01)). In this regard, **Article 35, Directive 2004/38** allows Member States to refuse, terminate, or withdraw rights in cases of abuse or fraud, including marriages of convenience.

Other situations have provided the necessary EU element, for instance the return to the home state after time spent in another Member State as a student (*D'Hoop v Office national de l'emploi* (Case C-224/98)) and, in a claim by a non-EU national, her husband's exercise of the right to provide services under **Article 49 EC** (now **Article 56 TFEU**) (*Carpenter v Secretary of State for the Home Department* (Case C-60/00)). Other cases have affirmed the EU rights of persons who had always been resident in one Member State but held the nationality of another (*Avello v Belgian State* (Case C-148/02); *Zhu and Chen v Secretary of State for the Home Department* (Case C-200/02)).

Free movement of workers

Overview of the legislation

EU migrant workers have primary free movement rights under the **TFEU** both as Union citizens (**Article 21**) and as workers (**Article 45**).

Article 45 TFEU: rights for workers

Article 45(1) embodies the fundamental principle of free movement for workers. Free movement entails the abolition of any discrimination based on nationality between the nationals of the Member States as regards employment, remuneration, and other conditions of employment (**Article 45(2)**). It also entails the right to move freely and stay in another Member State for the purposes of employment and, subject to conditions laid down in secondary legislation, to remain after employment has ceased. The right to enter and remain is made subject to limitations on grounds of public policy, public security, or public health (**Article 45(3)**).

Secondary legislation

Directive 2004/38 defines the precise scope of workers' rights of entry and residence, of family members' rights, and of the limits on those rights. **Regulation 492/2011** codifies former **Regulation 1612/68** and elaborates on workers' primary right to non-discrimination on grounds of nationality, incorporating provisions concerning equal access to employment and equal treatment in employment.

Who is a 'worker'?

Worker status is of immense importance because, if an individual is a worker, he or she has available the whole range of worker rights contained in the primary and secondary legislation. Whilst it is generally straightforward to establish worker status, there are a number of cases in which a claim to worker status has been challenged.

There is no Treaty definition of 'worker'. The Court of Justice has emphasized that the term may not be defined by national laws but has an EU meaning (*Hoekstra (née Unger) v Bestuur der Bedrijfsvereniging voor Detailhandel en Ambachten* (Case 75/63) and *Levin v Staatssecretaris van Justitie* (Case 53/81)). Clarification was provided in *Lawrie-Blum v Land Baden-Württemberg* (Case 66/85): '[the] essential feature of an employment relationship . . . is that for a certain period of time a person performs services for and under the direction of another person in return for which he receives remuneration'. Since worker rights relate to one of the fundamental freedoms of the EU, the Court of Justice has interpreted 'worker' broadly.

Part-time work

. . . .

Levin v Staatssecretaris van Justitie (Case 53/81) [1982] ECR 1035

Levin, a British national, lived in the Netherlands where she worked part-time. Her income was small but she was supported financially by her husband, a non-EU national. The Dutch authorities refused her a residence permit, claiming that she was not a worker because her wage was lower than the nationally recognized minimum subsistence level. The Court of Justice held that, provided work is an 'effective and genuine' economic activity and not 'purely marginal and ancillary', a part-time worker is entitled to [EU] free movement rights as a worker. Further, a person's motives in seeking employment in another Member State are irrelevant.

Kempf v Staatssecretaris van Justitie (Case 139/85) [1986] ECR 1741

Kempf, a German national living in the Netherlands, worked 12 hours per week as a music teacher. Like Levin, his earnings were below the minimum subsistence level but, unlike Levin, he relied on welfare to supplement his income. The Court of Justice held that persons undertaking genuine and effective part-time employment cannot be excluded from the free movement rights accorded to workers merely because their income falls below the minimum subsistence level and is supplemented by welfare benefits.

Fixed-term contracts

Again in **Ninni-Orasche**, the nature of the work, rather than its extent, was the determining factor.

Franca Ninni-Orasche v Bundesminister für Wissenschaft, Verkehr und Kunst (Case C-413/01 [2004] 1 CMLR 19

The Italian applicant had lived in Germany since 1993, taking up employment some years after her arrival and working for only two and a half months under a fixed-term contract. Meanwhile, she had gained qualifications for university entry and had sought other work between the expiry of her fixed-term contract and starting her course. The Court of Justice held that none of these factors would be relevant in determining worker status, provided the employment activity was not purely marginal and ancillary.

Unpaid work

Even where no formal wages are paid, an individual may still be a 'worker'.

Steymann v Staatssecretaris van Justitie (Case 196/87) [1988] ECR 6159

After a short period working as a plumber in the Netherlands, Steymann, a German national, joined the Bhagwan Religious Community. As well as doing plumbing and general household work, he participated in the Community's business activities. The Court of Justice held that the fact that Steymann received no formal wages but only his 'keep' and pocket money did not rule out his work as effective economic activity.

Can rehabilitation constitute 'work'?

The limits to the scope of 'worker' may be reached when the purpose of the employment is rehabilitation.

Bettray v Staatssecretaris van Justitie (Case 344/87) [1989] ECR 1621

The Court of Justice held that 'worker' did not include a person participating in a drug-rehabilitation programme aimed at reintegration into the workforce, although the work undertaken was paid and supervised. Since the objective was rehabilitation, the work could not be regarded as 'effective and genuine economic activity'.

Nonetheless, a person following a 'social reintegration programme' would be entitled to worker status if the work involved could be regarded as 'effective and genuine' economic activity.

Trojani v Centre public d'Aide Social de Bruxelles (Case C-456/02) [2004] ECR I-7574

Trojani, a French national, lived in a Salvation Army hostel in Belgium where, in return for board, lodging, and pocket money, he worked for around 30 hours per week as part of a 'personal socio-occupational reintegration programme'. The Court of Justice found that the benefits in kind and money received by Trojani were consideration for work for and under the direction of the hostel. The Court left the national court to decide whether that work was real and genuine, by ascertaining whether the services performed were part of the 'normal labour market'. This could entail consideration of the status and practices of the hostel, the content of the reintegration programme, and the nature and detail of the work.

Retaining worker status

Article 7(3) of Directive 2004/38 provides that a Union citizen who is no longer working or self-employed may nevertheless retain worker or self-employed status. Economic status is retained if the individual is temporarily unemployed through illness or accident; or is involuntarily unemployed after working for over a year or on expiry of a fixed-term contract, if registered as a jobseeker; or embarks on vocational training. In the latter circumstance, that training must be related to the previous employment unless the individual is involuntarily unemployed. **Article 7(3)** is an important provision, since it guarantees continued worker rights.

Revision tip

Can you discuss this case law confidently, for an essay question? Would you be able to apply these cases to the 'characters' in a problem scenario?

Jobseekers

EU nationals are entitled to enter and remain in another Member State to seek work (***Procureur du Roi v Royer*** (Case 48/75)). ***R v Immigration Appeal Tribunal, ex parte Antonissen*** (Case C-292/89) established that there is no right to remain indefinitely, though an individual would be entitled to remain if making genuine efforts to find work, with a real chance of being employed. **Directive 2004/38** provides protection from expulsion for jobseekers who satisfy these conditions, and their family members (**Article 14(4)**). According to **Article 24**, jobseekers are not entitled to welfare benefits in the host state. This provision has been interpreted creatively by the Court of Justice.

Collins v Secretary of State for Work and Pensions (Case C-138/02) [2004] ECR I-2703

Collins, who had dual Irish and American nationality, had come to the UK to look for work. His application for jobseeker's allowance was refused on the grounds that he was not habitually resident in the UK and was not a 'worker' under [EU] law. The Court of Justice acknowledged that in earlier decisions it had denied jobseekers entitlement to financial benefits but referred to its more recent judgments on Union citizens' Treaty right to non-discrimination, under [**Article 18**]. The Court held that the equality principle in [**Article 45(2)**] included a right to a financial benefit 'intended to facilitate access to employment in the labour market of a Member State'.

Nonetheless, a residence requirement attached to a jobseeker's allowance may be justified by proportionate and non-discriminatory objective factors. The required residency period must be no longer than is necessary for the authorities be satisfied that the individual is genuinely seeking work.

Subsequently, the Court has reiterated that the principle of equal treatment for Union citizens must include a financial benefit intended to facilitate access to the host state's labour market, though it would be legitimate for a Member State to grant the allowance only after establishing a real link between the jobseeker and the labour market (*Vatsouras & another v Arbeitsgemeinschaft Nürnberg 900* (Cases C-22 & 23/08)).

Freedom of movement: right to enter and remain

Directive 2004/38 elucidates workers' free movement rights contained in **Article 45 TFEU**. It sets out the right of workers who are Union citizens to enter and reside in another Member State for more than three months (**Articles 5(1), 7(1)**) and the right of permanent residence after five years (**Article 16**). Family members, irrespective of nationality, accompanying or joining the Union citizen also have the right to enter and remain (**Articles 5(2), 7(1)(d)), and 7(2)**) and the right to permanent residence after five years (**Article 16**).

Freedom from discrimination

Workers' right to non-discrimination is enshrined in the **TFEU**. Freedom of movement entails the abolition of discrimination between workers of the Member States as regards employment, remuneration, and other conditions of employment (**Article 45(2)**). **Regulation 492/2011** clarifies the scope of the right, covering two main areas: eligibility for employment and equality of treatment in employment.

Regulation 492/2011, Section 1 (Articles 1–6): Eligibility for employment

Any national of a Member State has the right to take up and pursue employment in another Member State with the same priority and under the same conditions as host state nationals (**Regulation 492/2011, Article 1**). The Regulation prohibits national provisions limiting applications or offers of employment or laying down special recruitment procedures, advertising restrictions, and other impediments (**Article 3**), or limiting by number or percentage the employment of EU migrant workers (**Article 4**). **Article 4** was invoked in *French Merchant Seamen*.

> ### Commission v France (French Merchant Seamen) (Case 167/73) [1974] ECR 359
>
> Ministerial orders issued under the French **Code du Travail Maritime**, 1926 imposed a ratio of three French to one non-French crew members on ships of the merchant fleet. By refusing to amend the relevant provision, France was in breach of the Treaty [**Article 45(2)**] and **Article 4 of Regulation 1612/68** [now **492/2011**].

However, **Regulation 492/2011** permits language requirements, provided these are necessary 'by reason of the nature of the post to be filled' (**Article 3(1)**).

> ### Groener v Minister for Education (Case 379/87) [1989] ECR 3967
>
> Irish rules required lecturers in Irish vocational schools to be competent in the Irish language. Although the teaching post at issue did not entail the use of Irish in the classroom, the Court of Justice held that the requirement would be justified provided it formed part of national policy to promote the use of Irish as the first official language under the Irish Constitution.

However, a requirement to hold a particular language qualification would be unlawful, unless it could be justified by factors unrelated to nationality and was proportionate (*Angonese v Cassa di Risparmio di Bolzano SpA* (Case C-281/98)).

Access to employment in the public service

Member States may restrict or deny access to employment in the public service on grounds of nationality (**Article 45(4) TFEU**). This provision applies only to access to employment. Discriminatory conditions of employment infringe the free movement provisions (*Sotgiu v Deutsche Bundespost* (Case 152/73)). 'Public service' is an EU concept. Its meaning is not to be determined by Member States (*Sotgui, Commission v Belgium*).

> ### Commission v Belgium (Public Employees) (Case 149/79) [1980] ECR 3881
>
> Under Belgian law, certain work for local authorities and on the railways, including jobs such as electrician, joiner, trainee driver, loader, platelayer, and shunter, was reserved to Belgian nationals. Belgium argued that entry to public office was a matter for Member States. The Court of Justice

disagreed, insisting on the uniform interpretation and application of [**Article 45(4)**] throughout the [EU] and defining 'public service' posts as those involving 'the exercise of power conferred by public law' where there was a 'responsibility for safeguarding the general interests of the State'. The posts in question fell outside the scope of [**Article 45(4)**].

Subsequently, various kinds of post have been excluded from **Article 45(4)**, including teachers (*Bleis v Ministère de l'Education Nationale* (Case C-4/91); *Commission v Luxembourg* (Case C-473/93) and trainee teachers (*Lawrie-Blum v Land Baden-Württemberg* (Case 66/85)), university foreign language assistants (*Allué and Coonan v Universita degli studi di Venezia* (Case 33/88)), researchers at an Italian national research centre (*Commission v Italy* (Case 225/85)), nurses (*Commission v France* (Case 307/84)), and private sector security guards (*Commission v Italy* (Case C-283/99)).

Article 45(4) applies only where the activities are exercised on a regular basis and do not form only a minor part of the job (*Anker, Ras and Snoek v Germany* (Case C-47/02)).

Regulation 492/2011, Section 2 (Articles 7–9): Employment and equality of treatment

The Regulation extends the non-discrimination principle to conditions of employment, in particular pay, dismissal, and, should the worker become unemployed, reinstatement and reemployment. Workers are entitled to the same tax and social advantages and access to vocational training as national workers (**Article 7**), as well as to equality regarding membership of trades unions (**Article 8**) and housing, including home ownership (**Article 9**). 'Social and tax advantage' is interpreted broadly.

Cristini v SNCF (Case 32/75) [1975] ECR 1085

Cristini, an Italian national living in France and the widow of an Italian migrant worker, was refused a fare reduction card for large families, which her husband had previously claimed from French Railways (SNCF), on grounds of nationality. SNCF argued that the card was not a 'social advantage' because that term applied only to advantages attached to worker status. The Court of Justice disagreed. **Article 7 of Regulation 1612/68** [now **492/2011**] applied to all social and tax advantages, whether or not attached to the contract of employment.

'Social and tax advantage' includes any benefit available by virtue of worker status or residence on national territory, where the benefit facilitates free movement of workers, for instance a handicapped adults' allowance (*Inzirillo v Caisse d'Allocations Familiales de l'Arondissement de Lyon* (Case 63/76)); a discretionary childbirth loan (*Reina v Landeskreditbank Baden-Württemberg* (Case 65/81)); a guaranteed income for old people (*Castelli v ONPTS* (Case 261/83)); and a minimum subsistence allowance (*Hoeckx v Centre Public d'Aide Sociale de Kalmthout* (Case 249/83)).

Direct and indirect discrimination

Discrimination is prohibited, whether direct or indirect. **Direct discrimination**, entailing open differentiation between nationals and non-nationals, is normally easily identified. **Indirect discrimination** is less obvious. Measures which appear, on their face, to treat nationals and non-nationals alike but in practice have a discriminatory effect are indirectly discriminatory.

Marsman v Rosskamp (Case 44/72) [172] ECR 1243

German legislation giving employment protection to workers who were injured at work applied to national workers irrespective of state of residence but only to those non-national workers living in Germany. The Court of Justice found the measure to be directly discriminatory.

O'Flynn v Adjudication Officer (Case C-237/94) [1996] ECR I-2617

O'Flynn, an Irish national working in the UK, was refused a grant for the cost of his son's funeral in Ireland, because the grant was limited to funerals held in the UK. The Court of Justice found that indirect discrimination would arise where national rules might operate to the detriment of migrant workers. Here, since non-nationals were more likely than nationals to want their relatives to be buried outside the UK, the refusal was indirectly discriminatory.

Workers' families

An EU worker's free movement rights would have limited practical value if family members could not move around with the worker. Family members' free movement rights (irrespective of nationality), first granted by **Directive 68/360**, are now contained in **Directive 2004/38**. These are derived rights, as they are entirely dependent on the worker's rights, though family members who are Union citizens have independent EU rights if they satisfy the necessary conditions.

Revision tip

Workers: make sure you understand the legislative framework: **Article 45 TFEU** (Treaty rights); **Directive 2004/38** (entry and residence); **Regulation 492/2011** (employment, equal treatment, and worker's families).

Free movement for the self-employed

Overview of the legislation

Like EU workers, self-employed Union citizens derive primary free movement rights from the Treaty. In addition to their citizenship rights enshrined in **Article 21 TFEU**, **Articles 49 and 56 TFEU** set out, respectively, the right of establishment and the freedom to provide services, both applying to individuals and companies. Issues relating to companies lie outside the scope of this book. This chapter focuses on the rights of self-employed persons. It will be recalled that **Directive 2004/38** clarifies the scope of Union citizens' rights, including the rights of the self-employed.

Distinguishing 'establishment' and 'provision of services'

Freedom of establishment includes the right to pursue activities as a self-employed person in another Member State, for instance setting up and managing a business or practising a profession, on a permanent basis. Where a person is established in one state and provides services into another, this constitutes the **provision of services**.

Direct effect

Reyners v Belgium (Case 2/74) and *Van Binsbergen v Bestuur van de Bedrijfsvereniging voor de Metaalnijverheid* (Case 33/74) confirmed the **direct effect** of [**Articles 49 and 56**], respectively. These Treaty rights are not conditional on the adoption of directives defining their scope.

Rights of entry and residence and limitations on the rights

Directive 2004/38 reaffirms the rights of entry and residence of the self-employed. The rights are subject to limitations on grounds of public policy, public security, or public health (**Articles 52, 62 TFEU**). The self-employed have no right of access to activities connected with the exercise of official authority (**Articles 51, 62 TFEU**).

Freedom of establishment

Right of establishment and freedom from discrimination

Article 49 prohibits restrictions on the freedom of establishment of Member State nationals in another Member State. Under **Directive 2004/38** the rights of the self-employed to freedom of movement and equal treatment are identical to those applying to workers.

For persons exercising the right of establishment, the general non-discrimination provision in **Article 18 TFEU** is supplemented by **Article 49**, which includes the right to pursue activity 'under the conditions laid down for its own nationals by the law of the country where such establishment is effected'. Clearly, this provision prohibits direct discrimination on grounds of nationality. However, equal treatment can be problematic when applied to rules concerning professional conduct and qualifications, which may hinder or make less attractive the exercise of free movement rights, particularly where individuals who comply with home state requirements find a host state's requirements difficult or impossible to satisfy.

Rules of professional conduct

Gebhard set out the principles to be applied to rules of professional conduct.

Gebhard v Consiglio dell'Ordine degli Avvocati e Procuratori di Milano (Case C-55/94) [1995] ECR I-4165

Gebhard, a lawyer qualified in Germany, faced disciplinary proceedings for practising in Italy under the title avvocato, in contravention of Italian legislation. The Court of Justice confirmed that an EU national exercising the right of establishment in another Member State must comply with the relevant requirements, such as the use of a professional title. However, 'measures liable to hinder or make less attractive the exercise of fundamental freedoms guaranteed by the Treaty' must be non-discriminatory, justified in the general interest, and suitable for and proportionate to their objective.

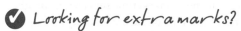 **✔ Looking for extra marks?**

Gebhard indicates that **Article 49** extends beyond inequality of treatment, to include restrictions raising unnecessary obstacles to freedom of establishment. Any measures hindering or making less attractive the exercise of rights, including those which are equally applicable to host state nationals, must be **objectively justified** and proportionate.

Professional qualifications

Like professional conduct rules, national professional qualification requirements can seriously hinder free movement, for they may not be easily met by non-nationals.

Thieffry v Conseil de l'Ordre des Avocats à *la Cour de Paris* (Case 71/76) [1977] ECR 765

Thieffry, a Belgian advocate, was refused admission to the Paris Bar because he did not hold the necessary French qualifications. The Court of Justice held that, since France officially recognized Thieffry's Belgian qualifications as equivalent, this was an unjustified restriction on freedom of establishment.

Where qualifications are not recognized as equivalent, they must be compared with national requirements and, if equivalent, accepted. If not, evidence of the necessary knowledge and experience may be required (***Vlassopoulou v Ministerium für Justiz*** (Case 340/89)).

Mutual recognition of qualifications

Alongside these case law developments, the EU is moving towards **harmonization** in this area. The harmonization programme is considered later.

Providers of services

Under **Article 56 TFEU** 'restrictions on freedom to provide services within the Union shall be prohibited in respect of nationals of Member States who are established in a Member State other than that of the person for whom the service is intended'.

'Services'

Services fall within the scope of the Treaty if 'normally provided for remuneration'. They include industrial, commercial, and professional activities (**Article 57 TFEU**); for instance legal services (*Van Binsbergen* (Case 33/74)), insurance services (*Safir v Skattemyndigheten i Dalarnas Lan* (Case C-118/96)), and medical services (*Geraets-Smits v Stichting Ziekenfonds and HTM Peerbooms v Stichting CZ Groep Zorgverzekeringen* (Case C-157/99)). Service provision includes the situation where the provider does not physically move from the state of establishment, for example the provision of telephone marketing services in another Member State (*Alpine Investments BV v Minister of Finance* (Case C-384/93)).

In *Grogan*, abortion services were held to fall within **Article 57** but a free 'information service' about London abortion clinics lacked the necessary economic dimension.

....

Society for the Protection of Unborn Children Ltd v Grogan (Case C-159/90) [1991] ECR I-4685

The SPUC challenged the practice of a students' union in Ireland, where abortion is illegal, to supply information, free of charge, about abortion services provided lawfully by London clinics. The Court of Justice held that, since the information was not distributed on behalf of the economic operators (the clinics), the students' 'information service' fell outside the scope of 'services'. Accordingly, the prohibition of the students' activity did not infringe EU law.

....

In view of the sensitive nature of the abortion issue in Ireland, it is likely that the Court's reasoning was strongly influenced by policy considerations.

Restrictions on freedom to provide services

Article 56 rights are, according to **Article 57**, exercised 'under the same conditions as are imposed by that state on its own nationals'. As with the right of establishment, Member States may impose restrictions on the freedom to provide services provided they are objectively justified. *Van Binsbergen* defined the scope of permissible justification.

....

Van Binsbergen v Bestuur van de Bedrijfsvereniging voor de Metaalnijverheid (Case 33/74) [1974] ECR 1299

A Dutch national, qualified as an advocate in the Netherlands, who was advising a client concerning proceedings in a Dutch court, was informed, on moving to Belgium, that he could no longer represent his client. Under Dutch rules only lawyers established in the Netherlands had rights of audience before certain tribunals. The Court of Justice held that requirements imposed on persons providing services – particularly rules relating to organization, qualifications, professional ethics, supervision, and liability – are compatible with EU law provided they are equally applicable to host state nationals, objectively justified in the public interest, and proportionate.

· ·

In *Criminal Proceedings against Webb* (Case 279/80), in the later 'insurance' cases (*Commission v Germany (Re Insurance Services)* (Case 205/84), *Commission v Ireland (Re Co-insurance Services)* (Case 206/84), *Commission v France* (Case 220/83), *Commission v Denmark (Re Insurance Services)* (Case 252/83)), and in *Säger v Dennemeyer* (Case C-76/90), the Court of Justice held that Member States must also take account of any relevant rules applying to the service provider in the state of establishment. Thus, a distinction is made between persons who are permanently established in a host state, who should in principle be bound by rules applying to nationals, and those who operate there on a temporary basis as service providers. In relation to the latter, 'double' regulation will be more difficult to justify.

Like restrictions on the right of establishment, measures that apply equally to national and non-national service providers will nonetheless infringe **Article 56** if they are likely to prohibit or impede the relevant activity, though such measures may be objectively justified.

· ·

Säger v Dennemeyer & Co Ltd (Case C-76/90) [1992] ECR I-4221

Under German legislation, licences for the provision of legal services were available to patent agents but not to persons who, like Dennemeyer (who was based in the UK) offered only patent renewal services. The Court of Justice held that [Article 56] not only requires the abolition of discrimination on grounds of nationality but also restrictions that are 'liable to prohibit or otherwise impede' the provision of services. Such restrictions are compatible with [EU] law only where they are justified by imperative reasons in the public interest, equally applicable to national and non-national providers insofar as the interest is not protected by rules applying in the non-national provider's state of origin, and proportionate.

· ·

Similar principles have been applied outside the context of professional rules of conduct and qualifications, for instance in *Schindler*.

· ·

HM Customs and Excise v Schindler (Case C-275/92) [1994] ECR I-1039

UK Customs and Excise confiscated invitations to participate in a German lottery on the grounds that they contravened national lotteries legislation. The Court of Justice, finding that lottery activities constitute services, held that, although the legislation applied without distinction to national and non-national lotteries, it was likely to 'prohibit or otherwise impede' the provision of lottery services and therefore infringed [**Article 56**]. Such legislation would however be justified by 'overriding considerations of public interest' (here, the protection of the consumer, the prevention of crime and fraud, and the restriction of demand for gambling), provided it was proportionate.

· ·

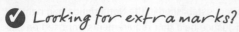 **Looking for extra marks?**

In developing the principles relating to equally applicable restrictions, objective justification, and pro-portionality under **Articles 49 and 56** the Court of Justice has moved towards a 'rule of reason' approach similar to that applied to restrictions on the free movement of goods under *Cassis de Dijon*. The focus has shifted towards the prohibition and potential for objective justification of rules, whether discriminatory or not, which prohibit or impede interstate trade or freedom of movement.

Recipients of services

The Treaty makes no reference to recipients of services. The right of Member State nation-als to enter and remain in another Member State for the purpose of receiving services, origi-nally contained in **Directive 73/148**, currently arises from the general provisions on entry and residence in **Directive 2004/38**. It will be recalled that, under the Directive, all Union citizens are entitled to enter and remain in another Member State for up to three months, without conditions, and to stay for more than three months, provided they have the required degree of financial independence.

The Court of Justice has recognized that **Article 56** includes the right to receive, as well as to provide, services. In early decisions, it held that 'recipients of services' included persons travelling to other Member States for medical treatment and for education and business pur-poses (*Luisi and Carbone v Ministero del Tresoro* (Cases 286/82 & 26/83)). *Cowan* concerned a recipient of tourist services.

··

Cowan v Le Trésor Public (Case 186/87) [1989] ECR 195

Cowan, a British national who had been violently attacked whilst on a visit to Paris, was refused the compensation to which a French national would have been entitled in these circumstances. He challenged this decision, relying on the Treaty right in [**Article 18**]. The Court held that tour-ism was a service and that tourists were entitled to equal treatment under [**Article 18**], including equal access to criminal injuries compensation.

··

The rights of recipients of services may be restricted, as for workers and others with free movement rights, on grounds of public policy, public security, or public health, considered later in this chapter.

Harmonization: rules relating to establishment and services
Mutual recognition of qualifications

To address the problems associated with the recognition of qualifications, an EU programme of harmonization was instigated, comprising the adoption of 12 sectoral directives setting out the requirements for particular trades and professions, such as doctors, dentists, pharmacists, and architects.

Progress was slow, so a new approach was taken with **Directive 89/48**, which related to professions other than those already covered by the sectoral directives. The Directive provided for mutual recognition of qualifications, on the basis that an individual who held a higher education diploma on completion of at least three years' professional education and had undertaken the necessary professional training was entitled to pursue that profession in another Member State. **Directive 89/48** was supplemented by **Directive 92/51**, covering diplomas awarded on completion of one-year post-secondary courses, and **Directive 99/42**, which extended the mutual recognition principle to a range of industrial and professional areas, replacing some of the earlier sectoral directives.

Almost all the existing harmonizing legislation was replaced and consolidated by **Directive 2005/36**. This Directive covers 'regulated professions' and applies to all EU citizens seeking to practise, as employed or self-employed persons, in Member States other than that in which their qualification was obtained. **Directive 2005/36** aims to liberalize the provision of services; it retains the existing systems of mutual recognition and recognition of qualifications covered by the previous sectoral directives and simplifies administrative procedures.

Directive 2006/123: the 'Services Directive'

Directive 2006/123, referred to as the '**Services Directive**', aims to remove barriers to cross-border service provision and to simplify associated procedures. The Directive, which covers both services and establishment, was adopted after a long and troubled process during which its opponents raised strong objections to the original proposals. The main opposition centred on the 'country of origin' principle, entailing the regulation of service providers by their state of origin rather than by the state in which services were provided.

The 'country of origin' principle was eventually abandoned and in its place the adopted text incorporates the principles on the provision of services established by the Court of Justice. **Article 16** provides for free access to and free exercise of a service activity within another Member State, subject to the application of non-discriminatory, necessary, and proportionate restrictions. **Article 16** adds to these existing principles a list of acceptable justifications for host state requirements – public policy, public security, public health, the protection of the environment, and rules on conditions of employment. It could well be that the Court of Justice will treat this list as non-exhaustive, permitting further justifications as it has done, for instance, in relation to the free movement of goods under the *Cassis* rule of reason.

Directive 2006/123 simplifies administration and procedures. In particular, businesses will be able to obtain information and complete administrative formalities through 'points of single contact' in the host state, instead of dealing with different authorities, and will be able to do this online. Customers will benefit from requirements concerning the quality of services, such as the availability of information on prices and quality. The Directive expressly excludes certain kinds of services from its scope, including some sectors already covered by legislation, such as financial services and transport, as well as other sectors such as social services and health care. **Directive 2006/123** had to be implemented by Member States by 28 December 2009.

Revision tip

Identify the key issues for self-employed persons: entry and residence rights; the three grounds of limitation; rules of professional conduct; qualification requirements; objective justification; harmonization.

Limitations on grounds of public policy, public security, or public health

Overview

As indicated throughout this chapter, free movement rights for Union citizens and family members are subject to various qualifications and limitations. Some of these have already been referred to, such as the provisions permitting Member States to restrict access to public service posts for migrant EU nationals on grounds of nationality. More particularly, **Articles 45(3), 52, and 62 TFEU** allow Member States to restrict rights of entry and residence, respectively, of EU migrant workers, persons exercising the right of establishment, and those providing services, on grounds of public policy, public security, or public health.

Directive 2004/38

The three grounds of limitation, originally contained in **Directive 64/221**, are now elaborated in **Directive 2004/38**, which repealed **Directive 64/221** but draws on its provisions, as well as consolidating the pre-existing case law. The limitations, which relate only to entry and residence, apply to all categories of persons exercising rights under **Directive 2004/38**, including family members, students, and persons of independent means as well as the economically active. In view of the fundamental importance of free movement in the internal market, the Court of Justice interprets the limitations very restrictively.

Directive 2004/38 refers to 'measures' taken by Member States (**Article 27**), defined as 'any action which affects the right of persons . . . to enter and reside freely in the Member States under the same conditions as nationals of the host state' (*R v Bouchereau* (Case 30/77)).

Public policy and public security

Directive 2004/38, Article 27 requires that measures taken on grounds of public policy or public security be proportionate and based exclusively on the personal conduct of the individual concerned. Here, no distinction is made between 'public policy' and 'public security'; indeed, 'public security' tends to be considered under the broader head of 'public policy'. These grounds may not be invoked for economic reasons.

Overview: limitations

TFEU

Rights subject to limitations of grounds of public policy, public security, or public health

Article 45(3) TFEU: workers
Article 52 TFEU: persons exercising the right of establishment
Article 62 TFEU: persons providing services

Directive 2004/38

Free movement of Union citizens subject to limitations on grounds of public policy, public security, or public health

Public policy and public security: Art 27

'Measures shall comply with the principle of proportionality and be based exclusively on the personal conduct of the individual concerned'

'Previous criminal convictions shall not in themselves constitute grounds'

'The personal conduct of the individual concerned must represent a genuine, present and sufficiently serious threat affecting one of the fundamental interests of society'

'Justifications that are isolated from the particulars of the case or that rely on measures of general prevention shall not be accepted'

- a 'present' threat: *Orfanopoulos & Oliveri*
- personal conduct: *Van Duyn* (association with an organization), *Calfa* (automatic expulsion)
- proportionality: *Orfanopoulos & Oliveri*
- general preventative measures: *Bonsignore* (deterrent measures)
- previous criminal convictions: *Bouchreau* (a 'present threat to the requirements of public policy', showing 'a propensity to act in the same way in the future')

Public health: Art 29

- diseases with epidemic potential as defined by WHO
- other infectious and contagious diseases if the subject of protection provisions in the host state
- diseases occurring after 3 months do not constitute grounds for expulsion

Partial restrictions: Art 22

- right of residence covers the whole territory
- partial restrictions acceptable only where they also apply to the host state's nationals
- *Rutili, Olazabal*

Limitations on grounds of public policy, public security, or public health
✱✱✱✱✱✱✱✱✱✱✱

Originally, whilst insisting on a strict interpretation of 'public policy', the Court of Justice allowed an area of discretion to Member States, permitting them to take account of national needs. Nonetheless, the Court insisted that the scope of 'public policy' must be subject to control by the EU institutions (*Van Duyn* (Case 41/74); *Rutili* (Case 36/75)). Later, in *Bouchereau* (Case 30/77) the Court moved to a narrower definition, now incorporated into **Directive 2004/38**: the conduct must represent a 'genuine, present, and sufficiently serious threat affecting one of the fundamental interests of society' (**Article 27**).

A 'present' threat

The personal conduct must represent a 'present' threat to the requirements of public policy. The public policy requirement must, as a general rule, be satisfied at the time of the expulsion, the national court taking account of matters demonstrating a diminution of the threat and occurring after the original decision, especially where a long time has elapsed (*Orfanopoulos and Oliveri* (Joined Cases C-482/01 & C-493/01)).

Personal conduct

Like the current provision in **Article 27 of Directive 2004/38**, **Directive 64/221** required that measures justified on grounds of public policy or public security be based exclusively on the personal conduct of the individual. *Van Duyn* and *Calfa* addressed the scope of 'personal conduct'.

....

Van Duyn v Home Office (Case 41/74) [1974] ECR 133

Yvonne van Duyn, a Dutch national, challenged the UK's refusal to allow her entry to work for the Church of Scientology, an organization considered by the UK to be 'socially harmful'. Van Duyn maintained that the public policy ground did not apply, arguing that her association with the Church did not constitute 'personal conduct'. The Court of Justice held that present association with an organization, reflecting participation in its activities and identification with its aims, constitutes personal conduct. In general, past association would not justify restrictions.

....
....

Criminal Proceedings against Donatella Calfa (Case C-348/96) [1999] ECR I-11

Ms Calfa, an Italian national, was convicted of drugs offences whilst on holiday in Crete, sentenced to three months' imprisonment, and, as required by national legislation applying to non-nationals, expelled from Greece for life. The Court of Justice emphasized that Member States may adopt against nationals of other Member States measures which they cannot apply to their own nationals, particularly on public policy grounds. However, automatic expulsion could not be justified on these grounds, since automatic expulsion took no account of the offender's personal conduct.

....

Similar reasoning was applied in *Oliveri*, which concerned German legislation requiring automatic expulsion for drugs offences (*Orfanopoulos and Oliveri* (Joined Cases C-482/01

& C-493/01). These principles are now incorporated into **Directive 2004/38**. Member States may not issue expulsion orders as a penalty or legal consequence of a custodial penalty, unless they conform to the conditions set out in **Articles 27** (proportionality, personal conduct, etc), **28** (protection against expulsion, considered later), and **29** (public health, considered later) (**Article 33**).

Proportionality

Restrictive measures must be proportionate to their legitimate aim. Expulsion would be a disproportionate penalty for purely administrative infringements (*R v Pieck* (Case 157/79)) and possibly also for more serious offences, as *Orfanopoulos* suggests.

....

Orfanopoulos and Oliveri v Land Baden-Württemberg (Joined Cases C-482/01 & C-493/01) [2004] ECR I-5257

Orfanopoulos, a Greek national, was living in Germany where he had worked intermittently. He was convicted of drugs offences and sentenced to imprisonment, followed by deportation. The Court of Justice held that, in assessing the proportionality of the penalty, the national court must take account of a range of factors, including the nature and seriousness of the offence, the length of residence in the host state, the time that had elapsed since the offences were committed, and the offender's family circumstances. Proper regard must be had to fundamental rights, specifically to the right to family life guaranteed by **Article 8 of the European Convention on Human Rights**.

....

These principles are now set out in **Directive 2004/38**, which provides guidance on the matters to be considered before an expulsion order is made, including how long the individual has lived in the host state, their age, health, family, and economic situation, social and cultural integration, and links with the state of origin (**Article 28**).

Further protection is afforded to Union citizens, and their family members, with permanent rights of residence. They may be expelled only on 'serious' grounds of public policy or public security. Expulsion decisions taken against those who have resided in the host state for at least ten years or who are minors (unless justified in the best interests of the child) must be justified by 'imperative' grounds of public security. This latter provision appears to rule out a public policy justification, though the Directive gives no guidance as to the distinction between 'public policy' and 'public security'.

General preventative measures

Directive 2004/38 precludes public policy and public security justifications that are 'isolated from the particulars of the case or that rely on considerations of general prevention' (**Article 27**). *Bonsignore*, which pre-dates the Directive, elucidates the meaning of 'considerations of general prevention'.

Limitations on grounds of public policy, public security, or public health
✱✱✱✱✱✱✱✱✱✱✱

Bonsignore v Oberstadtdirektor of the City of Cologne (Case 67/74) [1975] ECR 297

The German authorities had ordered the deportation of Bonsignore, an Italian national, following his conviction for unlawful possession of a firearm and causing death by negligence. The national court considered that the only possible justification for deportation would be 'reasons of a general preventive nature', based on 'the deterrent effect' on other non-nationals. The Court of Justice held that such reasons do not justify restrictive measures.

Previous criminal convictions

Like its predecessor, **Directive 64/221**, **Directive 2004/38** provides that previous criminal convictions shall not in themselves constitute grounds for measures taken on public policy or public security grounds (**Article 27**). *Bouchereau* provides guidance on previous convictions.

R v Bouchereau (Case 30/77) [1977] ECR 1999

Bouchereau, a French national working in England, was convicted of drugs offences. The magistrates proposed to recommend his deportation and sought clarification on whether previous convictions could be taken into account. The Court of Justice held that previous criminal convictions can only be taken into account when 'the circumstances which gave rise to that conviction are evidence of personal conduct constituting a present threat to the requirements of public policy'. This could only be the case where the individual showed 'a propensity to act in the same way in the future'.

Partial restrictions

Whilst the Treaty and **Directive 64/221** clearly allowed Member States to exclude or deport persons exercising EU free movement rights, it was less clear whether partial restrictions were permitted. *Rutili* and *Olazabal* addressed this issue.

Rutili v Ministre de l'Intérieur (Case 36/75) [1975] ECR 1219

Rutili, an Italian national resident in France, was a well-known trade union activist. Taking the view that he was 'likely to disturb public policy' the French authorities prohibited him from living in four particular *départements*. The Court of Justice held that prohibitions on residence may be imposed only in respect of the whole of the national territory, unless nationals are subject to the same limitations. Otherwise, they amount to inequality of treatment and a breach of the Treaty (now **Article 18 TFEU**).

The approach was different in *Olazabal*.

Ministre de l'Intérieur v Olazabal (Case C-100/01) [2002] ECR I-10981

Olazabal, a Spanish national of Basque origin, who had served a prison sentence in France following convictions for terrorism, was prohibited from residing in *départements* bordering Spain.

The Court of Justice declared that where nationals of other Member States are liable to deportation from the host state they are also capable of being subject to less severe measures consisting of partial restrictions, even though the host state cannot apply such measures to its own nationals.

Under **Directive 2004/38** the right of residence covers the whole territory of a Member State. Partial restrictions may be imposed only where the same restrictions apply to the host state's own nationals (**Article 22**). In the light of its judgment in *Olazabal*, it will be interesting to see how the Court of Justice interprets this provision.

Public health

The only diseases justifying restrictions on free movement are those with 'epidemic potential' (as defined by the World Health Organization) and other infectious or contagious diseases that are subject of 'protection provisions' applying to the host state's nationals. Diseases occurring beyond completion of three months' residence do not justify expulsion. During that period, Member States may insist upon a medical examination, free of charge, but not as a matter of routine (**Article 29, Directive 2004/38**).

Procedural rights

Important procedural safeguards supplement Union citizens' substantive rights, including the right to be notified of decisions; the grounds on which decisions are based; the right of appeal; and the right to remain pending an appeal. Persons excluded on public policy or public security grounds may, after a reasonable period and in any event after three years, apply to have the order lifted on the grounds that there has been a material change in the circumstances which justified the exclusion (**Articles 31, 32, Directive 2004/38**).

Revision tip

Be confident about the cases. Whilst they mostly pre-date **Directive 2004/38**, they are still relevant to the interpretation of the limitation provisions.

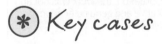 ✳ **Key cases**

Case	Facts	Principle
Sala v Freistaat Bayern (Case C-85/96) [1998] ECR I-2691	A Spanish national living in Germany challenged the refusal of a welfare benefit on the same basis as nationals.	As a Union citizen lawfully resident in another Member State, Sala could invoke [Article 18 TFEU] to claim entitlement to equal treatment with nationals.

Key cases

✳✳✳✳✳✳✳✳✳✳✳✳

Case	Facts	Principle
Baumbast v Secretary of State for the Home Department (Case C-413/99) [2002] ECR I-7091	A German national living in the UK challenged the refusal to renew his residence permit on the grounds that he was no longer economically active in the UK.	Baumbast had sufficient means and adequate sickness insurance. He had a continued right of residence in the UK, arising by direct application of [Article 21 TFEU].
Lawrie-Blum v Land Baden-Württemberg (Case 66/85) [1986] ECR 2121	The national court sought clarification of the meaning of 'worker'.	'[the] essential feature of an employment relationship . . . is that for a certain period of time a person performs services for and under the direction of another person in return for which he receives remuneration'.
Levin v Staatssecretaris van Justitie (Case 53/81) [1982] ECR 1035	Levin, a British national, lived in the Netherlands, where she worked part-time.	Provided work is 'effective and genuine' and not 'purely marginal and ancillary', a part-time worker is entitled to EU free movement rights as a worker. A person's motives in seeking employment in another Member State are irrelevant.
Franca Ninni-Orasche v Bundesminister für Wissenschaft, Verkehr und Kunst (Case C-413/01) [2004] 1 CMLR 19	The applicant was an Italian national working in Germany. When her fixed-term employment contract expired she had looked for work before starting a university course.	None of these factors would be relevant in determining worker status, provided the work activity was not purely marginal and ancillary.
Steymann v Staatssecretaris van Justitie (Case 196/87) [1988] ECR 6159	Steymann participated in the Bhagwan Community's business activities but did not receive formal wages.	The fact that Steymann received no formal wages but only his 'keep' and pocket money did not rule out his work as an effective economic activity.
Bettray v Staatssecretaris van Justitie (Case 344/87) [1989] ECR 1621	Bettray participated in a drug-rehabilitation programme aimed to reintegrate people into the workforce.	Since the objective was rehabilitation, the work was not an 'effective and genuine economic activity'.
Trojani v Centre public d'aide social de Bruxelles (Case C-456/02) [2004] ECR I-7574	Trojani worked for around 30 hours per week as part of a Salvation Army 'personal socio-occupational reintegration programme'.	To decide whether the work was real and genuine, the national court must ascertain whether the services performed were part of the 'normal labour market'.

Case	Facts	Principle
Procureur du Roi v Royer (Case 48/75) [1975] ECR 497	Royer, a French national, sought the right to remain in Belgium as a jobseeker.	Jobseeker rights of entry and residence were established.
Commission v France (French Merchant Seamen) (Case 167/73) [1974] ECR 359	French provisions imposed a ratio of three French to one non-French crew members on ships of the merchant fleet.	France was in breach of the Treaty [Article 45(2) TFEU] and Article 4 of Regulation 1612/68.
Groener v Minister for Education (Case 379/87) [1989] ECR 3967	Irish rules required lecturers in Irish vocational schools to be competent in the Irish language.	The requirement would be justified under Regulation 1612/68 provided it formed part of national policy to promote the use of Irish as the first official language under the Irish Constitution.
Commission v Belgium (Public Employees) (Case 149/79) [1980] ECR 3881	Belgian law reserved certain posts to Belgian nationals.	'Public service posts' defined as involving 'the exercise of power conferred by public law' where there is a 'responsibility for safeguarding the general interests of the state'.
Cristini v SNCF (Case 32/75) [1975] ECR 1085	Cristini, the Italian widow of an Italian migrant worker living in France was refused a French Railways fare reduction card on grounds of nationality.	Regulation 1612/68 applies to all social and tax advantages, whether or not attached to an employment contract.
Gebhard v Consiglio dell'Ordine degli Avvocati e Procuratori di Milano (Case C-55/94) [1995] ECR I-4165.	Gebhard, a lawyer qualified in Germany, faced disciplinary proceedings for practising in Italy under the title avvocato, in contravention of Italian legislation.	'Measures liable to hinder or make less attractive the exercise of fundamental freedoms guaranteed by the Treaty' must be non-discriminatory, justified in the general interest, and suitable for and proportionate to their objective.
Thieffry v Conseil de l'Ordre des Avocats la Cour de Paris (Case 71/76) [1977] ECR 765	Thieffry, a Belgian advocate, was refused admission to the Paris Bar because he did not hold the necessary French qualifications.	Since Thieffry's Belgian qualifications were officially recognized as equivalent in France, this was an unjustified restriction on freedom of establishment.

Key cases

****

Case	Facts	Principle
Van Binsbergen v Bestuur van de Bedrijfsvereniging voor de Metaalnijverheid (Case 33/74) [1974] ECR 1299	A Dutch advocate, qualified in the Netherlands, who was advising a client in relation to Dutch court proceedings, was informed, on moving to Belgium, that he could no longer represent his client. Under Dutch rules only lawyers established in the Netherlands had rights of audience before certain tribunals.	Requirements imposed on persons providing services are compatible with EU law provided they are equally applicable to host state nationals, objectively justified in the public interest, and proportionate.
Säger v Dennemeyer & Co Ltd (Case C-76/90) [1992] ECR I-4221	Under German legislation, licences for the provision of legal services were available to patent agents but not to persons who, like Dennemeyer (who was based in the UK) offered only patent renewal services.	The Treaty not only requires the abolition of discrimination on grounds of nationality but also restrictions that are 'liable to prohibit or otherwise impede' the provision of services. Such restrictions will be compatible with EU law only if justified by imperative reasons in the public interest, equally applicable to national and non-national providers insofar as the interest is not protected by rules applying in the state of origin and proportionate.
Cowan v Le Trésor Public (Case 186/87) [1989] ECR 195	Cowan, a British national who had been violently attacked whilst on a visit to Paris, was refused the compensation to which a French national would have been entitled in these circumstances.	Tourism is a service and tourists are entitled to equal treatment under [Article 18 TFEU].
Van Duyn v Home Office (Case 41/74) [1974] ECR 133	Van Duyn, a Dutch national, refused entry to the UK on public policy grounds, maintained that her association with the Church of Scientology did not constitute 'personal conduct'.	Present association with an organization, reflecting a participation in its activities and identification with its aims, constitutes personal conduct. In general, past association would not justify restrictions.
Criminal Proceedings against Donatella Calfa (Case C-348/96) [1999] ECR I-11	Calfa, an Italian national, was convicted of drugs offences in Greece, sentenced to three months' imprisonment, and, as required by national legislation applying to non-nationals, expelled for life.	Member States may adopt against nationals of other Member States measures which they cannot apply to their own nationals, on public policy grounds. However, automatic expulsion cannot be justified, since it takes no account of the offender's personal conduct.

Case	Facts	Principle
Orfanopoulos and Oliveri v Land Baden-Württemberg (Joined cases C-482/01 and C-493/01) [2004] ECR I-5257	Orfanopoulos, a Greek national, was living in Germany where he had worked intermittently. He was convicted of drugs offences and sentenced to a term of imprisonment, followed by deportation.	In assessing the proportionality of the penalty, the national court must take account of a range of factors, including the nature and seriousness of the offence, the length of residence in the host state, the time that had elapsed since the offences were committed, and the offender's family circumstances. Proper regard must be had to fundamental rights, specifically to the right to family life guaranteed by Article 8 of the European Convention on Human Rights.
Bonsignore v Oberstadtdirektor of the City of Cologne (Case 67/74) [1975] ECR 297	The German authorities had ordered the deportation of Bonsignore, an Italian national, following his conviction for unlawful possession of a firearm and causing death by negligence.	'Reasons of a general preventive nature', based on 'the deterrent effect' on other non-nationals do not justify restrictive measures.
R v Bouchereau (Case 30/77) [1977] ECR 1999	A French national working in England, was convicted of drugs offences. The magistrates proposed to recommend his deportation.	A previous criminal conviction can only be taken into account when 'the circumstances which gave rise to that conviction are evidence of personal conduct constituting a present threat to the requirements of public policy'. This could only be the case where the individual concerned showed 'a propensity to act in the same way in the future'.
Rutili v Ministre de l'Intérieur (Case 36/75) [1975] ECR 1219	Rutili, an Italian national resident in France, was a well-known trade union activist. The French authorities prohibited him from living in four particular *départements*.	Prohibitions on residence may be imposed only in respect of the whole of the national territory, unless nationals are subject to the same limitations. Otherwise, they amount to inequality of treatment and a breach of [Article 18 TFEU].
Ministre de l'Intérieur v Olazabal (Case C-100/01) [2002] ECR I-10981	Olazabal, a Spanish national of Basque origin, who had served a prison sentence in France following convictions for terrorism, was prohibited from residing in départements bordering Spain.	Where nationals of other Member States are liable to deportation from the host state they are also capable of being subject to less severe measures consisting of partial restrictions, even though the host state cannot apply such measures to its own nationals.

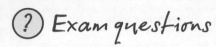 Exam questions

Problem question

Sally, a British national, is 20 years old. Sally had never travelled outside the UK, where all her family and friends live, until last year when she decided to settle permanently in Spain. She has been living in Madrid for the past nine months.

Shortly after her arrival in Madrid, Sally applied for unskilled work in the kitchens of a state-run secondary school. She was invited for interview but her application was unsuccessful because she failed a Spanish language test set at the interview. Eventually, Sally secured employment as a hotel chambermaid. However, after working in this job for a time, Sally began to feel very despondent about her low wages and she became involved in criminal activity. She has just been convicted of robbery with violence and the Spanish court is considering ordering her expulsion from Spain on public policy grounds.

Advise Sally as to the application of EU law on the free movement of persons to each aspect of this situation.

Essay question

With reference to relevant legislation and the case law of the European Court of Justice, critically discuss the significance of the status of Union citizenship for free movement rights.

Outline answers are available at the end of the book.

 Scan here

Scan this QR code image with your mobile device to see a full answer to these questions or log onto www.oxfordtextbooks.oc.uk/orc/concentrate/

#7

EU competition law: introduction and Article 101 TFEU

The examination

EU competition law is a huge topic. Some courses may cover only the basic concepts of **Articles 101 and 102 TFEU**, whilst others may incorporate more detail. Essay-type questions on **Article 101** may ask you to consider the aims of competition law and policy and the extent to which **Article 101**, and its application by the European Commission and the Court of Justice, have achieved these aims. Vertical restraints are a distinctive area and may feature in essay questions, particularly if your course has covered **Regulation 330/2010**. Again depending on your syllabus, you may be required to discuss the rule of reason and the extent to which **Article 101** incorporates such a rule, or **Regulation 1/2003** on enforcement. Problem questions may present general scenarios concerning arrangements between businesses and, if your course has covered **Regulation 330/2010**, could focus on distribution arrangements. Some courses may expect you to prepare for questions covering **Articles 101 and 102** together.

Chapter overview

Article 101 TFEU

Prohibition of anti-competitive agreements, decisions, and concerted practices

Article 101(1): prohibits

'All agreements between undertakings, decisions by associations of undertakings and concerted practice(s)

undertakings: 'legal or natural persons engaged in commercial activity' (*Höfner and Elser*)

which may affect trade between Member States:

'... an influence, direct or indirect, actual or potential, on the pattern of trade between Member States' (*STM*)

---

agreements:

- not only formal binding contracts but also less formal agreements or arrangements, for instance the so-called 'gentlemen's agreement'
- includes both horizontal and vertical agreements (*Consten*)

decisions by associations of undertakings include:

- non-binding recommendations if normally complied with (*IAZ*)
- decisions of professional associations if expressing the intention of members to carry out their economic activity in a particular way (*Wouters*)

concerted practice:

- 'a form of co-ordination between undertakings which, without having reached the stage where an agreement properly so-called has been concluded, knowingly substitutes practical co-operation between them for the risks of competition' (*Dyestuffs*)

but no concerted practice where:

- no evidence of communication between the companies and the behaviour (eg parallel pricing) is the result of the normal operation of the market (eg of an oligopolistic market) (*Woodpulp*)

Chapter overview

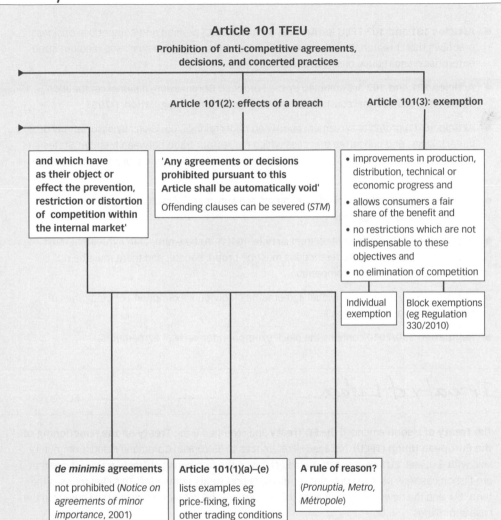

Article 101 TFEU

Prohibition of anti-competitive agreements,
decisions, and concerted practices

Article 101(2): effects of a breach

Article 101(3): exemption

and which have
as their object or
effect the prevention,
restriction or distortion
of competition within
the internal market'

'Any agreements or decisions
prohibited pursuant to this
Article shall be automatically void'

Offending clauses can be severed (*STM*)

- improvements in production, distribution, technical or economic progress and
- allows consumers a fair share of the benefit and
- no restrictions which are not indispensable to these objectives and
- no elimination of competition

Individual exemption

Block exemptions (eg Regulation 330/2010)

***de minimis* agreements**

not prohibited (*Notice on agreements of minor importance*, 2001)

Article 101(1)(a)–(e)

lists examples eg price-fixing, fixing other trading conditions

A rule of reason?

(*Pronuptia, Metro, Métropole*)

Key facts

- **Articles 101 and 102 TFEU** (ex **Articles 81 and 82 EC**) prohibit anti-competitive business practices that threaten the internal market, harm consumers and small and medium-sized enterprises, and reduce business efficiency.

- **Articles 101 and 102** are enforced by the European Commission, national competition authorities, and national courts under powers conferred by **Regulation 1/2003**.

- **Article 101(1)** prohibits agreements between undertakings, decisions by associations of undertakings, and concerted practices which may affect trade between Member States and which have as their object or effect the prevention, restriction, or distortion of competition within the internal market.

- Under **Article 101(2)** prohibited agreements are automatically void, though offending restrictions may be severed.

- **Article 101(3)** allows exemption from **Article 101(1)**. To be exempt, an agreement must have beneficial effects, the restrictions must be proportionate, and there must be no substantial elimination of competition.

- Exemption may apply to individual agreements ('individual exemption') or categories of agreement ('block exemption').

- **Regulation 330/2010** contains the block exemption for vertical agreements.

Treaty of Lisbon

The **Treaty of Lisbon** amended the **EC Treaty** and renamed it the **Treaty on the Functioning of the European Union (TFEU)**, replaced all references to 'European Community' and 'Community law' with 'EU' and 'EU law' respectively, and changed the numbering of Treaty articles. Note that pre-Lisbon case law uses the previous terminology and Treaty numbering. This chapter uses the term 'EU' and the new Treaty numbering throughout, placed in brackets where they appear in the case summaries.

Introduction to EU competition law

EU rules prohibiting barriers to trade, set out in **Articles 30, 36, and 110 TFEU,** continue to be fundamental to the effective operation of the internal market. They target restrictions adopted by Member States, usually in the form of national legislation. However, Member State action is not the only threat to the internal market. Restrictive business practices can also have harmful consequences. Indeed, not only do such practices prejudice the operation of the internal market, they can also have a detrimental effect on business efficiency, are likely to harm consumers, and, if engaged in by large and powerful companies, are likely to disadvantage small and medium-sized businesses.

Articles 101 and 102 TFEU prohibit anti-competitive business practices. The European Commission, national competition authorities, and national courts enforce **Articles 101 and 102** under powers conferred by **Regulation 1/2003.** From time to time, the European Commission issues non-binding notices providing clarification of the competition rules. This chapter focuses on **Article 101,** but begins with an outline of **Articles 101 and 102** and the rules on enforcement.

Article 101 TFEU

In broad terms, **Article 101** prohibits business agreements or arrangements which prevent, restrict, or distort competition within the internal market and affect trade between Member States. A fictitious illustration may be helpful.

Suppose that BigCo (a UK company) and GrandCo (a French company), two fridge manufacturers which together supply 70% of the fridges sold in the EU, tire of competing with each other. They agree that each will supply its products only within an agreed 'territory' (BigCo in the UK and 12 other Member States, excluding France, and GrandCo in France and the remaining Member States) and that they will charge the same prices.

This arrangement shields the companies from competition with respect to sales area and pricing that would normally be applied in a freely competitive market. The harmful effects of the arrangement on free trade, consumers, and business efficiency are evident. If the companies adhere to the 'market-sharing' agreement, their fridges will be prevented from moving freely in the internal market. If the 'price-fixing' arrangement is maintained and, as typically occurs in such circumstances, the prices are set artificially high, consumers will suffer. Without the threat of competition from each other, BigCo and GrandCo have little incentive to operate efficiently or maintain product quality. The arrangement prevents, restricts, and distorts competition and is likely to breach **Article 101.**

Article 102 TFEU

Whereas **Article 101** applies to arrangements between businesses, **Article 102** prohibits the abuse of market power, or 'dominance', normally by businesses acting unilaterally, within the internal market.

Suppose, for instance, that MightyCo, a UK fertilizer manufacturer, which supplies its products to independent wholesalers throughout the EU, has a 75% share of the market. It requires its customers to resell its products at a stated price ('price-fixing') and specifies the sales area to which each wholesaler's operations are restricted ('market-sharing'). Because of MightyCo's large market share, consumers have limited choice and may be unable to shop around for cheaper products. The fertilizers are prevented from moving freely around the internal market. MightyCo's behaviour is likely to infringe **Article 102**.

'Undertakings'

Articles 101 and 102 refer to businesses as 'undertakings'. The precise meaning of this term will be considered presently.

Revision tip

Remember that **Articles 101 and 102** concern the behaviour of businesses.

Regulation 1/2003: enforcement of Articles 101 and 102

A system of cooperation

The basis of the enforcement regime, set out in **Regulation 1/2003**, is a system of cooperation between the European Commission, national courts, and national competition authorities. The European Commission, through the Directorate-General for Competition, or D-G Comp, and national competition authorities, are empowered to investigate alleged infringements of **Articles 101 and 102**, issue decisions, and impose fines. The Commission can take over cases from the national authorities, in accordance with criteria set out in the *Commission notice on co-operation within the network of competition authorities*, 2004.

Cooperation with national authorities

To ensure consistency and effectiveness, **Regulation 1/2003** requires close cooperation between national competition authorities and the Commission and between national authorities themselves, including, for instance, the exchange of information.

Cooperation with national courts

Articles 101 and 102 are directly effective and so may be applied in national proceedings. National courts can request information or advice from the Commission and may refer questions of interpretation to the Court of Justice under the **preliminary rulings** procedure. National court proceedings and Commission proceedings may run in parallel and a national court may consider a case on which the Commission has already taken a decision. **Regulation 1/2003** requires national courts to avoid judgments that conflict with Commission decisions.

The European Commission's powers

Regulation 1/2003 empowers the European Commission to investigate alleged infringements, to require undertakings to terminate infringements, and to impose fines and penalties where breaches are established. The investigatory powers permit the Commission to request information from national governments and national competition authorities, to request or require undertakings to supply information, to interview individuals concerning its enquiries, and to inspect business premises. Inspections may be voluntary, conducted with an undertaking's agreement, or mandatory, the latter often being referred to as 'dawn raids'. Whilst the Commission has no power of forcible entry, it may require the necessary assistance from national authorities, usually the issue of a search warrant.

The Commission may levy substantial fines and daily penalties for infringements of **Articles 101 and 102** (up to 10% of the previous year's worldwide turnover plus daily penalties of up to 5% of daily turnover for continuing infringements), for supplying incorrect or misleading information (up to 1% of the previous year's turnover), or for failure to comply with a request for information (up to 5% of the previous year's turnover).

Safeguards for undertakings

Information collected pursuant to **Regulation 1/2003** may be used only for the purpose for which it was acquired. The Commission must have regard to the legitimate interests of undertakings in the protection of their business secrets, for instance when it publishes decisions. Before the Commission adopts an unfavourable decision, an undertaking must be offered a hearing. Commission decisions are subject to judicial review by the EU courts, being heard by the General Court (formerly the Court of First Instance), with appeal lying to the Court of Justice. Most cases comprise **Article 263** actions for annulment. Successful applicants are likely to secure reduced fines, rather than annulment.

It should be noted that **Articles 101 and 102 TFEU** are directly effective and can be relied upon by individuals in national courts. Indeed, there are a number of advantages for a complainant to pursue this course of action set out in paragraph 16 of the *Notice on the handling of complaints by the Commission*. *Courage Ltd v Crehan* (Case C-453/99) provides an example of such an action and makes it clear that EU law would not preclude a rule of national law (in this case English law) barring a complainant from relying on his own unlawful actions.

Revision tip
Even if your course does not cover enforcement, familiarity with the main provisions will help you understand the practical operation of the competition rules.

Outline of Article 101 TFEU

Article 101 is broad, covering formal agreements and also informal arrangements between undertakings. It prohibits, as incompatible with the internal market,

. . . all agreements between undertakings, decisions by associations of undertakings and concerted practices which may affect trade between Member States and which have as their object or effect the prevention, restriction or distortion of competition within the internal market . . . (**Article 101(1)**)

and lists examples of restrictions that are caught.

Under **Article 101(2)** agreements or decisions within **Article 101(1)** are automatically void, though if it is possible to sever (remove) restrictive clauses from an agreement, only those clauses will be void (*Etablissements Consten SA and Grundig – Verkaufs GmbH v Commission* (Cases 56 & 58/64)).

Article 101(3) provides for exemption. **Article 101(1)** may be declared inapplicable to an agreement, decision, or concerted practice if certain conditions are satisfied.

Revision tip

Be confident about this basic framework. You can then assimilate the detailed provisions and cases covered in the rest of this chapter.

Article 101(1): the prohibition

Article 101(1) prohibits:

- all agreements between undertakings, decisions by associations of undertakings, and concerted practices;
- which may affect trade between Member States; and
- which have as their object or effect the prevention, restriction, or distortion of competition within the internal market.

All three elements must be satisfied for a breach to be established.

Revision tip

Most problem questions will require you to set out and apply each of these elements in turn.

Agreements between undertakings, decisions by associations of undertakings, and concerted practices

Undertakings

The Treaty does not define this term. '**Undertaking**' has been interpreted broadly to include natural and legal persons (individuals and companies) engaged in commercial activity for the provision of goods or services (*Höfner and Elser* (Case C-41/90)).

Agreements

'Agreement' covers formal binding contracts and also less formal agreements or arrangements, for instance the so-called 'gentlemen's agreement' concluded simply by a handshake.

The broad scope of **Article 101(1)**, incorporating not only 'agreements' but also the much less formal 'concerted practices' means that it is unnecessary to identify the precise boundaries of 'agreement'.

Decisions by associations of undertakings

Article 101(1) is not confined to arrangements set up directly between undertakings, but also covers decisions of associations of undertakings. Anti-competitive activity might be coordinated through a trade association, for instance through a decision requiring its members to raise their prices to a specified level or to refuse supplies to particular categories of customer. Provided all the elements of **Article 101(1)** are satisfied, there is a breach. Even a non-binding recommendation to members may be caught.

IAZ International Belgium NV v Commission (Cases 96–102, 104, 105, 108 & 110/82) [1983] ECR 3369

A system regulating the connection of washing machines and dishwashers to the water supply, recommended to its members by a Belgian water suppliers' trade association, operated in such a way as to discriminate against imported machines. The Court of Justice held that a non-binding recommendation would fall within **Article [101](1)** if it was intended to be anti-competitive and was normally complied with, resulting in an appreciable effect on competition.

Decisions of professional associations may fall within **Article 101(1)**.

Wouters v Netherlands Bar (Case C-309/99) [2002] ECR I-1577

A regulation of the Dutch Bar Association prohibiting multi-disciplinary partnerships was a decision of an association of undertakings, since it expressed the intention of members to carry out their economic activity in a particular way.

Concerted practices

Like 'agreement' and 'decision', **'concerted practice'** has been interpreted broadly, though the outer limits of this concept have proved difficult to identify. Its meaning was first considered in *Dyestuffs*.

Imperial Chemical Industries Ltd v Commission (Dyestuffs) (Case 48/69) [1972] ECR 619

ICI challenged a Commission Decision finding that certain aniline dye producers, including ICI, had fixed prices through concerted practices. The producers maintained that their almost simultaneous and almost identical price rises did not amount to concerted practice but were a feature of an **oligopolistic market** (a market dominated by relatively few sellers in which, where pricing policies are transparent, rival companies tend to respond without **collusion** to each other's market strategy, a form of **'parallel behaviour'**).

The Court of Justice defined a concerted practice as 'a form of coordination between undertakings which, without having reached the stage where an agreement properly so-called has been concluded, knowingly substitutes practical cooperation between them for the risks of competition'. It held that, whilst parallel behaviour does not in itself constitute concerted practice, it may be strong evidence of it. That will be the case where the conduct 'leads to conditions of competition which do not correspond to the normal conditions of the market'.

Finding a concerted practice, the Court held that the companies had not reacted spontaneously to each other's pricing strategy. Advance announcements of price increases had eliminated all uncertainty between them as to their future conduct and their actions demonstrated a 'common intention' to fix prices.

Woodpulp also featured an oligopolistic market, but the outcome was different.

Ahlström & Ors v Commission (Woodpulp) (Cases C-89, 104, 114, 116–117, 125–129/85) [1993] ECR I-1307

The Court of Justice accepted that a system of quarterly price announcements operated by certain woodpulp producers did not amount to a concerted practice. There was no evidence of communication between the companies and the parallel pricing was the result of the normal operation of the oligopolistic woodpulp market.

✓ Looking for extra marks?

The Court of Justice's approach to parallel behaviour in oligopolistic markets is controversial, since it will generally be difficult to determine with any certainty what are 'normal conditions of the market'.

A concerted practice need not entail the existence of a plan (*Cooperatieve Vereniging 'Suiker Unie' UA v Commission* (*Sugar Cartel Cases*) (Cases 40–48, 50, 54–56, 111, 113, 114/73)). Moreover, there is a presumption that operators who have exchanged information and are still trading take account of that information in conducting their business. In such circumstances there will be a breach, even in the absence of anti-competitive effects on the market (*Huls AG v Commission* (Case C-199/92P)).

Cartels

Anti-competitive arrangements sometimes operate within **cartels**, on the basis of agreements and/or concerted practices. Typically, cartel members meet secretly to collude on prices or to exchange information. Their activity may be sustained over long periods, often many years, without detection. In recent years, the Commission has increased its efforts to root out cartels. To facilitate this, the Commission applies a leniency policy allowing 'whistleblower' cartel members to obtain immunity from fines or a reduction in fines for exposing the cartel or supplying information about its activities (*Commission notice on immunity from fines and reduction of fines in cartel cases*, 2002).

Vertical and horizontal agreements

Article 101(1) applies to both horizontal and vertical agreements. **Horizontal agreements** are concluded between parties operating at the same level of the production/distribution chain, for instance an agreement between manufacturers or between retailers. **Vertical agreements** operate at different levels, for instance a distribution agreement between a manufacturer and a distributor. *Consten* established that **Article 101(1)** applies to vertical agreements.

....

Etablissements Consten SA and Grundig – Verkaufs GmbH v Commission
(Cases 56 & 58/64) [1966] ECR 299

Under a dealership agreement, Grundig supplied its electronic products to Consten for resale in France. Consten challenged the Commission's finding of an infringement, arguing that **Article [101]** applied only to horizontal agreements. The Court of Justice disagreed, holding that both vertical and horizontal agreements are capable of falling within its scope.

....

✅ *Looking for extra marks?*

Restrictions in horizontal agreements are likely to affect **inter-brand competition** (competition between two or more brands of a particular product or service). By contrast, restrictions in vertical agreements (typically between non-competitors at different levels of the chain of distribution) are likely to affect **intra-brand competition** (competition within a particular brand).

Inter-brand restrictions pose a greater threat to the market than intra-brand restrictions. This can be illustrated by the potential effect on consumers. If two independent manufacturers of a particular product fix their prices for their respective brands, consumers' ability to shop around for a cheaper product is limited, particularly if these manufacturers together hold a large market share. On the other hand, if a manufacturer of a particular product imposes a fixed resale price on its distributors, consumers remain able to shop around for cheaper products of any other brand.

EU competition law formally recognizes the less harmful effects of vertical restrictions and their potential benefits, particularly in **distribution agreements**, through the vertical restraints block exemption **Regulation 330/2010**, considered later in this chapter.

Which may affect trade between Member States

There is no breach of **Article 101(1)** unless the agreement, decision, or concerted practice 'may affect trade between Member States'. This requirement concerns jurisdiction; arrangements that have no effect on trade between Member States fall to be considered under national law. Unsurprisingly, the Court of Justice has adopted a broad interpretation of the requirement. There would be an effect on trade wherever it is 'possible to foresee with a sufficient degree of probability on the basis of a set of objective factors of law or of fact that the agreement in question may have an influence, direct or indirect, actual or potential, on the pattern of trade between Member States' (*Société Technique Minière v Maschinenbau Ulm GmbH* (Case 56/65) (**STM**)). This broad test is easily satisfied.

Article 101(1): the prohibition

✳✳✳✳✳✳✳✳✳✳✳✳

As a potential effect is sufficient, agreements operating solely within one Member State may be caught by **Article 101(1)**.

....

Vacuum Interrupters Ltd (Commission Decision) OJ 1977 L 48/32, [1977] 1 CMLR D67

Two UK companies had entered into a joint venture research and development agreement to design and manufacture switchgear in the UK. The Commission found that, in the absence of an agreement, the companies would have developed the product independently and marketed it in other Member States. The agreement made it more difficult for potential competitors from other Member States to enter the UK market, given the combined economic and technical strength of the two manufacturers. The agreement was capable of affecting trade between Member States.

....

An effect on trade between Member States means any effect, even if it results in an increase in trade.

....

Consten contd

The dealership agreement between Grundig and Consten gave Consten the exclusive right to sell Grundig's electronic products in France. Consten agreed not to sell the goods outside France and, in return, Grundig agreed to obtain similar undertakings from distributors of its products in other Member States. Consten could enforce its exclusive rights in France through the GINT trademark, which Grundig had assigned to it. This network of agreements gave Consten total protection from competition in France ('**absolute territorial protection**').

When UNEF, a French company, began to sell Grundig products (bought in Germany) in France, undercutting Consten, the latter brought proceedings for infringement of its trademark. Following investigations, the European Commission decided that the Consten–Grundig agreement infringed **Article [101](1)**.

Consten's challenge to the decision was based not only on the vertical nature of the agreement (see earlier) but also on the Commission's finding of an effect on trade between Member States. Consten and Grundig argued that the agreement had increased trade between Member States and that therefore **Article [101](1)** did not apply. The Court of Justice rejected this argument, holding that 'effect on trade' includes both positive and negative effects.

....

The 'legal and economic context' of an arrangement will be taken into account.

....

Brasserie de Haecht SA v Wilkin (No 1) (Case 23/67) [1967] ECR 407

Under loan agreements with the brewery, Mr and Mrs Wilkin undertook to obtain all their supplies of beer and soft drinks exclusively from the brewery. When this obligation was breached, the brewery sought repayment of the loan in the national court. The couple argued that the agreements infringed **Article [101]** and were therefore void. Considering whether the agreements should be assessed in isolation or in the light of other similar agreements, the Court of Justice held that the effect on trade between Member States must be examined in the overall legal and economic context. The existence of similar contracts was a factor to be taken into account.

Guidance is provided by the Commission's *Notice: guidelines on the effect on trade concept contained in Articles 81 and 82 of the Treaty*, 2004. An agreement is not capable of affecting trade between Member States if the parties' aggregate market share on any relevant EU market affected by the agreement does not exceed 5% and (for horizontal agreements) their aggregate turnover does not exceed €40 million or (for vertical agreements) the aggregate EU turnover of the supplier does not exceed €40 million.

Revision tip

Be familiar with the cases demonstrating the Court of Justice's broad interpretation of 'agreements, decisions and concerted practices' and 'effect on trade between Member States'.

Object or effect: prevention, restriction, or distortion of competition

Object or effect

The agreement, decision, or concerted practice must have as its 'object or effect' the prevention, restriction, or distortion of competition. It is sufficient to establish either anti-competitive object or an anti-competitive effect (*STM*). The Commission has stated that with regard to particularly objectionable restrictions, such as horizontal price-fixing or market-sharing, it will be unnecessary to establish any actual effect on the market. The mere existence of such a restriction is sufficient (*Commission guidelines on the application of Article 81(3) of the Treaty*, 2004).

Agreements of minor importance

Early case law established that an agreement is caught by **Article 101(1)** only if it has an 'appreciable' effect on the market (*Volk v Établissements Vervaecke Sprl* (Case 5/69)). Agreements of minor importance (described as de minimis agreements) are not prohibited.

The *Notice on agreements of minor importance*, 2001 sets out the Commission's view of *de minimis* agreements. Agreements affecting trade between Member States do not appreciably affect competition if the parties' aggregate share of the relevant market does not exceed 10% (agreements between competitors, normally horizontal agreements) or if the market share of each of the parties does not exceed 15% (agreements between non-competitors, normally vertical agreements). *De minimis* does not apply to agreements containing **hardcore restrictions**, such as price-fixing and market-sharing, but otherwise, where the thresholds are not exceeded, the Commission will not institute proceedings. Where undertakings assume in good faith that an agreement is covered by the notice, the Commission will not impose fines.

Prevention, restriction, and distortion of competition

'Prevention', 'restriction', and 'distortion' of competition cover all forms of anti-competitive behaviour. **Article 101(1)(a)–(e)** provide examples. It should be noted that where an agreement infringes **Article 101(1)**, it might nevertheless be exempted under **Article 101(3)**.

Price-fixing or fixing other trading conditions (Article 101(1)(a))

Price-fixing includes horizontal price-fixing, which is deemed to have an anti-competitive object (*Dyestuffs* provides an example) and vertical price-fixing, illustrated by *Hennessy/Henkell*.

....

Hennessy/Henkell (Commission Decision) OJ 1980 L 383/11, [1981] 1 CMLR 601

An **exclusive distribution agreement** for the sale of Hennessy cognac in Germany contained a clause fixing the minimum and maximum resale prices to be charged by the distributor, Henkell. The Commission decided that the fixing of maximum and minimum price levels breached **Article [101](1)**.

....

Restrictions on imports and exports provide examples within the category 'fixing other trading conditions'. *Consten* provides an example.

Other restrictions (Article 101(1)(b)–(e))

These include agreements, such as the *Vacuum Interrupters* agreement, that control production, markets, technical developments, or investments (**Article 101(1)(b)**) and agreements that share markets or sources of supply (**Article 101(1)(c)**). Also included are agreements that apply dissimilar conditions to different trading parties (**Article 101(1)(d)**) and make the conclusion of contracts subject to supplementary obligations having no connection with the subject matter of the contract (**Article 101(1)(e)**). With respect to the latter category, for example, a clause in the Hennessy/Henkell agreement prohibiting Henkell from selling competing products was held to be acceptable, whereas a clause prohibiting the sale of any other products was not.

Rule of reason

The **rule of reason** originated in US antitrust (competition) law. Its application entails the balancing of the pro- and anti-competitive effects of restrictive agreements. Where the benefits outweigh the disadvantages, and therefore on balance the agreement is not anti-competitive, there is no breach. In EU competition law, some decisions, for instance *Pronuptia*, suggest that the Court of Justice has been willing to adopt a rule of reason approach in assessing agreements under **Article 101(1)**.

Pronuptia concerned a **distribution franchise**. Typically, distribution franchise arrangements are made between an established distributor of a product (the franchisor) and other independent traders (the franchisees). The franchisor grants the franchisees, for a fee, the right to establish themselves using its business name and methods. The franchisor derives financial benefit without investing capital; the franchisees gain access to successful business methods and benefit from the reputation of the franchisor's business name. In order to protect that reputation, the franchisor will insist upon the franchisee accepting specific obligations, such as those imposed in the *Pronuptia* agreement.

. . . .

Pronuptia de Paris GmbH v Pronuptia de Paris Irmgard Schillgalis (Case 161/84) [1986] ECR 353

The franchisor granted the franchisee the exclusive right to use the Pronuptia mark in the designated area. The franchisee agreed not to open a shop selling competing goods, not to sell its shop without the franchisor's prior approval, and to obtain stock only from the franchisor or from other suppliers selected by the franchisor. Despite the severity of these restrictions, the Court of Justice held that they did not breach **Article [101](1)** because they were indispensable to protect the franchisor's reputation and know-how and the uniform identity of the franchise outlets.

. . . .

A similar approach may be detected concerning **selective distribution agreements**. Here, goods or services are sold only through outlets chosen by the supplier according to its own criteria relating, for instance, to the suitability of the premises, the availability of after-sales service and the provision of adequately trained staff. Whilst the retailer's trading activity is restricted to some degree by the requirement to maintain these standards, in return the retailer gains protection from competition from unsuitable outlets and the quality and brand image of the product are upheld.

. . . .

Metro-SB-Grossmärkte GmbH & Co KG v Commission (No 1) (Case 26/76) [1977] ECR 1875

Restrictions in a selective distribution agreement relating to the technical qualifications of the retailer and the suitability of its trading premises, designed to ensure the quality of sales and service, would not breach **Article [101](1)** provided they were applied uniformly across the selective distribution network.

. . . .

The Court of Justice has not expressly referred to a rule of reason. Indeed, in *Métropole Télévision (M6) and Others v Commission* (Case T-112/99) the Court of First Instance (now the General Court) stated that judgments such as *Pronuptia* do not establish such a rule in [EU] competition law; whilst an assessment of the applicability of **Article [101](1)** to an agreement requires examination of the context in which the undertakings operate, this does not mean that it is necessary to weigh the pro- and anti-competitive effects of an agreement. If it were otherwise, the **Article [101](3)** exemption would lose much of its effectiveness.

Article 101(3) TFEU: exemption

Article 101(3) does entail assessment of an agreement's pro- and anti-competitive effects.

Article 101(3)

Article 101(3) provides that **Article 101(1)** may be declared inapplicable to any agreement, decision of an association of undertakings, or concerted practice or category of agreements, decisions, or concerted practices which

- contributes to improving the production or distribution of goods or to promoting technical or economic progress;
- while allowing consumers a fair share of the resulting benefit;

and which does not

- impose on the undertakings concerned restrictions which are not indispensable to the attainment of these objectives;
- afford such undertakings the possibility of eliminating competition in respect of a substantial part of the products in question.

For exemption to apply, all four conditions must be satisfied.

Revision tip

You must discuss and apply all four conditions in an answer to a problem question.

The reference to agreements, decisions, or concerted practices and categories of agreements, decisions, or concerted practices indicates that exemption can be 'individual' or 'block'.

Individual exemption

Originally, the Commission alone had power to grant **individual exemption**. Now, **Regulation 1/2003** allows **Article 101(3)** to be applied also by national courts and national competition authorities. Guidance on exemption is provided by the *Commission guidelines on the application of Article 81(3) of the Treaty*, 2004.

Improving production or distribution of goods or promoting technical or economic progress

According to the Commission guidelines, this condition requires efficiency gains (para 50). These may be quantitative, comprising reduced costs resulting, for instance, from improved production or economies of scale, or qualitative, generating better products or enhanced research and development. The causal link between the agreement and the claimed efficiencies must be demonstrated. *ACEC/Berliet* and *Prym-Werke* provide examples.

ACEC/Berliet (Commission Decision) OJ 1968 L 201/7, [1968] CMLR D35

The ACEC/Berliet agreement provided for technical cooperation and joint research on the development of a bus equipped with electric transmission. There were restrictive clauses controlling production and markets. Exemption was granted on the basis that the agreement allowed each party to concentrate on the areas within its own expertise, Berliet on research on vehicles and their manufacture and ACEC on research on electrical constructions.

Prym-Werke (Commission Decision) OJ 1973 L296/24, [1973] CMLR D250

Prym agree to stop making needles and instead to buy them from Beka, which agreed to supply Prym. This allowed Beka to specialize in needle production. The Commission granted exemption, stating that the concentration of manufacture improved production by increasing by at least 50% the quantity of needles manufactured at Beka's European factory, making it possible for the company to make more intensive use of existing plant and introduce production-line manufacture.

Allowing consumers a fair share of the resulting benefit

The Commission's guidelines state that 'fair share' implies that the resulting benefit must at least compensate consumers for any negative impact caused by the restriction of competition (para 85). For instance, if an agreement leads to higher prices, consumers must be compensated through better quality or other benefits.

No restrictions that are not indispensable

This condition requires **proportionality**. Restrictions must not go beyond what is necessary to achieve the beneficial objectives of the agreement. If the benefits can be achieved by less restrictive means, exemption will not apply.

CECED (Commission Decision) OJ 2000 L187/47 [2000] 5 CMLR 635

Domestic appliance manufacturers undertook to phase out washing machines with low energy efficiency. The agreement was found to breach **Article [101](1)** because it restricted consumer choice and raised production costs for some manufacturers. The Commission, interpreting economic efficiency to include environmental benefits as well as technical efficiency, considered whether there were less restrictive ways of reducing energy consumption, such as informing consumers about the energy costs of machines, allowing them to make a choice. The Commission concluded that this would not be the most effective means. Consequently the agreement was necessary to achieve the benefits.

Certain restrictions will rarely, if ever, be indispensable, notably clauses conferring absolute territorial protection or fixing prices.

Article 101(3) TFEU: exemption
****

No elimination of competition

There must be no elimination of competition in respect of the product in question. The Commission guidelines state that the 'protection of rivalry and the competitive process is given priority over potentially pro-competitive efficiency gains which could result from restrictive agreements' (para 105). In *CECED* the Commission found no elimination of competition because manufacturers could still compete on other features, such as price and technical performance. In *ACEC/Berliet* the Commission found that the buses would be competing with buses equipped with mechanical transmission produced by several other manufacturers.

Block exemption

Article 101(3) allows **Article 101(1)** to be declared inapplicable not only to individual agreements, but also to categories of agreement. The **block exemptions**, issued by the Commission in the form of regulations, cover agreements such as technology transfer agreements (relating to patent and know-how licensing), research and development agreements, and specialization agreements. An agreement which is drafted within the terms of the relevant block exemption is automatically exempt.

Most of the original regulations followed the same format, setting out the permitted restrictions, the 'white list', and the prohibited restrictions, the 'black list'. More recent block exemptions contain only 'black-listed' restrictions. The Commission considers that the removal of the 'white lists' will free business from the 'strait-jacket' effect of the earlier regulations, which limited the parties to using only the expressly permitted restrictions.

The following brief account of **Regulation 330/2010** provides an indication of the content and scope of a block exemption.

Regulation 330/2010: block exemption for vertical agreements

Regulation 330/2010, which replaces **Regulation 2790/99**, contains the block exemption for certain categories of vertical agreements and concerted practices.

In broad terms, **Article 2** of the Regulation exempts from **Article 101(1)** vertical agreements relating to the conditions under which the parties may purchase, sell, or resell certain goods or services, to the extent that these agreements contain otherwise prohibited restrictions. The Regulation covers, for instance, exclusive distribution, distribution franchise, and selective distribution agreements.

The exemption is subject to market-share thresholds. It applies only where both the supplier's market share does not exceed 30% on the relevant market on which it sells the contract goods or services, and the buyer's market share does not exceed 30% on the relevant market on which it purchases the contract goods or services.

The benefit of the block exemption does not apply to vertical agreements containing certain hardcore restrictions, set out in **Article 4**. They comprise restrictions by the supplier on the buyer's ability to determine its sale price, save for maximum or recommended sale prices, and restrictions on the territory into which the buyer may resell the goods or services, with some specified exceptions. The impact of **Article 4** is that an agreement containing hardcore restrictions is, in its entirety, outside the scope of the block exemption. The offending clauses cannot be severed (removed).

By contrast to **Article 4**, **Article 5** provides that the block exemption does not apply to certain obligations contained in agreements. Although the **Article 5** restrictions themselves fall outside the block exemption, they may be severed, allowing the remainder of the agreement to be block exempted. Severable restrictions comprise certain non-compete obligations (obligations on the buyer not to sell competing goods), including non-compete clauses exceeding five years.

Any restriction falling outside **Articles 4 and 5** is permitted.

 ✔ **Looking for extra marks?**

Before **Regulation 2790/99**, the predecessor to **Regulation 330/2010**, was adopted, the Commission had been criticized for its inflexible approach to vertical restraints, which it had tended to condemn without adequate analysis of their potentially beneficial economic effects. Moreover, the existing block exemptions for franchising and exclusive distribution agreements were form-based rather than effects-based, forcing parties into structuring their agreements in a particular way and constraining their commercial freedom. The adoption of **Regulation 2790/99** was an indication of the Commission's new economics-based approach to competition law.

 ✱ **Key cases**

Case	Facts	Principle
Etablissements Consten SA and Grundig – Verkaufs GmbH v Commission (Cases 56 & 58/64) [1966] ECR 299	Consten and Grundig challenged a Commission decision finding that their dealership agreement infringed Article [101](1).	If restrictive clauses can be severed, only those clauses will be void.
IAZ International Belgium NV v Commission (Cases 96–102, 104, 105, 108, & 110/82) [1983] ECR 3369	A recommendation to its members by a Belgian water suppliers' trade association discriminated against imported machines.	A non-binding recommendation falls within Article 101(1) if intended to be anti-competitive and normally complied with.
Wouters v Netherlands Bar (Case C-309/99) [2002] ECR I-1577	A Dutch Bar Association regulation prohibited multi-disciplinary partnerships.	'Decisions by associations of undertakings' can include decisions of professional associations.

Key cases

****

Case	Facts	Principle
Imperial Chemical Industries Ltd v Commission (Dyestuffs) (Case 48/69) [1972] ECR 619	ICI challenged a Commission Decision finding that certain aniline dye producers, including ICI, had fixed prices through concerted practices.	'Concerted practice': 'a form of coordination between undertakings which, without having reached the stage where an agreement properly so-called has been concluded, knowingly substitutes practical cooperation between them for the risks of competition'. Parallel behaviour does not in itself constitute concerted practice, but may be strong evidence of it, especially if the conduct 'leads to conditions of competition which do not correspond to the normal conditions of the market'.
Ahlström & Ors v Commission (Woodpulp) (Cases C-89, 104, 114, 116–117, 125–129/85) [1993] ECR I-1307	Challenge to a finding of a concerted practice in relation to a system of quarterly price announcements.	There was no concerted practice, since there was no evidence of communication between the companies and the parallel pricing was the result of the normal operation of the oligopolistic woodpulp market.
Etablissements Consten SA and Grundig – Verkaufs GmbH v Commission (Cases 56 & 58/64) [1966] ECR 299	(See earlier)	Both vertical and horizontal agreements can fall within Article 101(1).
Société Technique Minière v Maschinenbau Ulm GmbH (Case 56/65) [1966] ECR 235 (STM)	Agreement for the supply of heavy earth-moving equipment.	Effect on trade between Member States: wherever it is 'possible to foresee with a sufficient degree of probability on the basis of a set of objective factors of law or of fact that the agreement in question may have an influence, direct or indirect, actual or potential, on the pattern of trade between Member States'.
Vacuum Interrupters Ltd (Commission Decision) OJ 1977 L48/32, [1977] 1 CMLR D67	Joint venture research and development agreement between two UK companies to design and manufacture switchgear in the UK.	Agreements between undertakings operating solely in one Member State may have an effect on trade between Member States. A potential effect is sufficient.

Case	Facts	Principle
Etablissements Consten SA and Grundig – Verkaufs GmbH v Commission (Cases 56 & 58/64) [1966] ECR 299	(See earlier)	An 'effect on trade' includes both positive and negative effects.
Brasserie de Haecht SA v Wilkin (No 1) (Case 23/67) [1967] ECR 407	Mr and Mrs Wilkin claimed that their loan agreement with the brewery infringed Article [101](1).	Assessment of the effect on trade between Member States will take into account the 'legal and economic context' of an agreement.
Société Technique Minière v Maschinenbau Ulm GmbH (Case 56/65) [1966] ECR 235 (STM)	(See earlier)	It is not necessary to establish both the object and effect of an agreement. Either an anti-competitive object or effect will suffice.
Pronuptia de Paris GmbH v Pronuptia de Paris Irmgard Schillgalis (Case 161/84) [1986] ECR 353	Distribution franchise agreement.	A rule of reason approach? The restrictions did not breach Article [101](1) because they were indispensable to protect the reputation and know-how of the franchisor and the uniform identity of the franchise outlets.
Metro-SB-Grossmärkte GmbH & Co KG v Commission (No 1) (Case 26/76) [1977] ECR 1875	Selective distribution system.	A rule of reason approach? Qualitative restrictions in a selective distribution agreement would not breach Article [101](1) provided they are applied uniformly across the selective distribution network.
Métropole Television (M6) and Others v Commission (Case T-112/99) [2001] ECR II-2459	Challenge to a Commission decision concerning a pay-TV agreement.	Court of First Instance (now called the General Court): judgments such as Pronuptia do not establish a rule of reason in EU competition law.
ACEC/Berliet (Commission Decision) OJ 1968 L201/7, [1968] CMLR D35	Agreement providing for technical cooperation and joint research on the development of a bus equipped with electric transmission.	Exemption granted: the agreement allowed each party to concentrate on the areas within its own expertise.
Prym-Werke (Commission Decision) OJ 1973 L296/24, [1973] CMLR D250	Prym agree to stop making needles and instead to buy them from Beka, which agreed to supply Prym, allowing Beka to specialize in needle production.	Exemption granted: concentration of manufacture improved production.

Exam questions

Case	Facts	Principle
CECED (Commission Decision) OJ 2000 L187/47 [2000] 5 CMLR 635	Domestic appliance manufacturers undertook to phase out washing machines with low energy efficiency. The agreement was found to be anti-competitive because it restricted consumer choice and raised production costs for some manufacturers.	Exemption granted: there were less restrictive ways to reduce energy consumption, such as informing the consumer about energy costs. However, since this would not be the most effective means, the agreement was necessary to achieve the benefits.

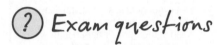

(?) Exam questions

Problem question

Blacksmiths plc ('Blacksmiths'), a UK widget manufacturer, has agreed to supply widgets to Marnier SA ('Marnier'), a French wholesaler, for resale. The agreement between them provides that Blacksmiths will supply its widgets only to Marnier in France and that Marnier, for a period of three years from the date of the agreement, will not sell goods which compete with the contract goods.

It has already been established that Blacksmiths has a 24% share of the relevant market and that Marnier has a 20% share of the relevant market.

Does this agreement fall within Article 101(1) TFEU and, if so, does it benefit from the block exemption under Regulation 330/2010?

Essay question

Because of its wide scope, Article 101(1) TFEU is an effective tool for the achievement of the fundamental aims of EU competition law. At the same time, the exemption provisions in Article 101(3) allow sufficient room for restrictions which, on balance, have beneficial effects.

Critically assess the accuracy of this statement, with reference to relevant cases.

Outline answers are available at the end of the book.

 Scan here

Scan this QR code image with your mobile device to see a full answer to these questions or log onto www.oxfordtextbooks.oc.uk/orc/concentrate/

#8

EU competition law:
Article 102 TFEU

The examination

As for **Article 101 TFEU**, the scope of questions on **Article 102 TFEU** will depend on the scope of your course. Problem-style questions on **Article 102** are likely to concern scenarios in which an allegedly dominant company has abused its position in the market, resulting in harm to another company or to consumers. You must apply all three elements of a breach: is there a dominant position, has that position been abused, and is the abuse capable of affecting trade between Member States? Essay-style questions may require discussion of all or part of this topic area. For instance, a question may ask you to critically discuss the concept of 'dominance' or of 'abuse', requiring analysis of the cases and the Court of Justice's interpretation and application of the terms.

Chapter overview

Article 102 TFEU

'Any **abuse** by one or more undertakings of a **dominant position** within the internal market or a substantial part of it shall be prohibited as incompatible with the internal market in so far as it **may affect trade between Member States**'

Must be established: Dominant positon – Abuse – Effect on trade between Member States

Dominant position

'A position of economic strength enjoyed by an undertaking that enables it to prevent effective competition ... on the relevant market by giving it the power to behave to an appreciable extent independently of its competitors, customers ... and consumers' (*United Brands*)

Relevant market: product, geographic, temporal

relevant temporal market
(*ABG Oil*)

relevant geographic market

' ... area where the objective conditions of competition...' are the same for all traders (*United Brands*) and (Art 102) 'within the internal market or a substantial part of it' (*Hilti, United Brands, Michelin, Sealink*)

relevant product market (RPM)

product substitutability

cross-elasticity of demand:

- characteristics (*United Brands*)
- use (*Hugin, Hilti*)
- price (SSNIP)

cross-elasticity of supply
(*Continental Can*)

Dominance in the relevant market

Market share (*Hiliti*); market structure (*United Brands*); duration of market position (*Hoffmann-La Roche*); financial and technological resources (*United Brands*); vertical integration (*United Brands*); intellectual property rights (*Magill, Hilti*); conduct (*United Brands*)

Chapter overview

Article 102 TFEU

'Any **abuse** by one or more undertakings of a **dominant position** within the internal market or a substantial part of it shall be prohibited as incompatible with the internal market in so far as it **may affect trade between Member States**'

Must be established: dominant positon – Abuse – Effect on trade between Member States

Abuse	Effect on trade between Member States

exploitative (targets consumers)	anti-competitive (targets competitors/potential competitors)

- **unfair prices** (*United Brands, British Leyland*)
- **discriminatory pricing** (*United Brands*)
- **discounting** (*Hoffmann-La Roche, Michelin, Hilti*)
- **tie-ins** (*Hoffmann-La Roche, Michelin, Hilti*)
- **predatory pricing** (*AKZO, Tetra Pak*)
- **refusal to supply** (*Commercial Solvents, Hugin, United Brands, Magill, Bronner, Sealink*)
- **import/export bans** (*Hilti*)

'... direct or indirect, actual or potential ...' (*STM*)

Key facts

- As noted in the previous chapter, **Articles 101 and 102 TFEU** prohibit anti-competitive business practices that threaten the internal market, harm consumers and small and medium-sized enterprises, and reduce business efficiency.

- **Article 102 TFEU** (ex **Article 82 EC**) prohibits abusive conduct by businesses ('undertakings') that have substantial market power.

- Whereas **Article 101** is concerned with anti-competitive agreements or arrangements between undertakings, **Article 102** targets behaviour by 'dominant' undertakings acting unilaterally.

- **Article 102** prohibits, as incompatible with the internal market, any abuse by undertakings in a dominant position within the internal market in so far as it may affect trade between Member States.

- Like **Article 101**, **Article 102** is enforced by the European Commission, national competition authorities, and national courts under powers conferred by **Regulation 1/2003**.

Treaty of Lisbon

The **Treaty of Lisbon** amended the **EC Treaty** and renamed it the **Treaty on the Functioning of the European Union (TFEU)**, replaced all references to 'European Community' and 'Community law' with 'EU' and 'EU law' respectively, and changed the numbering of Treaty articles. Note that pre-Lisbon case law uses the previous terminology and Treaty numbering. This chapter uses the term 'EU' and the new Treaty numbering throughout, placed in brackets where they appear in the case summaries.

Article 102 TFEU: what is prohibited?

Article 102 TFEU sets out the prohibition:

> Any abuse by one or more undertakings of a dominant position within the internal market or in a substantial part of it shall be prohibited as incompatible with the internal market in so far as it may affect trade between Member States.

'**Undertaking**' means any legal or natural person engaged in economic activity, in other words a company or an individual running a business.

To establish a breach of **Article 102**, three elements must be satisfied. The undertaking must have a dominant position; it must have abused that position; and that abuse must be capable of affecting trade between Member States.

Revision tip

Problem questions: these three elements make up your basic answer plan.

Dominant position

An undertaking that has a dominant position in a market has considerable economic strength or market power. The Court of Justice defined 'dominance' in *United Brands Co v Commission* (Case 27/76):

> A position of economic strength enjoyed by an undertaking that enables it to prevent effective competition . . . on the relevant market by giving it the power to behave to an appreciable independently of its competitors, customers . . . and consumers.

Revision tip

This definition should head up your discussion of 'dominant position'. Learn the definition, or be able to paraphrase it.

The *United Brands* definition refers to the 'relevant market'. In order to assess an undertaking's dominance, it is necessary first to identify the market in which it operates, the 'relevant market'.

Relevant market

There are three aspects to the relevant market: product, geographic, and temporal (or seasonal). In all cases, the Commission and the Court of Justice consider the product and geographical markets. In most cases, there will be no temporal (or seasonal) market and although this has occasionally been considered (for instance by the Commission in *Re ABG Oil* (1977)) a consideration of the temporal market will rarely be necessary.

Dominant position

****

An undertaking that is allegedly dominant will seek to establish the widest possible market as the relevant market. The wider the market, the smaller the undertaking's market share and the less likely it is to be dominant. If dominance cannot be established, there is no breach of **Article 102**. Conversely, the Commission will argue for a narrow market.

Relevant product market (RPM)

The relevant product market is the market for the undertaking's own product or service (**Article 102** applies to both products and services), plus the market for any substitutable products or services. The notion of **product substitution**, or product substitutability, has two elements, **demand substitutability** (or cross-elasticity of demand) and **supply substitutability** (or cross-elasticity of supply). Both must be considered to identify the relevant product market.

Demand substitutability concerns consumer behaviour. The question to be asked is whether a consumer would be willing and able to substitute one product for another or, to put it another way, to switch her/his demand from one product to another. Would a consumer consider the products to be substitutes? If the consumer would be willing and able to switch, there is said to be cross-elasticity of demand or demand substitutability. Substitutable products are in the same product market.

....

United Brands Co v Commission (Case 27/76) [1978] ECR 207

United Brands, a banana producer, challenged a Commission decision that it had abused a dominant position. Considering dominance, the Court of Justice first addressed the RPM. United Brands sought to define the RPM broadly, as fresh fruit. The Commission claimed that the RPM was bananas. Having considered product substitution and cross-elasticity of demand, the Court agreed with the Commission. It found that bananas are unique because of their appearance, taste, softness, seedlessness, and easy handling, all characteristics which make them a particularly suitable fruit for the old, the sick, and the very young. In these respects, no other fruits are acceptable as substitutes and there is little cross-elasticity of demand. The RPM was the banana market.

....

Whereas in *United Brands* the Court of Justice considered the product's unique characteristics and concluded that these characteristics placed bananas in a separate product market from other fresh fruit, in other cases, such as *Hugin* and *Hilti,* a product's specific use has ruled out substitutability, or interchangeability, with other products.

....

Hugin Kassaregister AB v Commission (Case 22/78) [1979] ECR 1869

Hugin, a Swedish company, challenged a Commission decision finding that it had infringed **Article [102]** by refusing to supply spare parts for Hugin cash registers to Liptons, a British company that repaired and serviced Hugin cash registers. The Court of Justice found that the only spare parts that could be used for the repair and maintenance of Hugin cash registers were Hugin spare parts. Since these were not substitutable with spare parts for other kinds of cash registers, this resulted in a specific demand for Hugin spare parts. Consequently, the RPM was the market for Hugin spare parts.

Similarly, in *Eurofix & Bauco v Hilti AG* (1989) the Commission, after examining the respective uses of nail guns and power drills, concluded that nail guns were in a separate product market.

Product pricing may be an important factor. In its 1997 *Notice on the Definition of the Relevant Market*, the Commission sets out a test for demand substitution based upon the consumer's response to a small but significant (between 5% and 10%) permanent increase in the price of a product. If such an increase would cause the consumer to switch from one product to another, this indicates that the two products are in the same product market. If the consumer would not switch, this indicates that the products are in separate product markets. This test for product substitution is known as the SSNIP (Small but Significant Non-transitory Increase in Price) test.

The RPM need not be the market for the supply of the product or service to the ultimate consumer. It can be an intermediate market, along the chain of production and supply, for instance the market for the supply of a raw material to a producer.

Istituto Chemioterapico Italiano SpA and Commercial Solvents Corporation v Commission (Cases 6 & 7/73) [1974] ECR 223

Commercial Solvents and its subsidiary Istituto challenged a Commission decision that they had infringed **Article [102]** by refusing to supply the raw material aminobutanol, used in the manufacture of an anti-tuberculosis drug, to Zoja, an Italian drugs manufacturer. They disputed the Commission's definition of the RPM, arguing that this was the market for the end product, the drug supplied to the ultimate consumer and not, as the Commission had found, the market for the supply of the raw material. The Court of Justice held that the RPM was Commercial Solvent's raw material, aminobutanol.

Supply substitutability, or cross-elasticity of supply, concerns the capability of other producers supplying similar products. To assess supply substitutability, it is necessary to determine whether any such producer could easily and cheaply enter the product market in question by simply adapting their production. If products are sufficiently similar to make this feasible, there is high cross-elasticity of supply and an allegedly dominant firm's market position is not so powerful as might appear at first sight.

In *Continental Can*, the Court of Justice found that the Commission had not assessed supply substitutability.

Dominant position
****

Europemballage Corp and Continental Can Co Inc v Commission (Case 6/72) [1973]
ECR 215

Continental Can made light metal containers for meat and fish and metal closures for glass jars.
The Court of Justice found that when the Commission defined the RPM, it had neglected to consider supply-side substitutability. The Commission had not determined how difficult it would have
been for potential competitors from other sectors of the market for light metal containers to enter
this market by switching their production by simple adaptation to substitutes acceptable to the
consumer.

Revision tip

RPM: discuss demand substitutability (characteristics, use, price) and supply substitutability
(feasible for producers of similar products to enter the market).

Relevant geographic market

The Court of Justice has defined the relevant geographic market as 'an area where the objective conditions of competition applying to the product in question' are the same for all traders
(***United Brands***). Here, the relevant geographic market consisted in all the Member States
except France, Italy, and the UK, since in these three Member States there were special
importing arrangements that disadvantaged United Brands' products.

The cost and feasibility of transportation can be a major factor in identifying the geographic market. Where goods can be easily and cheaply transported, the Court of Justice
may conclude, as it did in *Hilti*, that the geographic market is the whole of the EU.

A geographic market may be characterized in other ways, for instance as the area to which
customers are prepared to travel to buy the product or service, or in which they are prepared
to look for substitutes. It may be the geographical area to which use of the goods or services
is limited, as illustrated by the 'TV Listings' cases.

RTE v Commission (Case T-69/89) [1991] ECR II-485; BBC v Commission (Case T-70/89)
[1991] ECR II-535; ITP Ltd v Commission (Case T-76/89) [1991] ECR II-575; Radio Telefis
Eireann v Commission (Cases C-241 & 242/91P) [1995] ECR I-743) (Decisions upheld
on appeal to the Court of Justice in RTE & ITP v Commission (Joined Cases C-241 &
242/91P) [1995] ECR I-743))

Magill TV Guide claimed that RTE, BBC, and ITP abused a dominant position by refusing to allow
it to publish weekly listings for the companies' Irish television programmes, which were protected by copyright. The Commission's finding of an infringement, later upheld by the Court
of First Instance (now the General Court) and the Court of Justice, identified the relevant geographic market as Ireland and Northern Ireland, the area to which the use of the TV listings was
limited.

Article 102 provides that dominance must be 'within the internal market or a substantial part of it'. A geographic market need not be very extensive to satisfy this condition. An EU-wide market clearly qualifies, as in *Hilti*. So may a market comprising several Member States, as in *United Brands*. Even a single Member State is sufficient, as in *Michelin*.

. . . .

Nederlandsche Banden-Industrie Michelin NV v Commission (Case 322/81)
[1983] ECR 3461)

The Dutch company Michelin NV challenged a Commission decision finding that it had abused a dominant position in the market for replacement tyres for heavy vehicles. The Court of Justice upheld the Commission decision, confirming the latter's view that the Dutch market for these products was an isolated market, since Dutch dealers only obtained supplies within the Netherlands. This was the geographic market and a substantial part of the internal market.

. . . .

In some cases, particularly in the air and sea transport sector, the geographic market has been drawn very narrowly.

. . . .

Sealink/B and I – Holyhead: Interim Measures (Commission Decision)
[1992] 5 CMLR 255

The port of Holyhead was held to be the relevant geographic market and a substantial part of the internal market.

. . . .

Relevant temporal (or seasonal) market

Whilst the product and geographical markets will always feature in **Article 102**, a temporal market will rarely be identified. In *United Brands*, it was suggested that there were two seasonal markets. During the summer months, when supplies of fresh fruit were plentiful, the company's market power was reduced, whereas during the winter season, when substitutes were not available, its market power was greater. Despite this, both the Commission and the Court of Justice identified a single temporal market. By contrast, in *Re ABG Oil* (1977) the Commission defined the temporal market for oil by reference to the oil crisis precipitated by the action of the OPEC states in the early 1970s.

Dominance in the relevant market

Once the relevant market has been identified, it is next necessary to determine whether the undertaking is dominant in that market.

Revision tip

Remember to discuss dominance in the market, before moving on to consider 'abuse'.

Dominant position

****

Indicators of dominance

Several factors may combine to indicate dominance, though market share is the primary indicator. Other relevant factors include market structure, the length of time that the undertaking has held its market share, its financial and technological resources, vertical integration, intellectual property rights, and behaviour.

Market share

In practice, total monopoly situations (comprising a 100% market share) are rare. The Court of Justice has stated that very large market shares held for some time are, save in exceptional circumstances, evidence of a dominant position. In *Microsoft Corporation v Commission* (Case T-201/04), Microsoft were found to have a market share of over 90% of one of the identified markets. This was clear evidence of dominance.

However, the importance of market share varies from market to market, according to the structure of the market (*Hoffmann-La Roche v Commission* (Case 85/76)).

Market structure

Market structure is an important factor. United Brands was held to be dominant with a market share of between 40% and 45%. That share was several times greater than that of its nearest rival. Other competitors were even further behind. The Commission has indicated that, in a fragmented market, a market share as low as 20% might be sufficient to constitute dominance.

Financial and technological resources

Extensive financial and technological resources may allow a company to maintain – or 'entrench' – its market position, for instance through persistent price-cutting, perhaps selling below cost. With financial resources, an undertaking can retain market power by developing technological know-how, investing in product development, and providing technical services to customers. United Brands had used its wealth to reduce cross-elasticity of demand by widespread advertising. It had invested in research to improve productivity and perfect new ripening methods.

Vertical integration

An undertaking that is vertically integrated exerts control in the production and supply chain. This may include 'upstream' control, for instance in the raw materials market and/or 'downstream' control, for instance the control of distribution. The greater the vertical integration, the more likely there is to be dominance. The Court of Justice described United Brands' operations as 'vertically integrated to a high degree'. The company owned plantations in Central and South America, controlled loading operations, had its own transportation systems, and controlled banana ripeners, distributors, and wholesalers through an extensive network of agents. Similarly, in *Hoffmann-La Roche* the Court of Justice recognized that the company's highly efficient sales network was a factor indicating a dominant position.

Intellectual property rights

The possession of intellectual property rights, such as copyright and patents, may indicate market power. These rights can be enforced under national law to prevent competitors from reproducing information or making products which the rights protect. BBC, RTE, and ITP held copyright in the TV listings for their television programmes. Hilti held copyright and patents for its products. In both cases, the Court of First Instance (now the General Court) took these factors into account when assessing the respective companies' dominance.

Conduct

United Brands confirmed the Commission's view that an undertaking's conduct can indicate dominance. For instance, the fact that a company has charged unfair prices can be evidence of its dominance in the market. This view has been criticized, since the scheme of **Article 102** envisages that dominance be established before the existence of an abuse is considered. Nevertheless, the Commission continues to take conduct into account when assessing dominance.

Revision tip

Problem questions – having identified the relevant market, next consider dominance. Start with market share, then consider any other indicators.

✔ Looking for extra marks?

Factors indicating dominance are '**barriers to entry**' if they prevent potential competitors from entering the market. Such factors may also weaken the position of existing competitors or drive them out of the market. Conversely, factors indicating dominance can have positive effects. Consumers may benefit from a company's efficient distribution systems or from higher quality products, made possible through research and development. For these reasons, the Court of Justice's approach to assessing dominance can be controversial. Nonetheless, it should be noted that dominance in itself does not amount to an infringement of **Article 102**. There must also be an abuse which may affect trade between Member States.

Revision tip

Discussion of 'dominance' – consider the complexities of market definition and the controversy surrounding indicators of dominance.

Abuse

Dominance in itself is unobjectionable. An infringement occurs only where there is an abuse of a dominant position that may affect trade between Member States. **Article 102** provides that abuse . . . may, in particular, consist in:

(a) directly or indirectly imposing unfair purchase or selling prices or other unfair trading conditions;

(b) limiting production, markets or technical development to the prejudice of consumers;

(c) applying dissimilar conditions to equivalent transactions with other trading parties, thereby placing them at a competitive disadvantage;

(d) making the conclusion of contracts subject to acceptance by the other parties of supplementary obligations which, by their nature or according to commercial usage, have no connection with the subject of such contracts.

This list is not exhaustive, but gives examples of abusive behaviour. Often, abuses are classified into two categories, exploitative and anti-competitive. **Exploitative abuses** exploit consumers. **Anti-competitive abuses** prevent or weaken competition or potential competition from other undertakings. Many kinds of abusive conduct can be described as both exploitative and anti-competitive.

Unfair prices

Imposing unfair, or excessively high, prices is perhaps the most obvious exploitative abuse. However, the definition of an 'unfair' or 'excessive' price is not straightforward.

In *United Brands*, the Court of Justice defined an excessive price as one which 'has no reasonable relation to the economic value of the product'. Unfortunately, the assessment of economic value may be problematic. However careful the economic analysis, decisions on unfair or excessive pricing are likely to be controversial. Where prices rise to a higher level than the market will bear, the incentive for other firms to enter the market becomes very strong. These market forces can provide protection for the consumer, but such forces may not operate where there are significant barriers to entry, as illustrated by *British Leyland*.

··

British Leyland plc v Commission (Case 226/84) [1986] ECR 3263

The Court of Justice upheld a Commission decision finding that British Leyland had charged excessive prices for issuing type-approval certificates for left-hand drive British Leyland cars imported from the continent of Europe. The company had been able to impose prices that were disproportionate to the service provided, since its exclusive right to issue such certificates in the UK constituted a complete barrier to entry to this market, the market for the issue of the certificates.

··

In **British Leyland** the unfair pricing policy had an anti-competitive intent, as its purpose was to reduce competition in sales of British Leyland cars on the home market by discouraging imports into the UK.

Discriminatory pricing

In its simplest form, discriminatory pricing consists in charging different customers different prices for the same product without justification. This amounts to the application of 'dissimilar conditions to equivalent transactions with other trading parties, thereby placing them at a competitive disadvantage' (**Article 102(c)**).

United Brands Co v Commission (Case 27/76) [1978] ECR 207

United Brands charged different prices according to the Member State in which customers were established. There was no justification for this, since 'Chiquita' bananas were of almost consistent quality, unloading costs at the European ports of entry were similar, and transport costs from the ports to the ripening facilities were generally borne by the customer. The company's pricing policy was based purely on what the market would bear and was an abuse.

If differential pricing can be **objectively justified**, for instance on the basis of different transport costs, different labour costs, or different market conditions, there is no abuse.

Discounting

Abusive discounting is a more sophisticated kind of price discrimination. It exploits consumers and may also target competitors by undercutting their prices. This abuse takes various forms, such as discounts offered to customers who buy minimum quantities ('quantity' discounts), who agree to purchase all or most of their requirements from the supplier ('loyalty' or 'fidelity' discounts), or who reach specific sales targets ('target' discounts). Quantity discounts are unobjectionable provided they apply without discrimination to all purchasers and are justified, for instance if linked directly to the volume of goods supplied and the savings achieved by bulk production. Other kinds of discount are likely to be caught by **Article 102**.

Hoffmann-La Roche & Co AG v Commission (Case 85/76) [1979] ECR 461

Fidelity discounts offered by Roche obliged or induced customers to buy all or most of their vitamin requirements exclusively or in preference from the company. Most contracts also contained the so-called 'English clause', which allowed customers, if they discovered cheaper prices elsewhere, to ask Roche to reduce its prices. If Roche did not do so, customers could buy from other suppliers. In so far as the agreements enabled purchasers to buy at the lowest price, they were not exploitative. However, customers' commercial freedom was limited because the fidelity discounts induced them to buy from Roche. The arrangements also gave Roche access to information about its rivals' pricing policies, allowing it to react quickly, reducing its prices, and undermining competition. The Court of Justice found that the company's practices were abusive.

Michelin and *Hilti* provide further examples. The target discounting practised by Michelin was abusive because it tied in dealers to purchasing tyres from Michelin. *Hilti* had abused its dominant position by offering favourable terms to its competitors' major customers and withholding quantity discounts from customers who also bought from competing manufacturers.

Tie-ins

Tie-ins require or induce the purchaser of goods or services to buy other goods or services from the same supplier. Such arrangements make 'the conclusion of contracts subject to acceptance by the other parties of supplementary obligations which, by their nature or according to commercial usage, have no connection with the subject of such contracts' (**Article 102(d)**). Inducements can comprise price discounting or rebates, for instance those offered by Hoffmann-La Roche, Michelin, and Hilti, considered earlier. Hilti's tie-ins were extensive. As well as withholding quantity discounts from customers who bought nails from competitors, the company required purchasers of its patented nail cartridges also to buy nails and refused to honour guarantees on its tools where non-Hilti nails were used. Microsoft abused its dominant position in the personal computer market by bundling together its Windows operating system and Windows Media Player (*Microsoft Corporation v Commission* (Case T-201/04)). This case is particularly interesting as although customers did not have to use Windows Media Player (other streaming devices could be used) customers were not given the opportunity to obtain Windows Operating System without Windows Media Player. This amounted to an abuse.

Predatory pricing

Predatory pricing consists in price reduction below the cost of production. A dominant undertaking with sufficient resources to withstand short-term losses can use this strategy to target its smaller, less prosperous rivals. This is an anti-competitive abuse, designed to drive existing competitors out of the market or prevent market entry by potential competitors. Ultimately, predatory pricing also harms consumers. Whilst price reductions provide temporary consumer benefit, consumers suffer in the longer term, as the dominant company, having excluded its competitors, regains control of the market and becomes free to raise prices without constraint.

A certain level of price competition is clearly beneficial. It encourages efficiency and favours consumers. At what point, then, does 'normal' price competition become predatory pricing? This question was addressed in *AKZO*.

AKZO Chemie v Commission (Case C-62/86) [1991] ECR I-3359

AKZO produced organic peroxides for use in the plastics industry and for flour bleaching. When Engineering and Chemical Supplies (ECS), which had supplied organic peroxides for flour, decided to begin supplying to the plastics sector, AKZO reduced its prices in the flour sector. AKZO challenged a Commission decision finding predatory pricing. The Court of Justice held that prices are predatory if they are intended to eliminate competition. There is a deemed intention if prices fall below average variable costs (costs which vary depending on the quantities produced). An undertaking has no interest in applying such prices, save to eliminate competition and then subsequently increase prices, to the detriment of consumers. Where prices fall below average total costs (variable costs plus fixed costs), but above average variable costs, prices are abusive 'if . . . determined as part of a plan for eliminating a competitor'.

A finding of abuse is not confined to successful predation. Predatory pricing is to be penalized wherever there is a risk that competition will be eliminated, even without proof that a dominant undertaking has a realistic chance of recouping its losses (*Tetra Pak International SA v Commission* (Case C-333/94P)).

Refusal to supply

As a general principle of contract law, parties are free both to enter into agreements and to refuse to deal. An undertaking might justifiably refuse supplies, for instance, because a customer has not paid for goods previously supplied, or because of stock shortages or problems with production. If not objectively justified, a dominant undertaking's refusal to supply goods or services may be abusive. It will be an abuse if it is intended to eliminate competition.

Istituto Chemioterapico Italiano SpA and Commercial Solvents Corporation v Commission (Cases 6 & 7/73) [1974] ECR 223

Commercial Solvents refused to supply Zoja, an Italian drug manufacturer, with the raw material used for the manufacture of an anti-tuberculosis drug. The anti-competitive nature of Commercial Solvents' behaviour was apparent, since at the same time as it was refusing further supplies to Zoja, its own subsidiary, Istituto, was emerging as a competitor in the same market as Zoja, the market for the manufacture and supply of the drug.

United Brands' refusal to supply was retaliatory rather than anti-competitive.

United Brands Co v Commission (Case 27/76) [1978] ECR 207

United Brands discontinued supplies of green bananas to Olesen, a Danish ripener and distributor, because Olesen had taken part in an advertising campaign for one of United Brands' competitors. In condemning this as an abuse, the Court of Justice described the conduct as 'a serious

interference with the independence of small and medium-sized firms in their commercial relations with the undertaking in a dominant position'.

. . . .

Commercial Solvents and *United Brands* concerned refusals to supply existing customers. The *'TV Listings'* cases demonstrate that refusal to supply products or services to new
customers may also constitute an abuse. Here, the television companies' refusal to supply
weekly TV listings to Magill prevented the introduction of a new product, a general television guide, for which there was a potential consumer demand. That refusal was likely to have
the effect of excluding all competition in the market for television guides. The Court of First
Instance (now the General Court) recognized a similar risk in *Microsoft*.

. . . .

Microsoft Corporation v Commission (Case T-201/04) [2007] ECR II-1491

Microsoft's refusal to provide its competitors with 'interoperability information' that would have
enabled them to develop competing products was condemned as an abuse, since there was a real
risk that Microsoft would succeed in eliminating all effective competition on the relevant market.

. . . .

The conclusion was different in *Bronner*.

. . . .

Oscar Bronner GmbH & Co KG v Mediaprint Zeitungs- und Zeitschriftenverlag
GmbH & Co KG and others (Case C-7/97) [1998] ECR 1-779

A media company's refusal to allow a rival daily newspaper (in return for payment) to have access
to its nationwide home-delivery scheme did not constitute an abuse under **Article [102]**. An
abuse would be established only if the refusal could not be objectively justified and was likely to
drive the rival newspaper from the daily newspaper market because the service was indispensable to its carrying out its business. The Court of Justice found that there were no technical, legal,
or economic obstacles preventing the company from setting up its own nationwide home-delivery
service.

. . . .

Where a refusal to supply entails refusal of access to a facility, the conduct is assessed
under what is known as the 'essential facilities' doctrine. A dominant undertaking which
owns or controls a facility that is essential to conducting a business abuses its position if it
refuses access to another undertaking which cannot feasibly set up a facility of its own to run
its business. Sealink, for instance, which controlled the port of Holyhead, restricted B&I's
access to sailing facilities there and was found to have infringed **Article [102]** (*Sealink/B
and I – Holyhead: Interim Measures* (1992)).

Import and export bans

In order to maintain control of the market a dominant undertaking may seek to impose
importing/exporting restrictions on the companies it supplies. *Hilti* provides a good example

of this abuse. The company had exerted pressure upon its distributors in the Netherlands not to supply Hilti's cartridge strips in the UK. It did this because it wished to reserve the UK market to itself. Such practices not only restrict competition but are also incompatible with the internal market because they prevent the free flow of goods between Member States.

Revision tip

In discussing 'abuse' (essay questions) or applying 'abuse' to a fact scenario (problem questions), remember to discuss 'objective justification'.

Effect on trade between Member States

There is no infringement of **Article 102** unless a dominant undertaking's abuse 'may affect trade between Member States'. This term has the same meaning as under **Article 101**, namely a 'direct or indirect, actual or potential . . .' effect (*Société Technique Minière v Maschinenbau Ulm GmbH* (Case 56/65)). Since an indirect or potential effect is sufficient, this element of **Article 102** is generally easily established. Evidence that abusive behaviour might affect trade between Member States will be enough, as will an effect on the competitive structure of the internal market (*Commercial Solvents*).

Hugin is one of the few cases in which an effect on interstate trade was not established. The Court of Justice endorsed the Commission's view that Hugin, a Swedish company, was dominant in the market for its own spare parts. However, the company's refusal to supply its spare parts to Liptons in London had no effect on interstate trade. Liptons operated within a very limited area in and around London and there was no indication that it intended to extend its activities further. Moreover, the 'normal' pattern of movement of the spare parts was not between Member States but between Liptons in the UK and Hugin in Sweden, which at that time was not an EU Member State.

✅ *Looking for extra marks?*

In 2005 the Commission initiated a consultation on the policy underlying **Article 102** and in February 2009 it adopted *Guidance on its enforcement priorities in applying Article 82 EC to abusive exclusionary conduct by dominant undertakings*. This sets out a general framework for analysing exclusionary conduct by a dominant company – conduct that has the effect of excluding actual or potential competitors from the market, to the detriment of consumers. The focus is the protection of competition for the benefit of consumers, rather than for the benefit of competitors operating in the market. The guidance describes the Commission's effects-based approach, entailing an assessment of the effects of behaviour on the market, rather than a form-based approach which identifies particular forms of conduct as abusive.

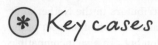 Key cases

Case	Facts	Principle
United Brands Co v Commission (Case 27/76) [1978] ECR 207	Challenge to the Commission's finding of a breach of Article [102].	Dominance: 'A position of economic strength enjoyed by an undertaking that enables it to prevent effective competition . . . on the relevant market by giving it the power to behave to an appreciable independently of its competitors, customers . . . and consumers'.
United Brands	Identification of the RPM: bananas or fresh fruit?	Demand substitutability assessed on the basis of product characteristics.
Hugin Kassaregister AB v Commission (Case 22/78) [1979] ECR 1869	Hugin had refused to supply spare parts for its cash registers.	Demand substitutability assessed on the basis of product use.
ICI SpA and Commercial Solvents Corporation v Commission (Cases 6 & 7/73) [1974] ECR 223	CSC had refused to supply a raw material used for producing an anti-tuberculosis drug.	RPM can be an intermediate market.
Europemballage Corp and Continental Can Co Inc v Commission (Case 6/72) [1973] ECR 215	Challenge to a Commission decision finding an infringement.	Decision annulled: the Commission had not considered supply-side substitutability.
RTE & ITP v Commission (Joined Cases C-241 & 242/91P) [1995] ECR I-743	RTE, BBC, and ITP had refused to allow Magill to publish weekly listings for their television programmes.	The relevant geographic market was the area to which the use of the product was limited.
Nederlandsche Banden-Industrie Michelin NV v Commission (Case 322/81) [1983] ECR 3461	Michelin challenged the Commission's finding of an abuse in the market for replacement tyres for heavy vehicles.	One Member State was the geographic market and a substantial part of the internal market.
Sealink/B and I – Holyhead: Interim Measures (Commission Decision) [1992] 5 CMLR 255	The Commission found that Sealink had abused a dominant position in its operation of the port of Holyhead.	The geographic market, the seaport of Holyhead, constituted a substantial part of the internal market.

Case	Facts	Principle
Hoffmann-La Roche v Commission (Case 85/76) [1979] ECR 461	Roche induced its customers, through fidelity discounts, to buy their vitamins from Roche.	A very large market share creates a position of strength which may in itself amount to a dominant position.
Hilti v Commission (Case T-30/89) [1991] ECR II-1439	Hilti had abused a dominant position in relation to the supply of nail guns and nails.	A share of between 70% and 80% in the relevant market was 'in itself a clear indication of a dominant position'.
United Brands	United Brands had a market share between 40% and 45%.	Market structure may indicate dominance.
United Brands	United Brands had used its wealth for advertising and for research and development.	Financial and technological resources indicate dominance.
United Brands	United Brands had upstream and downstream control of the market.	Vertical integration indicates dominance.
RTE & ITP v Commission (Joined Cases C-241 & 242/91P) [1995] ECR I-743	BBC, RTE, and ITP held copyright in their TV listings.	Intellectual property rights are taken into account in assessing dominance.
United Brands	United Brands was accused of charging excessive prices.	Excessive price: one which 'has no reasonable relation to the economic value of the product supplied'.
British Leyland plc v Commission (Case 226/84) [1986] ECR 3263	BL had the exclusive right to issue type-approval certificates for imported left-hand drive BL cars.	The prices charged were disproportionate to the service provided and therefore excessive.
United Brands	United Brands charged different prices according to the customer's state of establishment.	Pricing was based purely on what the market would bear, and therefore an abuse.
Hoffmann-La Roche v Commission (Case 85/76) [1979] ECR 461	Roche offered fidelity discounts. Its 'English clause' allowed customers who discovered cheaper prices elsewhere to ask for a price reduction.	Customers' commercial freedom was limited. The 'English clauses' gave Roche access to information about rivals' prices, allowing it to react quickly to reduce prices and undermine competition.

Exam questions

✳✳✳✳✳✳✳✳✳✳

Case	Facts	Principle
Hilti v Commission (Case T-30/89) [1991] ECR II-1439	Hilti withheld discounts from customers who bought from competitors; required purchasers of nail cartridges to buy nails; and refused to honour guarantees if non-Hilti nails were used.	Tying-in practices: an abuse.
AKZO Chemie v Commission (Case C-62/86) [1991] ECR I-3359	AKZO reduced its prices below cost to target a market entrant.	Pricing below cost is predatory and an abuse if intended to eliminate competition.
Commercial Solvents	Commercial Solvents refused to supply an Italian drugs manufacturer with a raw material.	Refusal to supply: an abuse.
United Brands	United Brands refused to supply Olesen because it had taken part in an advertising campaign for a competitor of United Brands.	Refusal to supply: an abuse.
Hilti	Hilti exerted pressure on its Dutch distributors not to supply Hilti's cartridge strips in the UK.	Import/export restrictions: an abuse.
Société Technique Minière v Maschinenbau Ulm GmbH (Case 56/65) [1966] ECR 235	Application of Article [101] to import restrictions.	Effect on trade between Member States: a 'direct or indirect, actual or potential . . .' effect is sufficient.

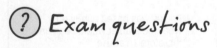 **Exam questions**

Problem question

Smartco plc ('Smartco') is a UK manufacturer of roofing tiles, which it supplies to building contractors in the UK, France, and Belgium. Because of the high cost of transportation of roofing tiles, Smartco has not extended its sales operations beyond these three Member States.

Smartco supplies more than 80% of the roofing tiles sold in the UK, France, and Belgium, but the company has only a 6% share of the EU market for roofing tiles ('the roofing tiles market'). Smartco's share of the wider market for general roofing materials in the UK, France, and Belgium, which comprises the market for roofing tiles and for sheet roofing materials used on flat roofs ('the roofing materials market'), stands at around 10%.

Using its extensive financial resources generated from healthy profits over the past five years, Smartco has developed a very efficient distribution system. The company's strong market position has also enabled it to offer discounts to some of its UK customers, negotiated separately with individual building contractors and based on the size of the orders placed.

Recently, one of Smartco's competitors, Simpleco plc ('Simpleco'), discovered that Smartco is offering huge discounts to Simpleco's existing customers if they agree to switch their custom to Smartco over the next 12 months.

Simpleco now questions the compatibility of all Smartco's discounting arrangements with Article 102 TFEU.

Advise Simpleco.

Essay question

In targeting both exploitative and anti-competitive abuses, Article 102 TFEU makes a significant contribution to the achievement of the aims of European Union competition law.

In the light of this statement and with reference to the interpretation of 'abuse' by the Court of Justice, critically discuss the extent to which Article 102 TFEU has succeeded in achieving the aims of European Union competition law.

Outline answers are available at the end of the book.

Scan here

Scan this QR code image with your mobile device to see a full answer to these questions or log onto www.oxfordtextbooks.oc.uk/orc/concentrate/

Outline answers

Full answers are available online at www.oxfordtextbooks.co.uk/orc/concentrate/

Chapter 1

Essay answer

- Meaning of 'undemocratic'.
- Consider the EU law-making institutions, in turn.
- *European Commission.* Describe its composition and the appointment of Commissioners. Consider the Commission's input into law-making. Conclusion: a lack of democracy – Commission is not democratically appointed but has considerable power.
- *Council.* Describe its composition and the appointment of members. Consider whether appointment is democratic. Discuss law-making procedures, the Council's extensive input, and its power of approval. Discuss voting methods – unanimity, simple majority, and qualified majority voting – and evaluate how far voting is democratic.
- *European Parliament.* Discuss its composition and the appointment of MEPs. Evaluate its input into law-making – consultation, co-decision, and consent. Trace the development of Parliament's power, from mere consultation to co-decision. Conclusion: the only directly elected EU institution but, arguably, the institution holding the least power.
- *Conclusion.* An evaluation of the composition and powers of the institutions supports the view that the EU is lacking in democracy, though this deficit has been partially addressed by the extension of co-decision, particularly by the Treaty of Lisbon, which further progressed the 'democratization' of the EU.

Chapter 2

Problem answer

Identify Fred's complaint. Consider compliance with the Act.

(a) Direct effect

- Explain meaning, conditions (*Van Gend, Van Duyn, Ratti*).
- Apply conditions: clear, precise, and unconditional, implementation deadline must have passed. Conditions appear to be satisfied.
- Directives only have vertical direct effect (*Marshall*). Claim is against the Home Office, an organ of the state.
- Conclusion: Fred can invoke the Directive against his employer.

(b) Direct effect

- Conditions regarding clarity, precision, unconditionality, and implementation deadline are satisfied (see answer to (a)).
- Directives are only directly effective vertically, against the state, a 'public authority' (*Marshall*), or 'public body' (*Foster*).
- Apply *Foster* to Fyso: a body providing a public service; under state control, with special powers. As a private company, Fyso is very unlikely to satisfy *Foster*.
- Fred cannot rely directly on the Directive.

Indirect effect

- Explain meaning: interpretation of national law in accordance with relevant [EU] law (*Von Colson*), including, as here, pre-dating national law (*Marleasing*).
- The duty of consistent interpretation applies only so far as possible (*Marleasing*). Harmonious interpretation is not always possible (*Wagner Miret*). No duty to adopt a *contra legem* interpretation (*Pupino*).
- Interpretation of the Act's overtime pay provisions in accordance with the Directive would be *contra legem*, but a national court would be willing to interpret 'health and safety training' to include 'sessions covering all new handling techniques relating to toxic substances'.

Conclusion

Fred can rely on the indirect effect of the Directive in relation to health and safety but not overtime pay.

Outline answers

✱✱✱✱✱✱✱✱✱✱

Essay answer

Supremacy

- Sovereignty: the Community is 'a new legal order . . . states have limited their sovereign rights . . .' (*Van Gend*). '. . . the EEC Treaty has created its own legal system . . .' (*Costa v ENEL*).

- Corollary of sovereignty is supremacy: EU law takes precedence over national law (*Costa v ENEL, Internationale Handelsgesellschaft, Simmenthal, Factortame II*).

Direct effect

Principle created by Court of Justice. Explain meaning.

Treaty articles

- Directly effective, subject to conditions (sufficiently clear and precise and unconditional), vertically and horizontally (*Van Gend, Defrenne*).

- Since *Van Gend, Defrenne*: numerous Treaty articles held to be vertically and horizontally directly effective.

- Significance: individuals can invoke Treaty rights in the national court.

Regulations

- Capable of vertical and horizontal direct effect (*Politi, Leonesio*).

Directives

- Originally not thought to be capable of direct effect: explain.

- *Van Duyn*: direct effect of directives, provided clear, precise, and unconditional and implementation deadline passed (*Ratti*) (explain rationale).

- Directives only directly effective vertically (*Marshall, Faccini Dori*). Rationale for limitation – discuss and evaluate.

- Effect of limitation mitigated: broad interpretation of 'public body', indirect effect, state liability.

- *Foster* test for 'public body' and application (*Becker, Fratelli Costanzo, Johnston*).

- Summary: significance of direct effect and supremacy.

Indirect effect

- Explain meaning (*Von Colson*). Can overcome the shortcomings of direct effect.

- Note limitations (*Marleasing, Wagner Miret, Pupino*).

State liability

- *Francovich*: damages for loss arising from a state's failure to implement a directive. Conditions.

- *Factortame III*: damages for other kinds of breach. Conditions and the factors indicating a 'sufficiently serious breach'.

- Application (*BT, Hedley Lomas, Köbler*).

- Significance: may be available in the absence of direct and indirect effect.

Conclusion

Direct effect, indirect effect, and state liability are crucially important for the protection of individuals' EU law rights in national courts.

Chapter 3

[References are to the TFEU unless otherwise indicated]

Problem answer

Court of Justice: jurisdiction

- Rulings on interpretation of EU law.

- Interpretation of 'permanent form' required.

- Dispute is genuine: Court of Justice unlikely to reject reference.

High Court

- Not a final court. No obligation to refer under Article 267(3) but has discretion if it considers a decision is necessary to enable it to give judgment (Article 267(2)).

- High Court considers itself bound by the House of Lords' earlier interpretation and precluded from referring. This is misguided. National rules of precedent do not apply (*Rheinmühlen*).

- High Court should determine relevance (*Dzodzi*). The meaning of 'permanent form' is relevant and conclusive.

• High Court should determine timing, first establishing the facts and legal issues (*Irish Creamery*).

• High Court has not considered whether 'permanent form' is clear, making a reference unnecessary. Discuss *CILFIT* on '*acte clair*'.

• Also discuss the English guidance (*Samex, Ex parte Else*).

Court of Appeal

• Court of Appeal may refer, on the same basis as the High Court. Although the meaning of 'permanent form' is now disputed and so not *acte clair*, this does not create an obligation to refer.

• Separate issue: when the Court of Appeal refuses leave to appeal, is it a 'court against whose decisions there is no judicial remedy under national law'?

• Court of Appeal's decisions: subject to appeal with leave of the Court of Appeal or the Supreme Court.

• A judicial remedy is not precluded because an appeal is subject to leave from a supreme court (*Lyckeskog*). Thus, the Court of Appeal is not a final court and has no obligation to refer.

Supreme Court

• However, if a question of EU law arises, a supreme court must refer either when considering leave to appeal, or later (*Lyckeskog*), subject to *CILFIT*.

Essay answer

Article 267

• Court of Justice's jurisdiction: interpretation of EU law.

• National courts' duty: to apply the Court's ruling.

• Scheme of Article 267: to ensure uniform interpretation of EU law.

• Any court may refer questions of interpretation (discretion to refer): Article 267(2).

• Courts against whose decision there is no judicial remedy under national law must refer (obligation to refer): Article 267(3).

• Accordingly, where necessary, references must be made at some stage.

Exercising discretion: guidelines

• If a question is irrelevant, a reference is unnecessary (*Dzodzi*).

• *Acte clair*: a reference is unnecessary if EU law is clear (*CILFIT, Samex, Ex parte Else*).

• A previous ruling by the Court of Justice does not preclude a reference, but may make it unnecessary (*Da Costa*).

• A previous ruling by a higher national court does not preclude a reference from a lower court (*Rheinmühlen*).

These guidelines do not prevent lower national courts from interpreting EU law themselves.

Obligation

Despite the Article 267 obligation, *CILFIT* provides exceptions, allowing final courts to avoid references where:

• The question is irrelevant, as there is no risk to consistent interpretation.

• The Court of Justice has already ruled on interpretation: consistency is not compromised, since the national court must apply that ruling (reiterating *Da Costa*), though a reference is not precluded. A developing system of precedent (*Da Costa, CILFIT*): changing relationship between the Court of Justice and national courts, from cooperation to a hierarchical system.

• The meaning is *acte clair*. *CILFIT* criteria for *acte clair* difficult to apply and, in practice, interpreted loosely by national courts, carrying the risk of liability in damages (*Köbler*).

Rejection of references

No cooperation when the Court of Justice refuses references (*Foglia, Meilicke, Telemarsicabruzzo*).

Conclusion

Generally, Article 267 ensures consistency of interpretation of EU law, though this outcome is not always guaranteed.

Chapter 4

[References are to the TFEU unless otherwise indicated]

Outline answers

****

Problem answer

Jurisdiction and *locus standi*

• The Court of Justice (and General Court): jurisdiction to review legally binding EU acts, such as the Commission decision of 1 February 2010.

• As a legal person and 'non-privileged' applicant, to establish *locus standi* to challenge the decision, Argenco must show direct and individual concern.

Direct concern

• No Treaty definition, but case law guidance: applicant must show unbroken chain of causation between the measure and the loss. No link if the measure leaves discretion to a Member State (eg *Municipality of Differdange*).

• The decision allows France discretion on the restriction of licences. The French authorities' exercise of discretion, not the decision, affected Argenco. No direct concern; the action is inadmissible.

• If the French authorities had sought permission to restrict licences for February 2010, the Court may conclude that France had already exercised its discretion (*Paraiki-Patraiki*). Thus, Argenco might persuade the Court that it is directly concerned by the decision.

Individual concern

• *Plaumann* test: applicant affected 'by reason of certain attributes which are peculiar to them . . . or . . . circumstances in which they are differentiated from all other persons'.

• Closed class: a class of applicants that was fixed and ascertainable at the date the measure was adopted (*Paraiki-Patraiki*). Argenco: as a member of the class of importers which made licence applications during January 2010, is individually concerned.

Time limit

• Two months.

Conclusion

Subject to the French authorities seeking prior permission to restrict licences, Argenco would probably succeed in establishing *locus standi*.

Essay answer

Elements of liability

• Article 340: '. . . the Union shall, in accordance with the principles common to the laws of the Member States, make good any damage caused by its institutions . . .'

• *Lütticke*: applicant must show wrongful or illegal act, damage, and causation.

Wrongful act

• Administrative acts (*Adams*).

• 'General legislative measures . . .': a 'sufficiently flagrant violation of a superior rule of law for the protection of the individual' required (*Schöppenstedt*).

• Court of Justice: broad interpretation of general legislative measures. Difficult to establish liability.

• Scope of 'superior rules of law'.

• 'Sufficiently flagrant violation': institution must have 'manifestly and gravely disregarded the limits on its powers' (*Schöppenstedt*). Difficult to establish and scope uncertain: may be the effect of the measure (*HNL*) or action 'verging on the arbitrary' (*Amylum*). Court of Justice: the risk of successful actions must not hinder legislative action. Claims rarely succeed.

• Different approach: application of *Factortame III* principles (*Bergaderm*).

Damage

• Must be quantifiable and exceed the loss arising from normal economic risks inherent in the business. Steps must be taken to mitigate the loss. Requirements may be interpreted very restrictively (*HNL*).

Causation

• Damage must be a sufficiently direct consequence of the institution's breach.

• Can be difficult to establish (eg *Dumortier*).

Concurrent liability

• Applicant must first exhaust all possible national causes of action: a further hurdle.

Time limit

• Generous: five years.

Conclusion

Whilst *Bergaderm* introduced a new and more generous approach to damages claims under Article 340 than had been previously adopted by the Court of Justice under *Schöppenstedt*, it is still the case that applicants face serious challenges in establishing liability in respect of acts of the EU institutions.

Chapter 5

[References are to the TFEU unless otherwise indicated]

Problem answer

Brief introduction

• Free movement of goods.

Identify the restrictions

• Import licence requirement, limit on imports, sales restrictions, requirement for external filtration system.

Import licence requirement

• Consider: MEQR and breach of Article 34?

• Apply *Dassonville*: 'all trading rules . . .' Requirement is a Portuguese trading rule hindering imports.

• Apply Directive 70/50, explain and apply 'distinctly' applicable measure.

• Requirement is an MEQR and breach of Article 34.

Limit on imports

• Consider: quantitative restriction and breach of Article 34?

• Definition of quantitative restrictions (*Geddo*): apply.

• Limit is a partial restraint of imports (import quota).

• Measure infringes Article 34.

Sales restrictions

• *Keck*: 'selling arrangements' outside Article 34 if they affect in the same manner the marketing of domestic and imported products.

• Restrictions on the kinds of retail outlets selling certain goods are 'selling arrangements' (*Commission v Greece*).

• No indication of greater impact on imported WGMs than on domestic WGMs.

• Provision likely to fall within *Keck*: no breach.

Requirement for external filtration system

• MEQR?

• Apply *Dassonville* and Directive 70/50: a hindrance to interstate trade; disparity between Portuguese rule and rules applying in other Member States (*Cassis, Walter Rau*).

• Requirement is an MEQR, breach of Article 34.

• Justification?

• Indistinctly applicable measure: *Cassis* and Article 36 apply.

• Principle of mutual recognition: apply (eg *Cassis, Prantl, Walter Rau*).

• Health justification? Requires evidence (*San Jose Scale*), proportionality and no arbitrary discrimination, disguised restriction (*Turkeys*). Facts suggest protectionism.

Conclusion

Requirements for licence and external 'vacuum filtration' units likely to breach Article 34. Import quota: a quantitative restriction, breach of Article 34. Limitation on sales appears to fall within *Keck*, compatible with EU law.

Essay answer

Introduction

• Internal market, four freedoms, Article 26.

Legislation, case law

• Negative integration. Prohibitions: Articles 30, 34/35, 110 (customs duties/CEEs, quantitative restrictions/MEQRs, discriminatory taxation). Court of Justice's broad interpretation, supporting economic integration.

• Positive integration: harmonization; mutual recognition.

Outline answers
✶✶✶✶✶✶✶✶✶✶

Article 30 prohibition

- Customs duties (*Diamonds* definition): easily identified.
- Wide scope includes CEEs (*Diamonds* definition).
- To escape prohibition: CEEs must benefit importer (*Statistical Levy*), be proportionate (*Customs Warehouses*).
- No derogation.
- Protectionist intent irrelevant (*Diamonds*).

Article 34 prohibition

- Wide scope.
- Quantitative restrictions: import/export quotas and bans (*Geddo*).
- Wide definition of MEQRs: *Dassonville*, Directive 70/50.
- But 'reasonable' restraints unobjectionable (*Dassonville, Cassis*).
- Further limit on 'MEQR'. *Keck*: excludes 'selling arrangements' where no greater impact on imports than domestic products (eg *Tankstation 't Heukske, Commission v Greece, De Agostini*).

Article 110 prohibition

- Discriminatory internal taxation (*Denkavit* definition).
- Direct, indirect discrimination (*Humblot, Lütticke*).
- Wide scope: equal taxation ('similar' products), no advantage to domestic products.

Harmonization

- Harmonizing directives (Article 115).
- Stricter standards for 'major needs' (Article 114).
- New approach: directives covering essential requirements (Council Resolution, 1985).

Impediments to free movement
Article 30

- No justifications for breaches.

Article 36, *Cassis*

- Only if no EU harmonizing measures.
- Distinctly and indistinctly applicable measures covered.
- Must be evidence of risk, proportionality, and no arbitrary discrimination/disguised restriction on trade. Justifications interpreted restrictively.
- Article 36 list is exhaustive, but covers distinctly and indistinctly applicable measures.
- *Cassis*: mutual recognition the underlying assumption.
- *Cassis* rule of reason: mandatory requirements wide, have been extended (eg *Danish Bottles, Oebel, Torfaen Borough Council*) but cover indistinctly applicable measures only.

Article 110

- Objective justification, provided proportionality (eg *Chemial Farmaceutici*) but no systematic policy.

Conclusion

Free movement through negative/positive integration. Restrictions broadly interpreted though note *Keck* limits. Justifications interpreted restrictively and subject to proportionality.

Chapter 6
....
[References are to the TFEU unless otherwise indicated]

Problem answer

Introduction

- Briefly explain: Articles 26, 18, 20, 21.

Entry and residence
Union citizen

- Sally: Member State national, Union citizen (Article 20).
- Article 21: right of free movement and residence in Spain 'subject to limitations and conditions'.

- Directive 2004/38: entry and residence rights, up to three months.

Jobseeker

- Right to enter and reside (Directive 2004/38, Article 14(4)(b), *Royer*).
- Must genuinely seek work, be capable of finding it (Directive 2004/38 Article 14 (4)(b), *Antonissen*). Apply: Sally has demonstrated both.

Worker

- No Treaty definition, but Court of Justice definition (*Lawrie-Blum*); entails genuine economic activity (*Levin, Bettray*). Apply: Sally is clearly a worker.
- Article 45(3): worker right to reside in Spain. Directive 2004/38 (Article 7(1)(a)): residency right for more than three months.

Access to employment

Freedom from discrimination

- Article 18: freedom from discrimination based on nationality 'within the scope of . . . Treaty'.
- Article 45(2): workers' right to non-discrimination in employment.
- Directive 2004/38 (Article 24): equal treatment with nationals.
- Sally: an EU migrant worker, entitled to these rights.

Access to employment

- Regulation 492/2011: right to take up employment under same conditions as nationals.
- Derogation: linguistic requirements (Regulation 492/2011, Article 3) but only where necessary 'by reason of the nature of the post'. Apply: language test may be beyond the job's requirements and disproportionate.

Expulsion

- Limitations, workers' residence rights: public policy, security or health (Article 45(3), Directive 2004/38, Article 27).
- Public policy: measures must be proportionate, based exclusively on personal conduct, represent a 'genuine, present and sufficiently serious threat affecting one of the fundamental interests of society'.
- Sally's criminal offence is personal conduct, recent and sufficiently serious.
- Directive 2004/38 (Article 28): before ordering deportation, the Spanish court must consider age, state of health etc. Apply: Sally is unlikely to qualify for protection against expulsion.
- Directive 2004/38 (Articles 30–32): procedural rights.

Conclusion

Despite Sally's right to enter and remain, given her criminal activity the Spanish court is justified in ordering deportation on public policy grounds.

Essay answer

Introduction

- Briefly explain: Articles 26, 18, 20, 21.

Position pre-Maastricht

- Rights largely tied to economic status: workers (Article 39 EC (now Article 45 TFEU)), self-employed (Articles 43, 49 EC (now Articles 49, 56 TFEU)) and families.
- But Court of Justice's broad interpretation: eg 'worker' (*Levin, Kempf, Steymann, Ninni-Orasche*).
- Extension of rights to jobseekers (*Royer, Antonissen*).
- Rights limited: public policy, security, health, though Court of Justice interprets narrowly.
- Directives 90/364/365/366: economic nexus partially broken.

Union citizenship

- Article 17 EC (now Article 20 TFEU): Union citizenship established (Member States' nationals).
- Article 18 EC (now Article 21 TFEU): right of free movement of Union citizens, subject to 'limitations and conditions'.

Outline answers
****

- Court of Justice used citizenship as basis for rights (*Sala, Grzelczyk, D'Hoop, Baumbast*).

Directive 2004/38

- Union citizens, families: right to enter and reside in another Member State, up to three months. No economic status required but no welfare entitlement unless economically active or family member.

- Economically active, students, persons of independent means, families: residency right for more than three months, but little change from previous provisions.

- Distinctions between family members who are Union citizens and those who are not: divorce, death, or departure of Union citizen.

- Scope of 'family member' extended: registered partners.

- New permanent residency right, after five years: significant, since no economic status required.

- Equality rights, but limits on welfare entitlement.

- Limitations: public policy, security, health. Court of Justice's restrictive interpretation (eg *Bonsignore, Calfa, Orfanopoulos and Oliveri, Bouchereau*).

- Protection against expulsion: after permanent rights acquired.

Conclusion

Union citizenship significant: extension of free movement rights, in case law and Directive 2004/38. However, qualifications, limitations remain.

Chapter 7
. . . .
[References are to the TFEU unless otherwise indicated]

Problem answer

Breach of Article 101(1)?

- Must establish: agreement between undertakings, which may affect trade between Member States and has as its object or effect the prevention, restriction, or distortion of competition within the common market.

Agreement between undertakings

- 'Undertaking': natural/legal persons engaged in commercial activity (*Höfner and Elser*). Blacksmiths, Marnier qualify and have an agreement.

Which may affect . . .

- Broadly interpreted: direct or indirect, actual or potential effect (*STM*).

- Blacksmiths (UK) to supply only to Marnier (France): agreement will have an actual, direct effect on trade between UK/France. The parties' aggregate market share exceeds the relevant threshold: an effect on trade is likely (*Notice: guidelines on the effect on trade concept*).

Which has as its object . . .

- *De minimis*: Both parties' market shares exceed the threshold (*Notice on agreements of minor importance*).

- Restrictive object or effect suffices (*STM*): agreement restricts Blacksmiths' ability to compete in France and Marnier's sales activity; is intentionally restrictive.

Agreement likely to breach Article 101(1).

Exemption

Article 101(3)

- Categories of agreement: block exemption, eg Regulation 330/2010.

Regulation 330/2010

- Article 101(1) does not apply to vertical agreements for sale/resale of goods, so far as they contain prohibited restrictions. Blacksmiths/Marnier agreement qualifies.

- Exemption applies provided neither party's market share over 30%.

- Both parties' market shares within threshold. Regulation 330/2010 can apply.

- Neither restriction is blacklisted.

Conclusion

Agreement likely to breach Article 101(1) but to benefit from Regulation 330/2010.

Essay answer

EC competition law: aims

• Internal market concept: free movement of goods and services.

• Targets anti-competitive business behaviour harming consumers, small/medium-sized businesses and efficiency.

• Article 101: prohibits restrictive business arrangements.

Article 101(1)

Wide scope

• Agreements, decisions, concerted practices. Discuss scope, with cases.

• 'Object' or 'effect' suffices (*STM*), including deemed object (market sharing, price-fixing).

• 'Restriction, prevention, distortion', including increase in trade (*Consten*).

• Covers horizontal and vertical agreements (*Consten*).

• 'Effect on trade between Member States' interpreted broadly: direct or indirect, actual or potential effect (*STM, Notice: guidelines on the effect on trade concept*). Includes agreements between undertakings operating within one Member State (*Vacuum Interrupters*). Agreements considered in market context: may breach even if, considered in isolation, they would not affect trade between Member States (*Brasserie de Haecht*).

• But *de minimis* agreements outside scope: an 'appreciable' effect on competition required (*Volk, Commission notice on agreements of minor importance*, 2001).

• List of Article 101(1) restrictions not exhaustive: Commission/Court of Justice can make case by case decisions, having regard to competition policy aims.

• Court of Justice may balance anti- and pro-competitive effects (*Pronuptia, Metro*), but a rule of reason not expressly recognized and denied by the Court of First Instance (now called the General Court) (*Métropole Television*).

• Possibility of severance (*STM, Consten*).

Achieving competition law aims

• Internal market: no absolute territorial protection (*Consten*).

• Harm to consumers, business efficiency: no price-fixing (*ICI, Hennessy/Henkell*).

• Harm to small/medium-sized undertakings: no disproportionate non-compete clauses (*Hennessy/Henkell*).

Exemption

• Article 101(3): balancing pro- and anti-competitive effects.

• Permissible restrictions: overall beneficial effects in distribution, production, technical, and economic progress, allow consumers a fair share of the resulting benefit, no unnecessary restrictions (*CECED*), and no substantial elimination of competition (*CECED, ACEC/Berliet*).

• Individual exemption: eg *ACEC/Berliet, Prym-Werke*.

• Block exemptions, eg Regulation 330/2010, cover categories of agreement normally satisfying Article 101(3).

Conclusion

Article 101(1): interpreted broadly, prohibits restrictive business practices with harmful effects. Article 101(3): allows exemption for agreements which, despite being restrictive, have overall beneficial effects.

Chapter 8

[References are to the TFEU unless otherwise indicated]

Problem answer

Establishing a breach

• Smartco must: have a dominant position, have abused that position, and the abuse must be capable of affecting trade between Member States.

Dominant position

• 'A position of economic strength enjoyed by an undertaking that enables it to prevent effective competition . . . on the relevant market by giving it the power to behave to an appreciable extent . . . independently of its competitors, customers . . . and consumers' (*United Brands*).

• Assessed in relation to the relevant market: relevant product, geographic and temporal markets.

Relevant product market (RPM)

• Smartco will argue a broad RPM: roofing materials (10% market share in UK, France, and Belgium).

• Simpleco will argue a narrow RPM: roofing tiles (80% market share in UK, France, Belgium. Smartco would be dominant).

• Product substitution: demand and supply substitution.

• Demand substitution: would the consumer substitute one product for another, regard sheet roofing and roofing tiles as substitutes, according to characteristics, use, price?

• Consider characteristics, use, price (eg *United Brands*, *Hilti*, *Hugin*). Apply SSNIP test.

• Supply substitution: could producers of roofing tiles/sheet roofing cheaply and easily switch production (*Continental Can*)?

• Likely conclusion: low cross-elasticity of demand/supply between the two products. RPM is roofing tiles.

Relevant geographic market

• Smartco will argue a broad geographic market, (whole EU, where its market share is small).

• Simpleco will argue the narrowest market (UK, France, Belgium, where Smartco has 80% share).

• Consider: cost and feasibility of transportation (*Hilti*) or other factors (eg '*TV Listings*').

Likely conclusion: geographic market is UK, France, Belgium; is a 'substantial part of the internal market' (*United Brands*, *Michelin*).

Temporal market

• Rarely relevant: seasonal nature of the building trade?

Dominance

• 80% share may be conclusive of dominance (*Hilti*, *Hoffmann-La Roche*).

• Other indicators: Smartco's financial resources (*United Brands*), vertical integration (*Hoffmann-La Roche*), conduct (*United Brands*).

Abuse

• Exploitative or anti-competitive (explain).

• Differential discounts (*Michelin*), discounts to Simpleco's existing customers (*Hoffmann-La Roche*).

Effect on trade

• Easily established: 'direct or indirect, actual or potential . . .' effect suffices (*STM*).

• Smartco trades across three Member States: its discounting arrangements will have an effect.

Conclusion

Smartco's conduct likely to infringe Article 102.

Essay answer

Identify the scope of the question

• Aims of EU competition law.

• Focus on 'abuse'.

• Exploitative and anti-competitive abuses.

Aims of EU competition law

• Set out aims of EU competition law.

'Abuse'

• Article 102 examples: unfair pricing/trading conditions; limiting production, markets, technical development to detriment of consumers; discriminatory treatment; imposition of supplementary obligations not connected to the subject of contracts.

- Court of Justice's interpretation: analysis of cases, referring to the aims of EU competition law.
- Distinction between exploitative and anti-competitive abuses, with definition/explanation.
- Exploitative abuses: protection of the consumer:
    - unfair pricing (eg *United Brands*, *British Leyland*);
    - price discrimination (eg *United Brands*).
- Anti-competitive abuses:
    - predatory pricing (eg *AKZO*, *Tetra Pak*): protection of small/medium-sized undertakings;
    - refusal to supply (eg *Commercial Solvents*, *Hugin*, *Sealink*, *United Brands*, *TV Listings*): protection of small/medium-sized undertakings, achieving internal market.
- Promotion of efficiency and the internal market through the protection of EU-wide competition.

- Exploitative and anti-competitive abuses:
    - target discounting (eg *Michelin*): protection of the consumer;
    - loyalty rebating (eg *Hoffmann-La Roche*): promotion of efficiency;
    - tie-ins (eg *Hoffmann-La Roche*, *Hilti*): protecting the consumer, promotion of efficiency;
    - import/export bans (eg *Hilti*): achieving the internal market.

Commission review

- Discussion paper, 2005 and Guidance, 2009 – focus on exclusionary conduct that harms consumer.

Conclusion

Court of Justice has addressed both forms of abuse and furthered the aims of EU competition law. The Commission's approach entails an increasingly effects-based regime, focusing on the protection of the consumer.

Glossary

Absolute territorial protection Complete protection from competition in a particular geographical area ('territory'), typically afforded to an undertaking through an exclusive distribution agreement which prevents parallel imports.

Acte clair Translated literally means 'clear act'. The term is applied to provisions of EU law whose interpretation is clear.

Anti-competitive abuse Abuse by an undertaking that prevents or weakens competition or potential competition from other undertakings.

Ban A 'total restraint', blocking the import or export of particular goods altogether.

Barriers to entry Factors that prevent or hinder entry to a market by an undertaking or undertakings.

Block exemption Exemption under Article 101(3) applied to categories of agreement.

Cartel A group of independent companies or businesses, operating in the same market, that collude to fix prices, share markets, or engage in other forms of anti-competitive behaviour.

CEE (charge having equivalent effect to a customs duty) A levy charged on goods by virtue of the fact that they cross a frontier, which is not a customs duty in the strict sense.

Co-decision (the 'ordinary legislative procedure') A legislative procedure involving the participation of the European Commission, the Council, and the European Parliament.

Collusion Coordination or communication between undertakings, without formal agreement, on the adoption of a common market strategy, for instance to fix prices.

Common customs tariff A common level of duty charged by all Member States on goods imported from third countries.

Common market (now known in the EU as 'internal market') An area within which goods, persons, services, and capital move freely without restriction.

Competence The power granted by the Treaties to the EU and the Member States, either respectively or jointly ('joint competence'), to enact legislation in a particular area.

Concerted practice A form of coordination between undertakings falling short of an agreement by which, through their cooperation, the parties eliminate or reduce competition between them.

Consultation procedure This legislative procedure requires only that the European Parliament be consulted before the Council adopts particular legislation.

Contra legem **interpretation** The interpretation of legislation against its clear meaning.

Customs duty A levy charged on goods by virtue of the fact that they cross a frontier.

Customs union A free trade area, together with a system whereby a common level of duty is charged on goods entering the free trade area from non-member countries.

Decision A form of EU secondary legislation which is addressed to one or a number of Member States or individuals and is directly applicable.

De minimis **agreement** An agreement of 'minor importance', with no 'appreciable' effect on competition.

Demand substitutability (or cross-elasticity of demand) There is demand substitutability if the consumer would be willing and able to substitute one product for another.

Derogation A permissible exception to a legal rule or principle.

Direct actions Proceedings brought directly before the Court of Justice or General Court. Distinguish from proceedings brought indirectly through preliminary references from national courts.

Direct discrimination A directly discriminatory measure openly discriminates on the basis, for instance, of nationality or product origin.

Direct effect If a provision of EU law has direct effect, it can be enforced by individuals (natural persons and businesses) in the national court.

Directive A form of EU secondary legislation which is not directly applicable but must be implemented by Member States.

Directly applicable (or 'self-executing') provisions of EU law are part of national law and automatically binding, without further enactment.

Distinctly applicable measures Measures that do not apply equally to domestic and imported products.

Distribution agreement Agreement for the supply of products for resale.

Distribution franchise An agreement between an established distributor of a product (the franchisor) and other independent traders (the franchisees). The franchisor grants the franchisees, for a fee, the right to establish themselves using its business name and methods.

Dual burden rules impose requirements on goods that are additional to requirements that may be applied in the state of origin, creating an extra burden for producers.

Dualist system A national legal system in which international law is not binding internally until it is incorporated by domestic statute.

Economically active persons comprise workers, the self-employed, and providers of services.

Economically inactive persons comprise persons other than workers, the self-employed, and providers of services.

Equal burden rules concern the marketing of goods. They impose an equal burden on domestic and imported products.

European Union law Comprises Treaty provisions, secondary legislation (regulations, directives, decisions), international agreements made by the EU, and the case law of the Court of Justice.

Exclusive distribution agreement An agreement under which a supplier appoints a sole distributor for a particular area.

Exploitative abuse Abuse by an undertaking that exploits consumers.

Force majeure Abnormal and unforeseeable circumstances, beyond the control of the person committing a breach, the consequences of which could not have been avoided through the exercise of all due care.

Four freedoms Free movement of goods, persons, services, and capital within the internal market.

Free trade area An area within which customs duties and other trade restrictions between the member countries are prohibited.

Freedom of establishment For individuals, this comprises the right to pursue activities as a self-employed person in another Member State, for instance conducting a business or practising a profession, on a permanent basis.

Hardcore restrictions The most serious restrictions on competition, notably price-fixing and market-sharing.

Harmonization The adoption of EU legislation with a view to eliminating any existing disparities arising from Member States' respective national provisions in the relevant areas.

Harmonizing legislation EU legislation adopted under the process of harmonization.

Horizontal agreement An agreement between parties operating at the same level of the production/distribution chain, for instance between manufacturers.

Horizontal direct effect If a provision of EU law has horizontal direct effect it can be enforced by an individual (a person or a company) in a national court against another individual.

Implementation The incorporation of EU law into national law by Member States, relating in particular to directives.

Indirect discrimination An indirectly discriminatory measure appears not to discriminate but its effect is to discriminate.

Indirect effect This principle requires that national law be interpreted in accordance with relevant EU law.

Indistinctly applicable measures Measures that apply equally to domestic and imported products (ie make no distinction between domestic and imported products).

Glossary

Individual exemption Exemption under Article 101(3) applied on a case-by-case basis to individual agreements.

Inter-brand competition Competition between two or more brands of a particular product or service.

Intergovernmental Describes decision-making entailing agreement between the Member States acting as independent sovereign states.

Internal market An area in which goods, persons, services, and capital move freely without restriction.

Intra-brand competition Competition within a particular brand, for instance between retailers selling the same brand of a particular product.

Legal base The legal base of a particular legislative measure is the Treaty article setting out the EU's power to legislate in the relevant policy area.

Legal certainty This principle incorporates the requirement that the distinction between what is lawful and unlawful should be reasonably clear.

Legitimate expectation This principle requires that law or action must not breach the legitimate expectations of those who are affected by it.

Locus standi (or 'standing') The right to bring proceedings before the Court.

Mandatory requirements Justifications that allow restrictions on the free movement of goods to escape the scope of Article 34 TFEU.

Measures having equivalent effect (MEQRs) Non-tariff barriers to trade which are not quantitative but have a similar effect to quantitative restrictions.

Monist system A national legal system in which EU law becomes binding from ratification, with no need for incorporating measures.

Mutual recognition (goods) Provided goods have been lawfully produced and marketed in one Member State, there is no reason why they should not be introduced into another without restriction.

National sovereignty The power of a state to regulate its own affairs, in particular through the enactment of legislation.

Non-retroactivity This principle dictates that the law should not impose penalties retroactively.

Non-tariff barriers Import, export, or other restrictions on the free movement of goods not involving direct payments of money, comprising quantitative restrictions and MEQRs.

Objectively justified A measure or action is objectively justified if it is based on a legitimate rationale.

Oligopolistic market A market dominated by relatively few sellers.

Parallel behaviour Behaviour of undertakings consisting in responding to each others' market strategy by adopting similar strategies, for instance on pricing.

Parallel imports The import of goods by a distributor into a sales area or sales areas allocated by the supplier to other distributors.

Parliamentary sovereignty A UK constitutional convention under which Parliament has the exclusive right to adopt and repeal national legislation and cannot bind its successors, so that subsequent Acts can either expressly or impliedly repeal a prior Act.

Preliminary reference A request from a national court to the Court of Justice for a ruling on the interpretation or validity of EU law.

Preliminary ruling Ruling on the interpretation or validity of EU law by the Court of Justice in response to a preliminary reference.

Product substitution Comprises demand substitutability (or cross-elasticity of demand) and supply substitutability (or cross-elasticity of supply).

Proportionality This principle requires that action or measures go no further than is necessary to achieve their objective or than is justified in the circumstances.

Proportionate An action or measure is proportionate if it goes no further than is necessary to achieve its objective or than is justified in the circumstances.

Protectionist motives A measure adopted with protectionist motives is intended to protect domestic products from competition from imports.

Provision of services This describes the situation in which an individual or company is established in one Member State and provides services into another.

Qualified majority voting (QMV) A majority voting system that is not based on a simple majority.

Quantitative restrictions Non-tariff barriers to trade that impose a limit on the quantity of goods that may be imported or exported, comprising quotas or bans.

Quota A 'partial restraint' placing a limit on the quantity of particular goods that can be imported or exported.

Reasoned opinion Issued to a Member State by the Commission under Article 258 TFEU setting out precisely the grounds of complaint and specifying a time limit for ending an infringement.

Reciprocity Non-compliance is justified because other Member States have not complied or an EU institution has failed to act. This defence has been rejected by the Court of Justice in Article 258 proceedings.

Regulation A form of EU secondary legislation which is directly applicable in all the Member States.

Rule of reason (competition law) This entails the balancing of the pro- and anti-competitive effects of a restrictive agreement. Where the benefits outweigh the disadvantages, there is no breach.

Rule of reason (free movement of goods) Restrictions on trade resulting from national provisions on product marketing, which differ from those applying in other Member States, are permissible if they are necessary to satisfy one of the mandatory requirements.

Selective distribution agreement An agreement under which goods or services are sold only through outlets chosen by the supplier according to its own criteria, such as the suitability of the premises.

State liability This principle gives rise to a right to damages against a Member State which has breached EU law, causing loss to the applicant.

Subsidiarity This principle requires that decisions be taken as closely as possible to the citizen and that action at EU level, rather than at national, regional, or local level, is justified.

Supply substitutability (or 'cross-elasticity of supply') There is supply substitutability if producers of similar products could easily and cheaply enter the product market in question by simply adapting their production.

Supranational Describes a level of government that operates above and independently of national governments.

Supremacy The doctrine of supremacy dictates that EU law takes precedence over conflicting provisions of national law.

Tariff barriers Import or export restrictions involving direct payments of money, comprising customs duties and charges having equivalent effect to customs duties (CEEs).

Third country nationals Persons who are not citizens of the EU.

Undertaking A natural or legal person (individual or company) engaged in commercial activity for the provision of goods or services.

Vertical agreement An agreement between parties operating at different levels of the production/distribution chain, for instance between a manufacturer and a distributor.

Vertical direct effect If a provision of EU law has vertical direct effect it can be enforced by an individual (a person or a company) in a national court against the state or a public body.

Index

**abuse of dominant position
(Art 102 TFEU)** 159–60
abuse 179, 188–93
refusal to supply 179,
191–2
see also prices
cross-elasticity of
supply 178, 183–4
discounting 179, 189–90
dominance
conduct 187
financial or technological
resources 186
indicators 186
intellectual property
rights 187
market-share 186
market structure 186
vertical integration
186–7
dominant position 178,
181–7
in relevant market 178,
185–7
exam questions 196–7
export bans 179, 192–3
import bans 179, 192–3
intellectual property
rights 187
key cases 194–6
key facts 158, 180
market-sharing 160
national authorities 160
national courts 160
overview 178–9
price-fixing 160
prices
discounting 179, 189–90
discriminatory
pricing 179, 189
predatory pricing 179,
190–1
SSNIP test 183
tie-ins 179, 190
unfair 179, 188–9
product substitutability 178

refusal to supply 179, 191–2
relevant market 178, 181–5
dominant position in 178,
185–7
geographic market
(RGM) 184–5
prices 183
product market (RPM)
182–4
temporal or seasonal
market 185
small but significant non-
transitory increase in
price test 183
supply substitutability 183–4
tie-ins 179, 190
trade between States 193
undertakings
meaning 160
safeguards 161
acquis communautaire 16
acte clair **doctrine** 56–7, 58
action for failure to act
Art 265 TFEU 77–8
declaration of failure to
act 78
locus standi 77–8
**agreements of minor
importance** 167
annulment actions
acts which may be
challenged 70–1
'closed class' test 63,75
effect of annulment 77
grounds 63, 76–7
illegality 78
individual concern 74–6
judicial review 63, 70, 71
key cases 84–5
locus standi 70, 71–6
'closed class' test 63, 75
direct concern 63, 73–4
individual concern 63,
74–6
non-privileged applicants
63, 72–6

Plaumann formula 74–5
privileged applicants 72
semi-privileged
applicants 72
non-privileged applicants
63, 72–6
Plaumann test 76
privileged applicants 72
reasons for judicial
review 71
regulations 76
semi-privileged
applicants 72
time limit 71
**anti-competitive agreements
(Art 101 TFEU)** 159,
161–73
affecting trade between
States 165–7
agreements of minor
importance 167
associations of
undertakings 163
block exemptions 172–3
cartels 164
concerted practices 163–4
distribution agreements
168–9
exam questions 176
exemptions 169–73
block 172–3
fair share of benefit to
consumers 171
improving production
170–1
individual 170–2
no elimination of
competition 172
proportionality 171
technical or economic
progress 170–1
fixing trading conditions
168
horizontal agreements 165
inter-brand competition
165

Index

****

**anti-competitive agreements
(Art 101 TFEU)** (*cont.*)
intra-brand
competition 165
key cases 173–6
key facts 158
legal and economic context
166–7
market-sharing
agreement 159
national authorities 160
national courts 160
object or effect 167
outline 161–2
overview 156–7
prevention, restriction,
distortion of
competition 168
price-fixing 159, 168
prohibition 162–9
Regulation 1/2003 160–1
rule of reason 168–9
undertakings 162
associations of 163
meaning 160
safeguards for 161
vertical agreements 165
**Area of Freedom, Security
and Justice** 10–11
Assembly *see* **European
Parliament**

cartels 164
Cassis de Dijon, **free
movement**
extension to mandatory
requirements
103–4
indistinctly applicable
measures 103
mutual recognition
principle 102, 112
no harmonizing rules 103
proportionality 104–5
rule of reason 102–5, 112
central banks 11
certainty 18
challenging EU law
acts which may be
challenged 70–1

annulment actions *see*
annulment actions
Art 263 TFEU 63, 70–7
judicial review 63, 70, 71
non-privileged
applicants 63
regulations 76
standing *see locus standi*
**Charter of Fundamental
Rights** 11
citizens
initiating proposals 10
Civil Service Tribunal 16
'closed class' test 63, 75
co-decision procedure 19
**Co-operation on Justice and
Home Affairs** 6
commercial property
protection 111
**Committee of Permanent
Representatives
(COREPER)** 11
Committee of the Regions
11, 16
Common Agricultural Policy 9
**Common Foreign and
Security Policy** 6, 10
common market 2, 3–4
competence
areas of 9
competition law
affecting trade between
States 165–7, 193
agreements 162–3
Art 101 TFEU *see* **anti-
competitive agreements
(Art 101 TFEU)**
Art 102 TFEU *see* **abuse
of dominant position
(Art 102 TFEU)**
cartels 164
Commission powers,
enforcement 161
concerted practices 163–4
enforcement 160–1
Commission powers 161
cooperation 160
inter-brand competition
165
key facts 158

concerted practices 163–4
contra legem
interpretations 35
copyright 111, 187
Council 4, 10
composition 12
powers 12
presidency 12
voting 12–13
Court of Auditors 11, 16
Court of First Instance *see*
General Court
**Court of Justice of the
European Union** 4,
11, 15
Advocates-General 15
chambers of three
judges 15
Grand Chamber 15
personnel 15
preliminary rulings *see*
preliminary rulings
role 15
courts
judicial panels 16
national *see* **national courts**
specialized courts 16
see also **Court of Auditors;
Court of Justice of
the European Union;
General Court**
criminal convictions
free movement
limitation 148
customs duties
CEE 92–3
pecuniary charge 92–3
customs union 4, 92

damages
administrative breaches 80
Art 340 TFEU 79–83
breaches of EU law 36–8
causation 79, 82
concurrent liability 83
discretion accorded to
institution 82
EU liability 79–83
key cases 85–6
legislative measures 80

non-contractual liability 79
non-implementation of
    directive 36–7
quantifiable damage 79, 82
sufficiently flagrant
    violation of superior
    rule 80–1
time limits 83
wrongful act 79, 80–2
decision-making
intergovernmental 6
supranational 6
decisions 17
**defences to enforcement
    actions** 67–9
actual compliance 68–9
force majeure 68
political or economic
    difficulties 68
reciprocity 68
democracy
Reform Treaty and 10
design rights 111, 187
direct action
action for failure to act
    77–8
annulment *see* **annulment
    actions**
challenging law *see*
    challenging EU law
enforcement actions *see*
    enforcement actions
illegality plea 78
judicial review 63
liability in damages *see*
    damages
direct actions
annulment action,
    grounds 63
exam questions 86–7
key cases 83–6
key facts 64
overview 63
direct applicability 27–8
direct effect 22, 49
conditions for 29
creation of principle of 28
direct applicability
    and 27–8
directives 30–3

horizontal 29–30, 31–2
limitations 36
public bodies 32–3
regulations 30
treaty articles 28, 29
vertical 29–30
directives 17
direct effect 30–3
incidental effect 33
incorrect implementation
    38–9
incorrect interpretation 39
national law implementing
    34–5
no horizontal direct effect
    31–2, 34, 35
non-implementation,
    damages 36–7
public bodies 32–3
Directorates-General 14
discounting 179, 189–90
discretion to refer
acte clair doctrine 58
guidance of exercise of 57
national precedent 58
preliminary rulings 58
previous ruling 58
relevance 58
validity references 57
discrimination
direct 137
eligibility for employment
    135
equal treatment 136
free movement and 134–7
freedom from 134–7
indirect 137
public service employment
    122, 135–6
self-employed persons 138
discriminatory pricing 179,
    189
discriminatory taxation
basis of assessment 95–6
collection methods 95–6
direct discrimination 95, 97
free movement of
    goods 91, 92, 94–8
harmonization of
    taxation 98

indirect discrimination
    95, 97
indirect protection to other
    products 96–7
objective justification
    96, 97
overview 97
'similar products' 96, 97
distribution agreements
    168–9
divorce
free movement and 128
double majority voting 13
dualist systems 26

**economic and monetary
    union** 9
**Economic and Social
    Committee** 11, 16
enforcement actions
against Member States
    administrative stage
    66–7
breach meaning 65
by Commission 65–9
by Member States 70
defences 67–9
defendants 66
failure to act 65
force majeure 68
identification of
    breach 66
interim measures 69
judicial stage 67
letter of notice 67
political or economic
    difficulties 68
procedure 66–7
reasoned opinion
    66–7, 70
reciprocity 68
effect of judgment 69
enlargement 4
equality 18
EU law 8, 25
challenging *see*
    challenging EU law
direct effect *see* **direct
    effect**
incorporation 26

Index

****

EU law (*cont.*)
  indirect effect *see* **indirect effect**
  preliminary rulings *see* **preliminary rulings**
  sovereignty and 25
  state liability *see* **state liability**
  supremacy 25–6, 27
  see also **national courts**
European Atomic Energy Community 4
European Central Bank 11
European Coal and Steel Community 3–4
European Commission 4, 11
  allocation of portfolios 14
  appointment of commissioners 13
  citizens' initiative 10
  composition 14
  Directorates-General 14
  'guardian' of law 14
  president 11, 13
  Reform Treaty and 10
  removal of commissioners 13
  role 14
  support staff 14
European Community 2
  enlargement 4
  institutions 4
  key facts 2
  origins 3–4
  treaties *see* **treaties**
  see also **European Union**
European Convention on Human Rights 11, 18
European Council 8, 11
  amendment of treaties by 9
  heads of states 11
  powers 9
  president 8, 11
  role 11
  summits 11
European Court of Justice *see* **Court of Justice of the European Union**

European Economic Community
  creation 2, 3
  institutions 4
European External Action Service 10
European law *see* **secondary legislation; treaties**
European Parliament 4, 11
  approval of commissioners 13, 15
  co-decision procedure (now ordinary legislative procedure) 15
  functioning 14
  membership 14
  powers 14–15
  Reform Treaty and 8, 9
  subsidiarity 9
'European summits' 11
European Union 4
  competence 9
  creation 2
  damages liability *see* **damages**
  enlargement 4
  exam questions 20
  external relations 10
  three-pillar structure 5–6
  treaties *see* **treaties**
external relations 10

failure to act *see* **action for failure to act**
family members
  death or departure of Union citizen 128
  divorce 128
  employment of 129
  equal treatment 129
  free movement 118, 119, 125, 126–7, 137
  marriages of convenience 127
  meaning 127
  spouses and partners 127
force majeure 68
foreign affairs
  External Action Service 10

High Representative of the Union for Foreign Affairs and Security Policy 10, 11
  solidarity clause 10
free movement of goods
  Art 36 TFEU derogation, grounds 109–13
  Cassis de Dijon 102–5
  extension to mandatory requirements 103–4
  indistinctly applicable measures 103
  mutual recognition principle 102, 112
  no harmonizing rules 103
  proportionality 104–5
  rule of reason 102–5, 112
  CEE 92–3
  copyright 111
  customs duties 92–3, 94
  customs union 92
  derogation 107–13
  design rights 111
  discriminatory taxation 91, 92, 94–8
    basis of assessment 95–6
    collection methods 95–6
    direct discrimination 95, 97
    harmonization of taxation 98
    indirect discrimination 95, 97
    indirect protection to other products 96–7
    objective justification 96, 97
    overview 97
    'similar products' 96, 97
  distinctly applicable measures 99–100
  restrictions 108
  exam questions 115–16
  harmonization 103
    derogations 111, 112–13
  health inspection fees 93
  health and life 110–11
  indistinctly applicable measures 99, 100–1

Cassis rule of reason 103
restrictions 108
industrial and commercial
property 111
internal market 92
Keck and Mithouard selling
arrangements 105–7
application of *Keck*
106–7
Keck judgment 106
key cases 113–15
key facts 89
measures falling outside
Art 34 TFEU 102–5
measures having
equivalent effect
(MEQRs) 98
Dassonville definition 99
definition 99
Directive 70/50 99
distinctly applicable
measures 99–100
indistinctly applicable
measures 99, 100–1
scope 99
mutual recognition
principle 102
restrictions 108
non-tariff barriers to
trade 90, 98
measures having
equivalent
effect 98–101, 112
overview 112
quantitative restrictions
98, 112
obligation to ensure 101–5
overview 90–1
patents 111
proportionality, restrictions
108, 112
restrictions 92
arbitrary discrimination
108, 112
Art 36 TFEU derogation
107–13
disguised 108, 112
distinctly applicable
measures 108
exhaustive list 107–8

harmonization 111,
112–13
indistinctly applicable
measures 108
mutual recognition 109
national treasures 111
no harmonizing rules
111
protection of health and
life 110–11
protection of industrial
and commercial
property 111
protection of national
treasures 111
public morality 109
public policy 109
public security 109–10
selling arrangements
application of *Keck*
106–7
dual burden 105
equal burden 105
Keck judgment 106
Keck and Mithouard
105–7
tariff barriers to trade 90
charges for services
rendered 93, 94
customs duties 92–3, 94
health inspection fees 93
overview 94
trade marks 111
free movement of persons
administrative
formalities 129
criminal convictions 148
Directive 2004/38 125–30
discrimination
direct 137
eligibility for employment
135
equal treatment 136
freedom from 134–7
indirect 137
public service
employment 122, 135–6
self-employed persons
138
divorce and 128

employment 122
eligibility 135
exam questions 154
family members 118, 119,
125, 126–7, 137
death or departure of
Union citizen 128
divorce 128
employment of 129
equal treatment 129
marriages of
convenience 127
meaning 127
spouses and partners 127
independent means 126
jobseekers 122, 133–4
key cases 149–53
key facts 120
limitations 121, 129–30,
144, 145
Directive 2004/38 144–5
general preventative
measures 147–8
partial 145, 148–9
personal conduct 146–7
'present' threat 146
previous criminal
convictions 148
procedural rights 149
proportionality 147
public health 145, 149
public policy 144, 145,
146
public security 144, 145,
146
non-economically active
citizens 124–5
overview 118–19
permanent residence 129
professional qualifications
119, 123, 139
mutual recognition 139,
142–3
public service employment
122, 135–6
re-entry rights 130
recipients of services 142
residency 124–5
rights 121
enter and remain 134

Index

****

free movement of persons
  (*cont.*)
  establishment 119, 123,
    138, 139, 142–3
  in state of origin 130
  self-employed persons 119,
    123, 125
  direct effect 138
  discrimination 138
  entry and residence 138
  establishment 119, 123,
    138, 139, 142–3
  legislation 137
  limitations 138
  professional conduct 123,
    139
  professional qualifications
    119, 123, 139, 142–3
  provision of services 138
  right of establishment
    119, 123, 138, 139,
    142–3
  service provision 140–2,
    143–4
  service provision 119, 123,
    140–2
  administrative formalities
    143
  harmonization of rules
    143–4
  meaning of services 140
  restrictions 140–2
  Services Directive 143–4
  students 126, 130
  third country nationals 9
  Union citizens *see* **Union
    citizens**
  workers 118, 122, 125
  Art 45 TFEU rights 131
  discrimination 134–7
  equal treatment 136
  families 137
  fixed-term contracts 132
  meaning of worker 131–3
  overview 122
  part-time work 131–2
  public service 122, 135–6
  rehabilitation as 132–3
  retaining status 133
  training 133

unemployment 133
unpaid work 132

General Court 15, 16
  direct actions 16
  judicial panels 16
  personnel 16
  preliminary rulings 59
glossary A12–15
goods
  free movement *see* **free
    movement of goods**

health inspection fees 93
**High Representative of the
  Union for Foreign
  Affairs and Security
  Policy** 10, 11
**horizontal direct
  effect** 29–30, 31–2
human rights 11, 18

illegality, plea of 78
indirect effect 23, 49
  individuals and 34
  limitations 36
  national law and 34–5
  principle 34
industrial property
  protection 111
institutions 11–16
  see also individual
    institutions eg
    European Council
intellectual property rights
  dominant position and
    187
  free movement of
    goods 111
internal market 2, 92
international agreements 18

jobseekers 122, 133–4
Judicial panels 16
judicial review
  challenging EU law
    63, 70
  reasons for 71
**Justice and Home
  Affairs** 10–11

Keck and Mithouard, **selling
  arrangements**
  application of *Keck* 106–7
  dual burden 105
  equal burden 105
  Keck judgment 106

law-making
  co-decision procedure 9,
    10, 15, 19
  legal base 18–19
  ordinary legislative
    procedure 9, 10, 19
  qualified majority
    voting 10
  Reform Treaty and 9
  special legislative
    procedures 9, 19
legal certainty 18
legitimate expectation 18
locus standi
  action for failure to act 77–8
  annulment actions 70
  'closed class' test 63, 75
  direct concern 63, 73–4
  individual concern 63, 74–6
  non-privileged applicants
    63, 72–6
  Plaumann formula 74–5
  privileged applicants 72
  semi-privileged
    applicants 72

markets
  market-sharing 159, 160
  relevant *see* **relevant
    market**
**marriages of
  convenience** 127
Marshall Plan 3
**measures having equivalent
  effect**
  Dassonville definition 99
  definition 99
  Directive 70/50 99
  distinctly applicable
    measures 99–100
  free movement of
    goods 98–101
  scope 99

indistinctly applicable
measures 99, 100–1
**minor importance,
agreement of** 167
monist systems 26
mutual recognition
free movement of
goods 102, 108
principle 102
restrictions 108

national courts
effectiveness 40, 41
equivalence 40
procedural autonomy 40
time limits 40
**national treasures,
protection** 111
non-privileged applicants 63,
72–6
non-retroactivity 18
non-tariff barriers to trade
free movement of
goods 90, 98–101
measures having equivalent
effect 98–101, 112
overview 112
quantitative
restrictions 98, 112

obligation to refer 53–7
acte clair doctrine 56–7
avoiding 54–5
previous ruling
exception 54–6
opinion, reasoned 66–7, 70
opinions 17

parliament
European *see* **European
Parliament**
national parliaments 9
subsidiarity 9
**parliamentary
sovereignty** 26
patents 111, 187
plea of illegality 78
**Police and Judicial
Co-operation in
Criminal Matters** 7

predatory pricing 179, 190–1
preliminary rulings
acte clair doctrine 56–7
Art 267 TFEU 45–60
binding effect 49
court or tribunal of
member state 50–1
courts of last resort
53–4, 55
delay in rulings 59
discretion to refer 58
acte clair doctrine 58
guidance of exercise
of 57
national precedent 58
previous ruling 58
relevance 58
validity references 57
exam questions 60–1
General Court 59
hypothetical questions 52
insufficient information 53
irrelevant questions 52
jurisdiction of court 49–50
jurisdiction of national
courts to refer 53–9
key cases 59–60
key facts 47
no genuine dispute 51–2
obligation to refer 53–7
acte clair doctrine 56–7
avoiding 54–5
previous ruling exception
54–6
outline procedure 46, 48
precedent 54–6
previous ruling exception
54–6, 58
reform 59
refusal to accept
references 51–3
timing of reference 48
**President of the European
Council** 8, 11
prices
discounting 179, 189–90
discriminatory pricing
179, 189
predatory pricing 179,
190–1

price-fixing 159, 160, 168
SSNIP test 183
tie-ins 179, 190
unfair 179, 188–9
principles of law
equality 18
human rights 18
legal certainty 18
legitimate expectation 18
non-retroactivity 18
proportionality 18
professional qualifications
free movement and 119,
123, 139, 142–3
harmonization 119
mutual recognition 139,
142–3
proportionality 18
anti-competitive agreement
exemptions 171
Cassis rule of reason
104–5
free movement of goods
108, 112
free movement of
persons 147
public bodies
directives and 32–3
**public health, limitation of
movement**
goods 110–11
persons 149
**public morality, limitation of
movement**
goods 109
**public policy, limitation of
movement**
goods 109
persons 144, 146
**public security, limitation of
movement**
goods 109–10
persons 144, 146
public service
employment 122,
135–6

qualified majority voting 9,
10, 12–13
distribution of votes 12–13

Index

****

reasoned opinion 66–7, 70
recommendations 17
reference for preliminary ruling
  refusal to accept references 51–3
  timing 48
  see also **discretion to refer; obligation to refer**
regulations 17, 18
  direct effect 30
relevant market 178, 181–5
  dominant position in 178, 185–7
  geographic market (RGM) 184–5
  prices 183
  product market (RPM) 182–4
  temporal or seasonal market 185
rule of reason
  competition and 168–9
  free movement of goods 102–5, 112

Schuman plan 3
secondary legislation
  adoption 18
  decisions 17
  directives 17, 30–3
  legal base 18–19
  opinions 17
  recommendations 17
  regulations 17, 30
  source of law 17
self-employed persons 125
  direct effect 138
  discrimination 138
  entry and residence 138
  establishment 119, 123, 138, 139, 142–3
  free movement 119, 123, 125
  legislation 137
  limitations 138
  professional conduct 123, 139
  professional qualifications 119, 123, 139, 142–3

right of establishment 119, 123, 138, 139, 142–3
service provision 140–2, 143–4
selling arrangements
  application of *Keck* 106–7
  dual burden 105
  equal burden 105
  free movement of goods 105–7
  Keck judgment 106
  Keck and Mithouard 105–7
service provision
  administrative formalities 143
  free movement and 119, 123, 140–2
  harmonization of rules 143–4
  meaning of services 140
  restrictions 140–2
  Services Directive 143–4
sources of law
  acquis communautaire 16
  case law 17–18
  human rights 18
  international agreements 18
  secondary legislation 17
  treaties 17
sovereignty 25
standing *see locus standi*
state liability 81–2
  administrative acts 39
  breaches of EU law 36–8
  expansions of 38–9
  Francovich 36
  incorrect implementation of directive 38–9
  incorrect interpretation 39
  non-implementation of directive 36–7
  principle 36
students
  free movement 126, 130
subsidiarity 9
supranational control 3
supremacy doctrine 25–6
  key facts 24
  national recognition 27

third country nationals
  free movement 9
trade marks 111, 187
treaties
  accession treaties 5
  amending treaties 5
  Constitutional Treaty (failed) 8
  EC Treaty 4, 5
    amendments 6
  ECSC Treaty 3–4
  EEC Treaty 3, 4, 5
  Euratom Treaty 4
  Maastricht *see* Treaty on European Union 1992
  Reform Treaty *see* Treaty of Lisbon 2007
  Single European Act 1986 5
  source of law 17
  Treaty of Amsterdam 1997 5, 7
  Treaty on European Union 1992 4, 5–6
    amendments to EC Treaty 6
    protocols 6
  Treaty on the Functioning of the European Union 8
  Treaty of Lisbon 2007 2, 8–11
    renumbering 11
  Treaty of Nice 2001 5, 7–8

undertakings
  concerted practices 163–4
  decisions by associations of 163
  meaning in competition law 160, 162
  safeguards for 161
Union citizens 118, 121, 122, 124
  death or departure of 128
  Directive 2004/38 125–30
  ECJ 124–5
  non-economically active 124–5
  residency 124–5

rights attached to
   citizenship 124–30
  welfare benefits 124, 126
  see also **free movement of
   persons**

vertical direct effect 29–30
veto 9, 12
**Visas, Asylum and
   Immigration** 7
voting
  Council 12–13
  double majority 13

qualified majority 9, 10,
  12–13
simple majority 12
unanimous 12
veto 9, 12

welfare benefits
  Union citizens 124, 126
workers
  Art 45 TFEU rights 131
  discrimination 134–7
  equal treatment 136
  families 137

fixed-term contracts 132
free movement 118, 122,
  125, 130–7
meaning of worker
  131–3
overview 130–1
part-time work 131–2
public service 122, 135–6
rehabilitation as 132–3
retaining status 133
training 133
unemployment 133
unpaid work 132